What Other Christian Leaders Are Saying About *CrossTalk* International

"I've known Randy for a long time and one of the things I have always appreciated, and one of the things I appreciate about having the program on the stations is the clarity of the message. He is one of the best teachers that I have heard in a long time. Every time that the program is on, I know that the people who watch that program are going to hear a clear voice of the Gospel in an understandable way."
    Jerry K. Rose, President & CEO
    Total Living Network
    Former Chairman of the of the Board (NRB)
    National Religious Broadcasters Association

"In my opinion, it's the greatest Messianic Jewish program that is available."
    Jamie Schmitz, General Manager & CEO
    WLMB TV-40
    NRB TV Station of the Year

"I've had the wonderful pleasure of bringing *CrossTalk* to our stations across the country. We are so happy that in a secular company, we can lift up the name of Jesus through Randy's ministry of *CrossTalk*."
    Suellen Roberts
    Tigereye Broadcasting Corp.

"One of our great programs on Sky Angel is *CrossTalk* with Dr. Randy Weiss. If you like ministry and the sharing of the Gospel with a little different flavor, then you will love *CrossTalk*. It's a wonderful program."
    Pelle Carlson, President
    Sky Angel Television

"We have carried *CrossTalk* from day one. We've loved it. It's ministered to our people. It's just a great way to bring the Gospel in a gentle loving ministerial way to our community."
    Brian Larson, President
    North East Gospel Broadcasting

"I really appreciate the ministry of *CrossTalk* with Dr. Randy Weiss. It's been a tremendous asset to our station in Wichita Falls, TX. We hear from people throughout our community that they enjoy Dr. Weiss' program. It gives us more insight into God's word. He shares valuable stories about what God is doing in the United States, as well as God's work in Israel."
    Rod Payne, President
    CFNT TV
    NRB LPTV Station of the Year

"I work with ministries all over the country. I want you to know that **CrossTalk** is a great program in Christian television. Dr. Randy Weiss is an incredible communicator that will help you understand the intricacies of the word of God. He provides insight into Jewish perspectives and idioms that make the Scriptures come alive."

> Mark Dreistadt, President
> Infinity Ministries
> Chairman NRB TV Committee

"We get great reception from our viewers in the San Francisco market. One of the reasons that we do is because of the programs that we run. One of our very choice, select programs is **CrossTalk** with Randy Weiss. We fully endorse what they are doing and their mission."

> Dave Scott, Vice President
> KTLN Television

"I would like to recommend Dr. Randy Weiss' program, **CrossTalk**, as a program that will help you to become familiar with the Jewish roots of the faith. Dr. Weiss has a great sense of humor. He presents his material in a fashion you will be able to relate to. He is a wonderful man of God. In fact, I count it a privilege to have him on the board of directors of our international organization."

> John Cathcart, President
> World Missionary Evangelism

"Dr. Randy Weiss is able to give insights that a non-Jewish believer would never see in Scripture. His insights on contemporary Christian issues, combined with his guests, provide a truly unique perspective to the viewer not available in any other program."

> Dr. David W. Clark
> Former President Family Net TV & Radio
> Former Chairman of the Board (NRB)
> National Religious Broadcasters Association

Contents

Foreword with A Jewish Rabbi's Perspective ... 9
Foreword with A Christian Leader's Perspective ... 10
Dedication ... 11
Prologue: A Jewish Guy's Concern About the Passion ... 12

SECTION 1
HISTORY & THE PASSION

CHAPTER I ... 20
Introduction
- What is Anti-Semitism? ... 21
- Arabs Not Anti-Semitic ... 22

CHAPTER II ... 27
Religion of Love—Legacy of Hate
- Pagan Philo-Judaism—Christian Anti-Semitism ... 28
- The "Roman Road" Began in Jerusalem ... 30
- Jewish Sects in the Age of Jesus ... 31
- The 1st 15 Popes Were Jewish! ... 32
- Jesus, A Jew; Christianity, A Jewish Sect; the New Testament, A Jewish Book! ... 35
- Judaism: a Vibrant Source of Faith ... 36
- Jews and Christians Divided By War ... 37

CHAPTER III ... 41
The Jewish/Christian Divide—a Religion in Revolution
- A Jewish Legend and a Roman Emperor ... 42
- Replacement Theology ... 43
- God Has Not Disowned His Firstborn ... 46

CHAPTER IV ... 49
Passion Plays & Other Examples of Medieval Anti-Semitism
- Shakespeare and Classical Anti-Semitism ... 50
- Medieval Passions and the Passion Play ... 50
- Drama and Art as Educational Tools ... 52

The Legend of Oberammergau	53
The Passion of Oberammergau	53
Addressing the Problem of Oberammergau	55
Separating Passion Fiction From New Testament Fact	56

CHAPTER V   **59**
The Passion Error

The Messiah and Public Opinion	60
The Church: God's Avenger for the "Blood Curse"?	62
Anti-Semitism and the Money-Changers	64
Greedy Moneychangers or Other Sins?	66
Packed Palestine and the Passover Pilgrims	69

CHAPTER VI   **72**
Conspiracy: The Deicide Alternative

A Per Capita Consideration	73
The Alternative Theory	74
Passover in the Last Supper	76
Mystery and the Upper Room	76
Arrested in Darkness—IT WAS A CONSPIRACY!	79
The Sound of Dawn	80
The Conspiracy Ignored by the Passion Play	82

CHAPTER VII   **85**
Sin in the Superstar

The Apostle's Greed	87
Judas: a Scripted Anti-Hero	88
Pilate: Pawn or Prefect?	91
Another Look at Ben Hur	92

SECTION 2
CHRISTIAN BIGOTS & THE PASSION

CHAPTER VIII   **96**
The Passion of Eureka Springs, Arkansas

An Unfair Portrayal	98
Wickedness Personified	99

Pilate & Claudius as Friends of Jesus   101
An Angel Beyond Imagination   102

CHAPTER IX   **104**
Legacy of Hate: Gerald L. K. Smith & Famous Friends
"The Voice of America"   105
Radio Priest or Renegade Religious Bigot?   107
Preacher, Politician, Man of Passion   108
Passion to Save America   109
The Divine "Call" of Hatred   111
Was the Preacher an Early Holocaust Denier?   112

CHAPTER X   **117**
Ford & Hitler: Anti-Semites, Fanatics or Respected Leaders?
#1–Christ, #2–Napoleon, #3–Henry Ford?   118
Have You Been Driven By a Ford Lately?   119
Hitler's Church Connection   120
The International Jew   122
Hitler's Helper?   125

CHAPTER XI   **128**
Stumbling Blocks to Passion
Jews Do Not Run the Banks!   128
Israel: A State, Not a Savior   129
Israel's Most Powerful Enemy—The U.N.   131
The "Missed" Weapons of Mass Destruction   132

SECTION 3
HOLOCAUST DENIAL & THE PASSION

CHAPTER XII   **136**
Holocaust Denial
A New Breed of Nazi   140
Prophecy of General Eisenhower   142

CHAPTER XIII   **145**
Politics of Hate
Pat Buchanan—Holocaust Denier?   146

It is Not Academic! 147
Europe's Denial 148
Is the world safe for Jews? 151
Asian Anti-Semitism 151
Russia's New Freedom to Hate 153

CHAPTER XIV   **157**
The Pope, Nazis, & Israel
The Pope's Insensitivity 161
Guilt Crosses Denominational Lines 163
Righteous Gentiles 164
Israel, the Pope, and *The Passion of the Christ* 165

CHAPTER XV   **168**
Rome and the Chosen People
Chosenness Discussed 169
Rome Sees No Evil 170
Nazis: Saved by Grace or Rome? 171
Conflicts of Conscience? 173

CHAPTER XVI   **175**
Passionate About the Passion?
Thumbs up & down: the film review by one Jewish guy 182
Is Gibson a Catholic Who Broke the Rules? 193

CHAPTER XVII   **196**
Did the Jews Kill Christ or Was He the Victim of Identity Theft?
WILL THE REAL JESUS PLEASE STAND UP? 198
Surviving the Beating in the Passion? 200

Conclusion   203

Epilogue   206

Bibliography   210

About the Author   214

Foreword with A Jewish Rabbi's Perspective

There has been a great deal of both enthusiasm and consternation in the Christian and Jewish communities as a result of Mel Gibson's blockbuster film, *The Passion of The Christ*. Christians hail the movie as a grand epic expressing the suffering of Jesus because of, and, on behalf of, all humanity. Jews, on the other hand, fear that this powerful film will lead to an upswing in virulent anti-Semitism. This has been the result of other Passion dramas presented by Christians for many centuries. And, on a very positive side, Christians and Jews of good will have been seeking a meaningful dialogue about the film, the actual events, and their interpretations. These are at the very core of Christian-Jewish relations. But there is a serious problem in obtaining this important dialogue.

JEWS AND CHRISTIANS DO NOT SPEAK THE SAME LANGUAGE

Jews have no frame of reference to understand the seminal event which is the Passion. Truly, without the Passion, there would be no Christianity. While there have been major events within Jewish history, there is nothing that defines Judaism's very existence as the Passion does for Christianity.

Likewise, the overwhelming majority of Christians have never suffered a genocide comparable to World Jewry. They have never experienced repercussions or fear at Easter after passionate sermons incited the faithful to murder Jews because they "killed Christ." They can watch *The Passion of The Christ* without noting the similarities with Nazi-era propaganda, and without thinking, "Sure, they are beating up on the Jewish kid, a lesson they have learned very well." How do we bridge this language gap?

Dr. Randy Weiss' *The Passion Conspiracy* is required reading for those who truly wish to span that gap. From his unique perspective, Dr. Weiss is able to explain the Passion so that both Jews and Christians can appreciate its importance. And with his keen historical perspective, Dr. Weiss can open the all-too-often blind eye that has allowed Christian anti-Semitism to run rampant for centuries.

Rabbi Stanley Halpern
Temple Israel
Gary, IN 2004

Foreword with A Christian Leader's Perspective

It is astonishing that a modern film made in two dead languages about the execution of an obscure religious teacher from two thousand year ago in a remote corner of the Roman Empire should cause such world-wide emotional reaction (both pro and con). By any reasonable standard, the story should be buried in the sands of history. Instead, it is so well known the movie can start at the end without explaining the beginning.

Who was this man? Opinion is divided. But were it not for this man, we should know little about the daily drama of life in an ancient Roman province. Were it not for this man, we should know little about old Jewish sects. Were it not for this man, numberless acts of bloody savagery would not have taken place across the centuries, nor would numberless acts of unselfish love and sacrifice been experienced. How can one man have generated such energy? How can one man have generated such dedication? It depends on whom he is seen to be.

This man and his nation are the flash-point of modern international politics and policies. He is a figure of contention from China where his spiritual followers are tortured and suppressed to the Middle East where his ethnic people are threatened with annihilation while the United Nations Security Council winks in assent. The strangest phenomenon of all, his spiritual followers and his ethnic people are often bitterly divided about his identity and each other's agendas.

In this book, a man, who is not only a spiritual follower of this teacher but also a member of his race, shares his thoughts and feelings from both sides of the "divide" at one and the same time. This presents a rare chance for Christians, Jews, and Secularists to gain some insight and understanding of each other and the issue of *The Passion of the Christ*.

John Cathcart, President
World Missionary Evangelism
Dallas, TX 2004

Dedication

In addition to my family (who endured their own suffering while I wrote this book), I want to dedicate this work to everyone who viewed *The Passion of the Christ*. To each believer who rejoices in His Resurrection and the finished work of the Cross, I pray God's peace will fill your heart.

To each viewer who failed to embrace the love expressed by my Jewish Messiah, I offer the following brief personal reflection:

In 1973, I had a hopeless marriage, a deadly drug problem, and a life without purpose. As a result of the suffering and passion of the man depicted in the film, His love healed my marriage, redeemed me from drugs, and revealed a purpose for my life that is both compelling and renewing. If you lack hope, if you lack peace, or if you lack purpose, please embrace God's love.

Trust and obey the man called Jesus the Messiah. Contrary to what you might think, He declared Himself to be God and He was worshipped by His early Jewish followers. I declare my allegiance and remind you of His words, "I am the way, the truth, and the life. No one comes to the Father except through Me" (John 14:6). I realize this implies a very exclusive membership. However, all are welcome and the price has been paid by the One Who gave the invitation. Jesus said, "Come to Me, all you who labor and are heavy laden, and I will give you rest" (Matthew 11:28). I know this is true because I came and I found rest.

I remain eternally grateful and eternally His.

Prologue:

A Jewish Guy's Concern About The Passion

I am an odd duck. I am Jewish and I believe that Jesus is the Messiah. For these reasons, and more, I don't fit in very well. I have odd interests and I think odd thoughts. Some may feel it was an odd thing I did in 1994 when I chose this topic of research for my doctoral dissertation. No one was really interested in the history of Christian art and drama as it related to anti-Semitism in the passion play.[1] Who was concerned with a medieval drama about the passion of the Christ as it related to Jews? At the time, it seemed that nobody cared. I held my own theory as to how typical passion play presentations were historically inaccurate. While most people were unfamiliar with the background of these Christian drama productions, for me, it became an obsessive concern. As my research developed, I saw a pattern of problems. I formulated a theory as to why the pattern existed. I also realized a more accurate interpretation could lead to a less inflammatory depiction. I became certain that the theory I proposed could be proven by the evidence and the research would support my conclusions. By the time that I completed my work, it was evident that anti-Semitic influences had negatively impacted the scripts of various passion plays. I was also certain that errant anti-Semitic biases had become embedded in the divisive patterns contained in passion plays. History revealed these to be detrimental to Jewish people.

In the 1990's proposing the theory that the passion play was anti-Semitic elicited a hearty yawn. Few cared whether the premise was true or false. Making the task of finding anyone to read my book more improbable, I invested nearly one quarter of the work discussing the tedious problem of Holocaust denial as a serious modern issue among Christian anti-Semites. This brought confused, glazed looks followed by another yawn.

The book project was hopelessly non-commercial. It would have been considered weird (even for an odd duck) were it not for the fact that I identified an obvious verifiable problem in the drama that had been repeatedly presented from the earliest dramas of the Church era through Jesus Christ Superstar and even into more recent Hollywood offerings. This ancient problem continues to affect uninitiated viewers in modernity.

The strange topic chosen for my dissertation gained a life of its own as the research progressed. When I realized that some of the most vociferous anti-Semites in history were drawn to this drama, my attention was riveted to its impact. I was shocked to learn that the founder of the largest passion play in America hated Jews to the degree that he became one of the first "Christians" in history to deny the existence of the Holocaust! Since the Holocaust defined the most violent form of anti-Semitism in human history, I could not remain silent in the face of so-called "Christians" who publicly denied the historicity of the Nazi Holocaust and the near destruction of my people.

At the time I had no answer as to how such theological and moral confusion could exist among people who named the name of Jesus as Lord. Yet what burned within me was an unshakable compulsion to sort it out for myself. And so I became engaged in the academic project from a prior millennium that led to this new book.

I completed that research, completed that book project, completed that degree program, and with an awkward sense of satisfaction, I placed it on a bookshelf in my office where it sat for ten years. It did not make the pain or disgust go away because I knew that nobody was interested in medieval Christian drama. I was keenly aware that many people had never even heard of the malady identified as "Holocaust denial." I had found the heart-breaking answers to the profound questions that had troubled my soul. My search was over—or so I thought.

Now, fast forward to 2004. It's amazing how a single decade and one enormously successful film by a Catholic action star can change the perception of what is relevant. During that entire prior decade, nobody ever asked for my considered opinion about the subject of the Passion of the Christ. Yet as soon as it was known that Mel Gibson was producing a film about the subject it became relevant. When it was publicized that Mel Gibson's father is alleged to be a Holocaust denier, all of a sudden, my research became very relevant.

Prologue

After reading my findings you still might feel that I am an odd duck. Some might be less kind and say that I am *meshuganeh*. Yet those among my Jewish peers who use that term to describe me in an unkind manner will probably find my research to be of interest. And those among my Christian peers who are staunch supporters of the film will find both added support and well-reasoned criticism for the work of Mr. Gibson.

By the way, if you are unfamiliar with the Yiddish word I used, suffice it to say that *meshuganeh* implies that I might be an odd duck to such an extent that I excessively cross the line of reason. It might also imply I am a "crazy" person. I am not *meshuganeh*. This book is an act of reason. It is the despicable behavior of certain anti-Semites described in this book that is *meshuganeh*.

Was the Passion of the Christ reasonable? I don't mean the Mel Gibson film. I mean the passion embraced by the One I call Messiah. I guess some might say that Jesus was *meshuganeh*—He was not! The action of Jesus was not reasonable. Acts of passion are often not reasonable. The courts in America have become familiar with "crimes of passion." Emotions have the power to inform an individual's reason to such an extent that one's actions become unreasonable to those not compelled by the same passion. The actions of Jesus were not crazy. He was obedient to the point of death. He was so in love with the object of His passion that it caused Him to act in a manner some might presume to be unreasonable. Why would anyone suffer and die the death of a miserable convict when a simple denial might have saved His life?

Maybe the better question is, "How could a Christian hate the Jews and follow the Jewish Messiah?" Is it possible? I must ask you to read my findings and draw your own conclusions. This is the only way that some folks will ever be convinced.

Permit me to point out that if you are reading this, you are an odd duck too. Let's be honest, who reads old doctoral dissertations for entertainment? Well ducky, research and documentation are the nuts and bolts of this book. I made many modifications to put it into a more popular format so this book does not mirror the style of the original. Nevertheless, it is inescapable that this book is the result of an amalgam of research done with academic purposes in view. I will not apologize for the fact that I did not produce this work to entertain anyone. I did it for me. I had some questions and I dug to find the answers. I approached the questions according to academic standards and reached my conclusions based on the same. It is not jammed with emotion. These pages will not teach you how to be wealthy. Do not presume that you will find any bizarre answers to presumed mysteries. I share no insights about when the Messiah will return or the identity of the Anti-Christ. I provide no decoder ring to unravel the "Bible Codes," nor a brush to paint over DaVinci's (though it would be useful.) This is not a work of fiction; it is a look at history. I pray you find it to be relevant. What I will present is a reasoned, logical alternative view about who is responsible for the death of Jesus. I will also explain my view as to why the event is typically presented erroneously.

I must confess that the main reason for this book is that too many people asked for my opinion about Mr. Gibson's film phenomenon. I am unable to answer them individually. I was confronted with the same questions from friends, relatives, and listeners of the weekly TV and radio show that I host—***CrossTalk***. Generally, people wanted to know my view about **The Passion of the Christ**. They asked if I believed the film to be anti-Semitic? Was it faithful to the biblical narrative? Was the film too violent? I have been asked all of the standard questions about the film. Did the Jews kill Christ? What do I think? A decade after I asked and answered those questions for myself, I have decided it is appropriate to publish this modified edition of my research for anyone who is interested.

I will answer the question posed in this book's subtitle in the final chapter. I will specifically answer the direct questions I have been asked about the film and provide a meaningful critique in the chapter appropriately titled, "Passionate About the Passion?" (To those of you who only wanted an opinion on the film, this book is offered on the honor system. It may self-destruct if you misbehave and read the later chapters before the beginning.) Ok, that was a misguided attempt at humor, however; suffice it to say that I do hope you will read the entirety of this research as presented. My opinion is best evaluated from the level playing field of an informed background of the genre of passion dramas. For it is only within that context that my closing opinion about the contemporary passion film will make sense when related to the ancient pattern that has been influenced by Christian anti-Semitism. I will also suggest you "stay tuned" for the epilogue. One personal experience with Christian anti-Semitism resulting from the passion play will explain the reason for my original interest in this subject.

If you can't play by the rules and wait until the end, I will simply say that I loved the film and I hated the film. It is too complex to reduce to a single exclusive emotion. I have very strong feelings about the film and I will share them before I am done. I must say that in my entire adult life, I have never seen anything create the stir about Jesus that this film has caused. People have talked about this film in the barbershop, the coffee shop, the tavern, and at bus stops. This film has caused newspapers, film critics, radio program hosts and televangelists to all get on the same page about the sensation it caused. I am grateful for the privilege of sharing my faith in my Jewish Messiah as a byproduct of Mr. Gibson's film.

To my delight, rabbis, pastors, priests, and even the Pope discussed the film in public forums. To my discomfort, it was extremely troubling that the film created cause for polarization. Deep divides along clearly partisan lines were quite evident from the earliest stages of the debate. Many months prior to the film's theatrical release, Jews tended to hate it and Evangelicals tended to love it. Secular critics seemed to recognize the purposeful use of violence. Most everyone had an eye-opening experience into the suffering of Jesus. The high cost of salvation was detailed in the Gospels and visually explained through Mr. Gibson's high tech cinematography. It is clear that the preponderance of viewers were moved to a place of reflection rarely experienced (if ever) in a movie house. I too, was deeply moved each time I viewed the film preparing for this book.

The greatest problem that I observed among those arguing about the film is that few of the opponents in the debate seemed willing to honestly consider the opposing arguments. Most troublesome was the fact that the opposing parties tended to vilify each other instead of listening to each other. It is my hope that this work will provide a perspective that has not been fully embraced heretofore by either side because it has not been presented from a friendly position to both sides. I am Jewish and I am a believer in Jesus. I am friendly to both sides. I see the value in the film and I see the problems of the film too. In an effort to seek common ground and to stimulate responsible dialogue, it is my hope that this book will help both sides recognize that love covers a multitude of sins. And without love for one another, it matters little who holds the theological high ground.

In concluding this prologue, I must state that I believe the Jewish people have been the butt of jokes and the focus of disgust because of a lie told from generation to generation. I am now certain that the ancient accusation of "deicide" (the Jews killed God) is the source of anti-Semitism in the world. It is a charge leveled against my people (the Jews) by my people (the Church). To all concerned, I declare that the suffering of Jesus cannot be overstated nor the depth of His love underestimated.

Who cares about the history of Christian art? Who cares about a drama from the Middle Ages performed every ten years in Bavaria or annually by middle-aged Sunday School teachers in homemade costumes? Who cares about facts when opinions are so much more prevalent? Well, I guess you do if you are reading this book for odd ducks. By the way, now would be a great time to remember the honor system and turn the page to keep reading. And with that, permit me to thank you for taking the time to consider my thoughts in this book. May God bless you and draw you near to Himself as you consider the love of Jesus revealed in "his passion" (Acts 1:3).

---

1 This is a common term used to describe the dramatic presentation of the final days in the life of Jesus. These staged productions typically include a depiction of His arrest, the trials, the execution of Jesus Christ, culminating in the Resurrection.

Section 1

History & the Passion

Chapter I

Introduction

Anti-Semitism is a sin! It is hatred birthed in ignorance. No one is immune to pain; no one is immune to hatred. Anti-Semitism is a form of heart disease but there is a vaccine. Everyone requires a dose of truth. Many have contracted the illness while in the company of those previously contaminated. Others have been infected when exposed to untreated ignorance. It is known to be an orally communicable social disease but it is not carried in the bloodstream. It is not a congenital disease because it is never present in children below the age of understanding; nevertheless, it is most often transmitted from generation to generation. Left untreated, it is terminal. Love is the only cure. It is hoped that this discussion of anti-Semitism will help to identify the problem. If successful, healthy souls will be better equipped to encourage infected individuals to seek the cure.

Society has failed to protect the public health and does not prohibit the behavior that leads to the transmission of the disease. This is not by design but by default. In a free society the freedom to love presupposes the freedom *not* to love. To society's detriment, anti-Semites have misconstrued the former, only to abuse the latter. They have developed a practice and philosophy of hatred. Christianity, unlike society, is not free. Christianity, unlike society, presupposes that its adherents sacrifice the freedom to hate and willingly commit to love. To Christianity's detriment, Christian anti-Semites have ignored the fundamental duty of the faith.

They deny the command to love. Christianity expresses itself in many ways. Some forms of Christian expression carry the germs of anti-Semitism and several insidious examples will be investigated in this study. To prohibit the spread of anti-Semitism, Christian expression should be cleansed. Christianity, the religion of love, must be purged of a deadly strain of viral hatred. Christian anti-Semitism is the sin of Gentile Christianity. Christian anti-Semitism ignores that Jesus came to and for the "lost sheep of the house of Israel" (Matthew 15:24).[2]

This research will define anti-Semitism and describe examples of its impact. Documentation will be provided to show that anti-Semitic influences within Christianity have damaged the Jewish people. What will not be shown is the resulting negative effect that anti-Semitism has had on Jewish people. How many Jewish people have been turned away from the love of Jesus by the hatred of His followers? That statistic will not be known until revealed by the Lord when the account books are balanced by His better measure. Yet the negative influences of Christian anti-Semitism must be examined so that the phenomenon can be correctly understood and the symptoms of this form of religious bigotry properly identified.

The problem is not new and forms of the problem are contained within medieval Christian literature and medieval Christian drama. The particular aspects of one such medieval Christian drama known as the passion play will be analyzed in several modern forms. Comparisons and contrasts with the text of the New Testament will be considered. The New Testament provides the most correct data to inform the script of the drama. It is necessary to test the accuracy of the passion play to prove that the presentation denigrates the Jewish people and should therefore be corrected or discontinued. Further, I will propose a theory presenting an alternative interpretation that attempts to correctly explain the involvement of the Jewish people related to the events generally portrayed in the passion play. Lastly, the Church, as the source of Christian anti-Semitism, will be examined to understand its actions during modern events such as the Nazi Holocaust and recent anti-Semitic trends in the United States and abroad. Although the concept of "Christian anti-Semitism" is an oxymoron, it exists in history, and it exists today.

What is Anti-Semitism?

Anti-Semitism is a form of bigotry that should not be hidden behind semantics. Therefore, it is necessary to define the topic to escape the academic fog surrounding anti-Semitism. Anti-Semitism is an inflammatory term that might easily be misunderstood. William F. Buckley, Jr. wrote a timely book on the subject, *In Search of Anti-Semitism*. A criticism that had previously been leveled against Buckley was due to his lack of definition of the term itself. In response, Buckley quoted an acceptable definition which he inserted into his book as a "dislike or disapproval a) even of Jews one has never met and b) of any corporate objectives identifiable as of special concern to prominent and vociferous Jews."[3]

I found the definition to be very interesting. It might explain some of the political positions that are often taken against Israel by many modern anti-Semites. I must admit that this is not always the case. Certain anti-Israel opinions may be completely justified when a national policy of Israel is objectively wrong.[4] It is therefore incorrect to assume that every position taken against Israel is an anti-Jewish gesture. More common, however, opponents of Israel are usually first opponents of Jews. Common to their anti-Jewish propensity, they often oppose the rights of Jews to expand or maintain control in Israel. The quality of specific Israeli policies is often incidental to the opposition. Hence the 1975 United Nations Resolution that proclaimed "Zionism is Racism." The United Nations is wrong. Zionism is <u>not</u> racism. In fact, I believe it should be declared that "anti-Semitism is racism," but the United Nations will not likely make such a declaration.

Arabs Not Anti-Semitic

The subject of anti-Semitism can be quite confusing. This is particularly true when dealing with Arab/Israeli or Muslim/Jewish conflicts. According to the lineages described in the Hebrew Bible, both Jews and Arabs are people of Semitic origins. In other words, both peoples can trace their roots to a son of Noah named Shem. They are therefore both Shemites, more commonly known as Semites. Therefore, Yasser Arafat could not be properly identified as an anti-Semite. It might be fair to say that he hated Jews, but it would be bad form to say that he hated all Semites. It would imply a form of self-hatred to say that Arabs (or Palestinians) are anti-Semitic. Of course, some might suggest that Palestinian self-hatred is appropriate based on the behavior of Yasser Arafat. That however is beyond the scope of this research. For the purposes of this study, it must be stated that many anti-Semites are not anti-Arab. It is more likely that they are best described as anti-Jewish.[5]

It is necessary to briefly remind my readers of one more distinction. Many people are opposed to Israel because of an anti-Jewish bias. Often, those same anti-Jewish attitudes are combined with a pro-Arab posture. Since September 11, 2001, the contrary might also be true. Some people hate Arabs and therefore exhibit a pro-Jewish bias in favor of supporting Israel. In truth, there is nothing inherently evil about Arabs or righteous about Jews. Politics aside, both peoples can produce positive and negative examples. The political considerations are often blurred by the preconceived attitudes one has toward the peoples of the lands. There are better ways to evaluate the politics and it is unwise to embrace a simplistic view about the peoples, religions, or the politics of the region. The troublesome problems that plague the Middle East are not as simple as the simpletons who often attempt to define the issues and propose the solutions over drinks at the local watering hole.

In truth, both ends of the polarized spectrum have legitimate concerns. One cannot dismiss the need Israelis have to maintain a Jewish homeland. Neither can one ignore the struggle and suffering endured by those Israeli-Arabs who continue to live in squalor as hopeless citizens of refugee camps. No one can honestly pretend that these legitimate problems should be ignored. However, it is also a mistake to overlook the fact that the so-called "Palestinian" refugees are in fact, mere political pawns of neighboring Arab brothers of the region dedicated to the proposition that Israel must be eradicated as a Jewish state.[6]

Since so many geo-political issues surround the sentiments facing Arabs and Israelis, it is often unclear where religious lines intersect political or economic concerns. More complex issues related to the philosophical differences between Judaism and Islam also distort the problems. The real issues often appear to be buried under the rhetoric of hatred. For this reason, I want my readers to be aware that the politicized anti-Israel form of anti-Semitism should not be confused with Christian anti-Semitism. Christians, unlike Muslims of the region, do not have the same incentives to promote hatred of Jews. Christians will gain no political or geographical advantage by vanquishing the Jews. Yet in spite of what seems to be a limited incentive, some Christians continue to be anti-Semitic.

Some would try to diminish the impact of the problem among Christians. Others have attempted to deflect blame. Irving Kristol, was quoted by William F. Buckley, Jr. in an article originally printed in the *National Review* suggesting that the recent forms of anti-Semitism that have been dangerous to Jews have <u>not</u> been the result of Christian anti-

Semitism. Rather, he believed it to be a neo-pagan form of anti-Semitism as exhibited by the Nazis, the fascists, and the Marxists. Of course, he also recognized the more contemporary forms of hatred of Jews as shown by Moslem fundamentalists. Call it what you will, the propensity for people of other religions and philosophical views to hate Jews exists. Kristol would have us believe that Jews are essentially safe in the midst of modern Christians.

I believe that the *National Review* article was wrong to suggest that Jews will find relative safety because in that author's view, the future of Christianity will be determined by the liberal-modernist-secular forms of Protestant Christianity. Kristol went so far as to declare, "that never again would Christians want to be *devout*." The more liberal forms of the Christian faith, in his opinion, are safer for Jews. He also pointed out that the American Jewish community is very concerned about the Christian revival that seems to be growing among the Evangelical Protestants. Kristol contends that Jews are "anxiously looking for signs of anti-Semitism among 'born-again' Christians." He also warned that it is likely that Jews will "exaggerate the few such expressions they do find, and wait for this phenomenon to pass." Buckley held a vastly different view. He wrote, "I don't think it will pass. *I believe the secular era is fading*, that Jews (at least those who remain Jews) will become more Jewish, Christians more Christian, Moslems more Moslem, Hindus more Hindu, etc., [emphasis mine.]"[7]

I have asked my readers to consider these views because I believe both Irving Kristol and Mr. Buckley's basis for their bold conclusions are wrong. I vehemently disagree with the suggestion that the "secular era" is fading. Liberalism may be fading but that might lead to nothing more than a conservative secular era. If one listens to "talk radio," political conservatism seems to be growing. This does not automatically equate to a growth in Christian orthodoxy or dedication to Christian values. Christians may remain innocuously silent toward Jews. Still, one assumption must be disputed. There is no basis for the presupposition that "devout" Christians are *not* or will not become anti-Semitic. Nothing tangible prohibits a reoccurrence of the same form of historical errors that birthed the Crusades among the devout. The Crusader's devotion should not be questioned. They were willing to die for their convictions. Devotion to one religion (not even versions of Christianity) does not equate to proper attitudes and actions toward people of other religions. The problem of the Crusaders was not a lack of devotion; it was that they maintained perverse convictions. They believed strongly. But what they believed was wrong. The Crusaders were neither the first nor the last Christians to love Jesus and persecute Jews.

Neither Kristol nor Buckley nor any scholar familiar with Church history can offer any assurances that the Church will not be led into new or revised forms of Christian anti-Semitism. It is possible for Christendom to lose its tolerance toward Jews at any time. Of course I recognize that anti-Semitism is not a public priority at this time. The purpose of this investigation is not to suggest that Jews are under siege at the hands of violent Christian hate-mongers. A decade ago, one Jewish scholar suggested that, "Today antisemitism in the United States is neither virulent nor growing. It is not a powerful social or political force. Moreover, prejudicial comments are now beyond the bounds of respectable discourse and existing societal restraints prevent any overt antisemitic conduct."[8] Outward anti-Semitic pronouncements are generally viewed as unacceptable but nobody knows how people *really* feel. More to the point, neither Jews nor Christians should be deceived about the reality of Christian anti-Semitism. At this time, it is a concern to many Jews in America and around the world. The theatrical release of the film, *The Passion of the Christ*, has raised the level of concern felt by large numbers of Jewish people.

---

2 Unless otherwise noted, all New Testament Scripture references are from the New King James Version. King James Version references will be identified by KJV. Unless otherwise noted, all Hebrew Bible (Old Testament) Scripture references used are from *The Holy Scriptures According to the Masoretic Text*, (The Jewish Publication Society of America, Philadelphia, 1955).

3 Excerpt from a reader's criticism published by William F. Buckley, Jr., *In Search of Anti-Semitism*, (New York: The Continuum Publishing Company, 1992), 92.

4 In general, I do support Israel's right to make their own independent decisions regarding their own national security without regard to the political expediencies of other nations. This is particularly true when defending their right to survive surrounded by anti-Jewish enemy nations dedicated to the eradication of the independent Jewish State in the Middle East.

5 It is necessary to explain the specific choice of terminology. In this study, anti-Semitism will be generally used as an expression referring specifically to hostility against Judaism, and Jewish people. No other Semitic peoples are included within the usage of the term in this study. Further, anti-Semitism appears to be understood by

most moderns in the form used throughout this work as a form of animosity directed against Jews, Jewish issues, Jewish beliefs, or the Jewish nation.

6 For an insightful, fact-filled analysis of the outrageous claims of so-called "Palestinians" being the rightful owners of the land of Israel, see Joan Peter's <u>From Time Immemorial</u>, Chicago, IL, JKAP Publications, 1985.

7 Buckley, 81

8 Leonard Dinnerstein, *Antisemitism in America*, (New York: Oxford University Press, 1994), 243.

Chapter II

Religion of Love– Legacy of Hate

Understanding the history of the term "anti-Semitism" helps to address the phenomenon it describes. Many will be surprised to learn that the word did not exist in antiquity before Christianity had become a dominant force. I assume that many of my readers will be shocked to learn that "anti-Semitism" did not exist in antiquity. The usage of the word did not occur until the middle of the nineteenth century. Not surprisingly, it was a German writer who coined the term "to bestow 'scientific' respectability upon the hatred of Jews by arguing that Jews and Germans belonged to different species of humanity ('races'). But the ancients did not have anything resembling a racial theory."[9]

In ancient times, anti-Judaism existed among the Gentiles, though it was a much different form than is generally understood. "Furthermore, the social and economic tensions that produced the virulent anti-Semitism of nineteenth-and twentieth-century Europe did not exist in antiquity. There were no 'nation-states' in antiquity in which the Jews were an unassimilable foreign element."[10] Jews lived near or among their non-Jewish neighbors wherever they resided. In antiquity, the Jews tended to make their living in diverse ways. One could expect to find Jewish farmers, Jewish laborers, Jewish craftsmen, Jewish artists, and even Jewish soldiers functioned among the many nations where Jews put down roots. The important issue herein is that most Jews were not wealthy. That is a terrible myth. In fact, most Jews were just as poor as the vast majority of the their neighbors in the ancient world. "Not a single ancient text says or implies that the Jews are hated or feared because of their economic power. Money-lending was still centuries in the future, and the rise of the Jewish middle classes did not begin until the nineteenth century."[11]

It will be clearly shown that anti-Semitism did not exist in the ancient world! There was a form of anti-Judaism that existed among pagans, but it had nothing to do with the horrendous stereotypes and false accusations characterized by Christian anti-Semites of later eras. To understand the anti-Judaism of antiquity, one must recognize that the cause of the problem was due to the unwillingness of ancient Jewish people to accept the gods in vogue among their pagan neighbors. Jews believed and lived differently than their pagan contemporaries.

> Pagan hostility toward the Jewish people was aroused, above all, by the refusal of the Jews to join the ecumenical consensus of paganism . . . Thus pagan anti-Jewishness can be regarded as a specific form of xenophobia, the fear and dislike of the stranger simply because he or she is seen as strange.[12]

Had the Jews been willing to worship their own God in conjunction with the wider categories of gods of Rome, they would have been accepted in the Roman world. This distinction is not minor. Ancient anti-Judaism was a result of an unwillingness of Jewish people to accept pagan gods. The allegations against Jews by the ancients had nothing to do with character assassinations or the types of accusations brought by later Christian anti-Semites.

Pagan Philo-Judaism–Christian Anti-Semitism

It would be a mistake to suggest that Judaism was abhorred by all of their pre-Christian contemporaries. Among some segments of the ancient population, Judaism was highly respected. This truth is imperative to understanding a correct view of the relationship between ancient Judaism, ancient paganism, and ancient Christianity. Between the second century BCE[13] and the end of the first century CE, although anti-Judaism existed, some Gentiles had a view toward philo-Judaism. That era brought much admiration and respect from pagan neighbors who found great value in many of the Jewish practices and beliefs. There was both love and disdain. It was truly a time of philo-Judaism as well as anti-Judaism. Many pagans were converting to Judaism. This had a corresponding effect that stimulated a different type of hatred of Judaism. Jewish people attempted to remain separate and identifiable in their lifestyles and views. However, they also wanted to "accept and retain gentile converts. Indeed, some of the anti-Jewish literature of this period is motivated . . . by a desire to discourage conversion to Judaism. The literature that evinces a dislike of Judaism paradoxically confirms Judaism's powerful attraction.[14] In the simplest terms, the anti-Judaism of antiquity was little more than sour grapes. Jews were growing in effectiveness as promoters of Judaism. In the process, disenchanted pagans drew near to Judaism and many embraced the religion of Israel. The resulting animosity among pagans was due to the success of the competition. The Jews did gain some ground in the marketplace of ideas. This was quite different from the later forms of Christian anti-Semitism that have plagued the Jewish people for nearly 2,000 years. It was completely unlike the form of anti-Semitism caused by the Church.

Christianity carries the primary responsibility for developing and expressing the concept of modern anti-Semitism. This would seem implausible and horrible; nevertheless, the Church is guilty. Christian leaders developed and spread anti-Semitism as it has been practiced for many centuries. "An unmistakable component of modern anti-Semitism is its theological justification developed by Christianity."[15] Christianity, with all of its claims to be the religion of love, invented a platform of hatred against the Jews. Pagans of the same era were not as "creative." Christian hatred was not based on rational disputes, such as political, economic, social, or philosophical issues. Christianity's basis for hatred was based on the accusation of deicide. The view declares that the Jews killed God. The result let to the alleged eternal condemnation of the Jewish race.

Few would argue that the practices of paganism were often despicable, however, the pagans were not the people of antiquity who taught their children to believe that the Jews were cursed by the gods. Neither did they promote the vicious lies that the Jews were in league with the devil. Pagans did accuse the Jews of *atheism*, but this was because the Jewish people flatly refused to worship the pagan gods who were revered in that ancient culture. The Jews rejected the religion of the state. The gods of Rome were not accepted by the children of Israel. That was the primary basis for animosity exhibited by the Greeks and Romans. The same cannot be said for the Christians. "When the Christians accused the Jews of being 'Christ-killers' and of denying the Trinity, they meant something much more serious. In their eyes the Jews were cursed by God, doomed to Hell, and denied salvation in the hereafter, concepts that are foreign to the perception of Judaism by pagans. In sum, "anti-Semitism" did not exist in antiquity.[16]

The "Roman Road" Began in Jerusalem

Christian anti-Semitism can be traced back to the transitional shift in Church power from Jerusalem to Rome. This phenomenon may have begun as an adverse response to the original Jewish Church leaders' efforts to superimpose certain Jewish practices and traditions on the earliest Gentile Christians. Possibly, anti-Semitism grew out of a reactionary trend against perceived Jewish elitism in the Jerusalem Church. By the beginning of the second century CE the demographics of the Church changed from a Jerusalem-based Church of Jewish believers, into a growing, diverse, kinetic population of Rome-oriented Gentile believers. The Acts of the Apostles presents this trend of leadership and growth away from Jerusalem on the path to Rome. Nonetheless, Jewish Christians were still a major factor within the Church. Though often ignored, Jewish Christian sects survived for several centuries within the history of the Church.

The views of modern theologian, William G. MacDonald, have been included in an excellent text edited by Clark H. Pinnock, *The Grace of God, The Will of Man*. One extremely discomforting view is espoused that must be emphatically rejected. MacDonald proposes a common misconception about the demographics in the early days of Christianity.

> By the third decade after Jesus' resurrection the overwhelming constitution of the church was internationals. At that time only a small remnant-sized percentage of his church was also descended from father Abraham. What we see, therefore, in the middle of the first century is the emergence of a new society polarized around the Lord Jesus Christ.[17]

This suggestion may seem believable, but it is too simplistic. Prior to the first Jewish Revolt nearly *four decades* after the resurrection, the Church still predominantly held a Jewish perspective. After the Second Temple was destroyed, many shifts occurred within Judaism. The Church was also impacted by that event. Labeling people or events as Jewish or Christian is rather imprecise. The body of information that is being developed through the study of the Dead Sea Scrolls suggests that lines of demarcation are not as distinct as MacDonald's assumptions (or commonly accepted Christian thought) might suggest. Qumran researchers suggest that as more information becomes available to the theological community, more comparisons may prove stunning similarities between early Christianity and the Judaism of the Second Temple era.

Judaism was quite varied prior to the destruction of Jerusalem by the Romans. I heartily agree with the view of James C. Vanderkam in this regard. He appropriately declared it "inaccurate to talk about Judaism. Many scholars talk about Judaisms."[18] And rightly so. There were many competing streams within the flow of so-called "mainstream Judaism." Some groups were focused on strict adherence to their interpretations of the Jewish Law. While others were concerned with the messianic expectations that were rife in the apocalyptic era in which they lived. Many Jews believed they were living in the end of days. This led to variations of mysticism and dualism in addition to a strange variety of views. These systems of beliefs among Jews also influenced early Christians. Palestinian Judaism was is no manner monolithic. There were a variety of Judaisms at work at that time. And it is certain that one left its imprint on the other. The scholarship that is emerging through the study of the Dead Sea Scrolls is proving what many of us believed to be true. Early Christianity was simply a form of ancient Temple Judaism. "The picture that is emerging is that after the destruction of 70 C.E. by the Romans, both rabbinic Judaism and messianic Christianity emerged with their roots in different pre-70 strains of Judaism. In that sense, they are sister religions, both going back to Second Temple Jewish sources of which Qumran documents are the greatest contemporaneous exemplars that we have."[19]

Jewish Sects in the Age of Jesus

The distinctive sects of Judaism that existed during the formative years of Christianity provide rich ground to harvest valuable insights about ancient Judaism and nascent Christianity. To some degree, the Pharisees have survived within the traditions of Rabbinic Judaism. Since the New Testament offers popular (though certainly not comprehensive) insights into the beliefs and behavior of both the Sadducees and the Pharisees, these two groups have somehow come to be equated to "Judaism" as understood by Gentile Christians. This is an absolute fallacy. Further, tremendous insights can be gained by open-minded students of Christianity by delving into the faith and practices of those more obscure Jewish sects of the New Testament era such as the Essenes, Ebionites,

Zealots, Sicarii, Herodians, and the Therapeutae. (For more information about the forms of Judaism in existence during the time of Jesus, please see the book titled, <u>Jewish Sects of the New Testament Era</u>, by Randy Weiss published by Excellence in Christian Books and in electronic form through Logos Research Systems, Inc.)

It is well established that much division existed between the diverse groups within Judaism. "They were anything but united at the time of the death of Jesus." In fact, as it related to the animosity toward Jesus felt by some Jewish leaders, they "were in profound disagreement. Many looked upon the High Priests as appeasers, collaborators with the Romans."[20]

It is certainly not correct to reduce the Jews of the first century to Pharisees and Sadducees. The former being the legalistic Jewish enemies of Christ and the latter being the more secularized Jewish enemies of Jesus. That reductionist view of the Children of Israel is based on flawed positions or a lack of information. It is often a result of the Christian view that perceives Judaism as having been repudiated by the New Testament. Among some Christians, denominational doctrine and dogma define "all" that is relevant. That view often suggests that Judaism can only inform the Church about that which is nebulous. Shallow views of Judaism are often based upon a surface reading of the New Testament, to the exclusion of readily available outside sources of information.

No excuse exists for ignoring a more correct view. Judaism is neither nebulous nor extraneous. It is the source of messianism from which Christian beliefs developed. The Judaism from which Jesus, Paul, and the apostles grew was more meaningful than concerns about the "tithe of mint and anise" (Matthew 23:23), yet, unfortunately, that is often how ancient Judaism is perceived. Even worse, from that mistaken vantage, it is possible for some modern Christians to fall into the error of believing ridiculous propositions about Jews and Judaism. Christian anti-Semitism thrives in ignorance, as does most prejudice.

The 1st 15 Popes Were Jewish!

Judaism brought much to the world of first century Christianity. I want to consider one bold claim that I regularly make in my own efforts to cause Christians to reconsider the facts. I have been quoted many times for a declaration that sounds odd, yet is a fact of history. I make the following declarative statement without hesitation. <u>The first fifteen popes were Jewish</u>! I state this unashamedly to establish the fact that those who assume the Church was not inhabited by Jews are sadly mistaken. In fact, it causes me to pose a question. We used to run the show and fill the pews. How did we get left out of modern Christianity? Eusebius, one of the most famous ancient historians of the early Church, details that the Church was led by Jewish bishops in Jerusalem until the Roman invasion under Hadrian (approximately one hundred years after the death of Jesus). Permit me to quote his record and provide the names of the first fifteen Jewish leaders of the Church. It seems that their identity and their Jewishness have been forgotten by most Gentile Christians. The historian provides the details proving my declaration.

> There were fifteen successions of bishops in that church, all which, they say, were Hebrews from the first, and received the knowledge of Christ pure and unadulterated; so that, in the estimation of those who were able to judge they were well approved, and worthy of the episcopal office. For at that time the whole church under them, consisted of faithful Hebrews who continued from the time of the apostles, until the siege took place . . . The first, then, was James called the brother of our Lord; after whom, the second was Simeon, the third Justus, the fourth Zaccheus, the fifth Tobias, the sixth Benjamin, the seventh John, the eighth Matthew, the ninth Philip, the tenth Seneca, the eleventh Justus, the twelfth Levi, the thirteenth Ephres, the fourteenth Joseph, and finally, the fifteenth Judas. These are all the bishops of Jerusalem that filled up the time from the apostles until the abovementioned time, all of the circumcision.[21]

Each name of each Jewish bishop going all the way back to James, the brother of Jesus is listed in an unbroken line of Jewish bishops that lasted until the early decades of the second century. In the earliest era of the Church, the leaders of the Church were called bishops. The term "pope" was not used until later in Church history. It is the lineage detailed by Eusebius that the Church of Rome uses to trace the line of Popes allegedly unbroken all the way back to Saint Peter. Of course I do not accept that specific Catholic doctrine. Nonetheless, the Jewish leadership of the Early Church is undeniable and should be remembered.

Jewish bishops in Jerusalem were obviously the norm when the primary population of the Church consisted of Jewish people. What some might find interesting is that now after nearly 1,900 years, Jerusalem once again has a Jewish bishop. During Pope John Paul's visit to Israel in the spring of 2000, he appointed Benedictine Abbot Jean-Baptiste Gourion to the position of bishop at a Catholic church near Jerusalem. He was born in 1934 to a Jewish family in Algeria.[22] This book does contain some critical comments about Pope John Paul II. However, I believe he deserves recognition for his foresight in appointing a Jewish bishop to the region at this critical time in history. I can only hope that the next pope also grows in sensitivity to the Jewish people and the problems facing modern Israel.

Some Christian scholars continue to misinterpret the circumstances whereby Jewish leadership of the Early Church dissipated. William MacDonald presumes that the "internationals" hastily took over from the children of "faithful Abraham." He is not exactly correct. "Father Abraham" had many sons; some of them ran the Church. He ignores that "in the middle of the first century" the New Testament was not yet written. Paul was still in the middle of his evangelistic efforts. It should not be presumed, as is often accepted, that the Temple and the Church were "polarized around the Lord Jesus Christ" immediately following Pentecost. Unquestionably, this polarization occurred, however, it was nearly a century after that first Pentecost of the Church age featured in the Book of the Acts of the Apostles.

The dictates of Rome during that century show how the prevailing worldview differentiated Jews from Christians—they did not! The Jews of the era were not separate and distinct from the Christians of that time. When the Jews of Rome were expelled by Claudius, the Christians and Jews were all viewed the same—*as Jews*. The behavior of Rome against the Jews affected the Christians exactly as it did the rest of the Jews in the empire. In the eyes of Rome, Christianity was "indistinguishable from the synagogue."[23]

One need not look beyond the New Testament account in the Acts of the Apostles to understand the situation. When Paul came to Corinth in Acts 18:2, he visited with two Jewish Christians, Aquila and Priscilla. They had recently left Rome. Their exit was due to an edict by Claudius demanding that all the Jews of Rome be expelled. F.F. Bruce makes clear that they were not converts of the Apostle Paul. Rather, they had become Christians while living in Rome. In fact, the edict by Claudius to expel the Jews was likely the result of the propagation of Christianity among the ranks of the Jewish community in Rome. This conclusion is justified by "the natural inference from the statement of Suetonius that 'because the Jews of Rome were indulging in constant riots at the instigation of Chrestus (*impulsore*

Chresto) he expelled them from the city'."[24]

The early Jewish Christians were certainly included as one category of Jews among many sects of Judaism. "Christianity was indistinguishable from Judaism in the time of Claudius." However, this condition did not remain stagnant. "It was perfectly distinguishable by the time Suetonius wrote (*c*. A.D. 120), and it was well known that it had been founded by Christ (*Christus*, not unnaturally confused with the common slave-name *Chrestus*, which was pronounced in practically the same way).[25]

Jesus, A Jew; Christianity, A Jewish Sect; the New Testament, A Jewish Book!

It is foolish for Christians to present Jesus or his early followers as anything other than Jews. No doubt exists about the fact that Jesus and his followers were observant Jews. They never attempted to "convert" out of Judaism. They did not separate themselves from the religion of biblical Judaism. "Historical scholarship now permits us to affirm with confidence that Jesus of Nazareth was a faithful and observant Jew, who lived by the Torah, and taught nothing against his own people and their faith."[26] Many proof texts exist to assure this truth in the New Testament. If Jesus or his followers had wanted to separate themselves from Judaism they would not have been engaged in following various Jewish traditions. Jesus would not have celebrated *Chanukah* (Feast of the Dedication, John 10:22), *Succoth* (Feast of Tabernacles, John 7:2, which included the water libation ceremony referred to in John 7:37), *Pesach* (Passover), or *Shavuot* (Pentecost, Acts 2:1-4). When Paul was on the mission field, he regularly went to the synagogues (in Salamis, Acts 13: 5; in Antioch, Acts 13:14; in Iconium, Acts 14:1; in Thessalonica, Acts 17:1; in Berea, Acts 17:10; in Athens, Acts 17:17; in Corinth, Acts 18:4; in Ephesus, Acts 18:19). Additionally, it is recorded that Paul kept specific Jewish vows (Acts 18:18).

I like to tell folks that if you removed the Old Testament quotes, paraphrases, and references from the New Testament, you could write what was left on a dinner napkin. Perhaps that might be a slight exaggeration. Yet any responsible representation of the New Testament clearly shows that it is predominantly dependent on the ancient Jewish writings for its primary sources. Merely looking at the impact of the book of Isaiah on the New Testament proves how dependent the early Church was on the Jewish texts. "Isaiah greatly influenced John the Baptist, Jesus, and certainly, the New Testament writers whose works include 411 quotations from Isaiah."[27]

The New Testament writers also relied heavily on the texts from Psalms, Genesis, and Exodus. Texts ascribed to the other ancient Hebrew prophets were not ignored by the apostles either. Zechariah was quoted seventy-one times, while Ezekiel was quoted directly or indirectly sixty-five times. It is worthy of note that additionally, secondary sources also seem to be dependent on the same ancient Jewish writings. Those sources include the Jewish works such as the *"Book of the Maccabees"* and *"The Assumption of Moses"* found in the Pseudepigrapha or Apocrypha. "In the New Testament, the Epistle of Jude explicitly quotes Enoch and introduces the quotation with the formula 'Enoch, the seventh from Adam.'"[28] This reference, also pseudepigraphic in nature, verifies the importance of the earlier Jewish texts that were studied and revered by the writers of the New Testament.

Since some non-Catholic readers may be unfamiliar with the genre of literature mentioned above, the term "Apocrypha" includes the collection of Jewish religious texts not included in the Jewish or Protestant canon. Some later New Testament era apocrypha have also been discovered. "Pseudepigraphal" writings are other ancient works ascribed to ancient Jewish biblical luminaries (e.g., Enoch, Abraham, Moses) whose names were intended to lend credibility to the works. In some instances, the use of pseudonyms was also intended to protect the true writers from reprisals by either oppressive religious leaders or the tyrannical reigning regimes of the wicked governments that were often the subject of the literature. It is however, well known that the original writers were not those cited as the authors.[29]

Judaism: a Vibrant Source of Faith

It is negligent for Christians to limit Judaism to the once-thought characterizations of a monolithic, legalistic, or otherwise easily stereotyped "dead" religion. Judaism was vibrant and distinctive in its variety. The manner in which some Gentile Christians typify ancient Judaism is simply too erroneous to ignore. The errors also constitute part of the reason that Christian anti-Semitism exists. The commonly held view of ancient Jewish stereotypes is inaccurate.

Ancient Judaism has left a rich legacy that transcends itself. Both Rabbinic Judaism and Gentile Christianity remain as successful examples of modern religions whose origins grew from the matrix of ancient Judaism. Rabbinic Judaism may be viewed as the surviving evolutionary example of ancient Judaism, whereas Gentile Christianity represents the hybridization of first century Jewish messianism. In essence, they are the fruit of several discarded ancient Jewish sects. Religious sects, within this context, refer to smaller groups of like-minded believers who are identifiably distinct from the larger body of believers within a religion. Although the term "sect" usually suggests a negative concept, as used herein it is neutral. Therefore, the sects discussed are not seen as distorted forms of normative religion. More correctly, they should be understood and treated as differing forms, or, competing philosophies within one religion—Judaism.

"The heyday of Jewish sectarianism was from the middle of the second century B.C.E. to the destruction of the temple in 70 C.E."[30] Judaism was distinctive during the Second Temple era. During that period it had many sects that claimed to be the rightful practitioners of the Jewish faith passed down through their forefathers from ancient Israel. "This was the age of sects (Pharisees, Sadducees, Essenes, the Qumran community, Christians, Sicarii, Zealots, and others) and of sectarian literature.[31] It can be seen as far back as the period of the Second Temple that "Talmudic literature states there were 24 sects in Israel."[32]

Jews and Christians Divided By War

It has already been shown that ancient Rome officially classified Christianity as a Jewish sect among other Jews. As was discussed, Rome expelled the Christians along with all the other Jewish residents. Their welcome came "to an end with Claudius's edict in A.D. 49. Christian and non-Christian Jews alike were expelled from the city."[33] It is wrong for modern Christians to impose lines of demarcation between ancient Judaism and early Christianity that did not exist. Certainly there were differences; the issue lies in the manner with which those differences have been unquestioningly presumed. The walls between the ancient beliefs and the ancient believers have never been as clear-cut as assumed within some Gentile Christian circles. James H. Charlesworth, a respected (though liberal) Christian scholar has opined, "It is simply impossible today to apply the adjective "Jewish" or "Christian" to some phenomena prior to approximately 135 C.E."[34] History reports that "Roman Christianity was thoroughly Jewish, and long after the apostolic age it continued to exhibit certain . . . features, moreover, which seem to be more characteristic of nonconformist Judaism than of the main stream.[35]

In the broader scope of Judaism and Christianity, several hundred years of development may have allowed a wide variety of Christian segmentation and sects to develop before the complete transfer of Church power shifted from Jerusalem to Rome. Recent archeological finds confirm this view that Jews and Christians were not separated by the wide gaps generally imagined. Some of the early Christian groups can now be identified as extremely Jewish in their orientation. It can also be shown that the Jewishness of the sects were not mysteriously "gentilized," nor did they disappear with the advent of Pauline soteriology. As early as 70 CE, when the Temple was destroyed, several sects of Jewish Christians had already begun reformatting their theological views. It is now recognized that Jewish forms of Christianity existed long after Gentile Christianity became the norm.

> From their disputations at Pella in the hills opposite Beit She'an, a host of Judeo-Christian sects would emerge.
>
> Now, Dr. Claudine Dauphin, a French archeologist who spent years surveying sites on the southern Golan Heights, has produced evidence that at least one of these Judeo-Christian groups, the Ebionites, survived into the fourth century as a thriving community.
>
> Her findings tend to support the hotly disputed contention by Franciscan scholars that Judeo-Christians were responsible for preserving the tradition of Christian sites in the Holy Land for centuries until gentile Christians took over. . . . The Franciscans held, for instance, that it was Judeo-Christians who preserved the tradition of sites like the Grotto of the Annunciation in Nazareth until the Church of the Gentiles took over in the second half of the fourth century.[36]

"Belief in Jesus' resurrection and status as messiah was the focal point of differentiation between Christian and non-Christian Jews."[37] Presumably, all would agree with that basic overview of the distinctions. The timing of the separation and the events that incited the division is not quite so distinct.

When did Early Christianity cease to be a Jewish sect? One Jewish scholar, Shaye J.D. Cohen suggests it occurred "when it ceased to observe Jewish practices. It abolished circumcision and became a religious movement overwhelmingly gentile in composition and character."[38] Cohen suggests, and I heartily agree, that the Church opted out of its Jewish character early in the second century. He says, "Its practices no longer those of the Jews, its theology no longer that of the Jews, and its composition no longer Jewish, the Christianity of the early second century c.e. was no longer a Jewish phenomenon but a separate religion."[39]

Admittedly, Jewish influence diminished in the Church but the imprint remained. The Jews within the early Christian Church did not evaporate at the end of the second century CE. Different Jewish-Christian sects continued to exist in decreasing numbers for several hundred years. As Gentile Christianity expanded, Jewish Christianity became a less acceptable form of religion to mainline Jews and the emerging Church. The fact of their existence is unquestionable. The level of their influence may have diminished proportionately to their numbers. They did not automatically assimilate into the Gentile Church, nor return to Judaism, instead, they "persisted through the first five or six centuries c.e."[40] To discard their existence is as illogical as denying the Jewishness of early believers in Christ.

Jewish Christians led the Church for many years after the ascension of Jesus, and their influence has not been fairly understood since that time. Misunderstandings about the Jewish nature of early Christianity has led to profound misunderstandings about the actions and attitudes of the various groups of Jews described in the New Testament. When a correct historical perspective of first century Jews, Jewish Christians, and the other people of the New Testament is understood, then a proper view of the events described can be ascertained with more clarity.

---

9 Shaye J. D. Cohen, *From the Maccabees to the Mishnah*, (Philadelphia: The Westminster Press, 1987), 47-48.
    10 Ibid., 48.
    11 Ibid.
    12 William Nicholls, *Christian Antisemitism: A History of Hate*, (Northvale, New Jersey: Jason Aronson Inc., 1993), xix.
    13 As generally preferred by Jewish writers, the abbreviations BCE and CE will be used respectively indicating "Before the Common Era" and "Common Era" in place of BC and AD, except as used by other writers in quotes.
    14 Cohen, 49.
    15 Ibid., 48.
    16 Ibid.

17 William G. MacDonald, "The Biblical Doctrine of Election," in *The Grace of God, The Will of Man*, Clark H. Pinnock, Editor, (Grand Rapids, MI: Academie Books, 1989), 215.

18 James C. Vanderkam, "Implications for the History of Judaism and Christianity," *The Dead Sea Scrolls: After Forty Years*, (Washington, DC: Biblical Archaeology Society, 1992), 16.

19 Ibid.

20 Robert Gorham Davis, "Passion at Oberammergau," *Commentary* 29 (March 1960), 203.

21 Eusebius, Pamphilus, *The Ecclesiastical History of*, Translated by Christian Frederick Cruse, (Grand Rapids, Michigan: Baker Book House, 1992), 130.

22 Aviel Schneider, Editor, *Israel Today*, Jerusalem, January 2004, 20.

23 F. F. Bruce, *New Testament History*, (Garden City, NY: Doubleday & Company, Inc., 1980), 297.

24 Ibid.

25 Ibid.

26 Nicholls, xxvi.

27 William Sanford La Sor, David Allan Hubbard, and Frederic William Bush, *Old Testament Survey*, (Grand Rapids, Michigan: Wm. B. Eerdmans Publishing Company, 1982), 365.

28 H. F. D. Sparks, Editor, *The Apocryphal Old Testament*, (Oxford: Oxford University Press, 1990), 169.

29 Jeffrey, D. L. (1992). *A Dictionary of Biblical Tradition in English Literature*. Grand Rapids, Mich.: W.B. Eerdmans.

30 Cohen, 143.

31 Ibid., 17.

32 David Flusser, *The Spiritual History of the Dead Sea Sect*, (Tel-Aviv, Israel: MOD Books, 1989), 15.

33 Bruce, 299.

34 James H. Charlesworth, Editor, <u>Explorations</u>, *"Jews," "Pagans," and "Christians" in Antiquity and Our Search for "The Next Step,"* Volume 8, Number 1 1994, 1.

35 Ibid.

36 Abraham Rabinovich, *The Jerusalem Post International Edition*, "The Judeo-Christians in Israel," December 11, 1993, 9.

37 Cohen, 168.

38 Ibid.

39 Ibid.

40 Ibid.

Chapter III

The Jewish/Christian Divide–a Religion in Revolution

The Jewish people left an indelible mark on Roman history. The Jews were the first subjects to revolt against the Roman oppressors and they were not satisfied mounting only one revolution. They enacted two separate failed revolts. The first Jewish revolt of approximately 70 CE brought the destruction of the Temple. The Second Jewish Revolt of approximately 132 CE brought Rome's "scorched earth" policy, which resulted in the utter annihilation of Jerusalem.

Hadrian led this devastating second Roman invasion of Jerusalem. Many believe the fateful Second Jewish Revolt was a direct result of Hadrian's ban on circumcision. This was the action that precipitated the uprising led by Ben-Kosebah. It was also this event that ultimately led to the final separation between Jewish Christians from the remaining Jews who joined in the revolution.[41] Both groups undoubtedly remained connected to the Abrahamic covenant as well as to the specific sign of the covenant evidenced in male circumcision. The schism developed because the Jewish Christians could not take part in the latter revolt against Rome. This was not because of any unwillingness to fight alongside their brothers in the Jewish military. Rather, it was exclusively a result of the misguided messianic claims of Jewish leadership. The Christians could not serve two masters.

Regardless of the cost socially, politically, or otherwise, Jewish Christians could not join their friends, families, and neighbors in their final fight against Rome. They could not follow Ben-Kosebah into battle because he had been widely acknowledged as the messiah of Israel. This Second Jewish revolt was therefore a dramatic turning point for the early Jewish Church. The obvious lack of support by Jewish Christians at that critical time in Jewish history led to the disintegration of relations between non-Christian Jews and the Jewish Christians of the era. Jewish Christians could not join in a revolt led by a messianic pretender. They believed Jesus was the Messiah. The result led to the great divide between Jews and Jewish believers in Jesus.

Ben-Kosebah was better known as Bar Cochba, meaning "the son of the star." His title referred back to Balaam's prediction in Numbers 24:17 depicting a "star out of Jacob." His detractors stylized his name into an insult, Bar-Koziba, "the son of falsehood." The revolt changed the relations between Jews, Romans, and Christians forever. Though Bar Cochba was not the messiah, as proclaimed by Judaism's famous Rabbi Akiba, he definitely ushered in a new age—an age of terror from Rome.

A Jewish Legend and a Roman Emperor

An interesting Jewish legend has developed around Onkelos, a nephew of Hadrian. This ancient Jewish story might help to inform modern Gentile Christians about the beauty of Judaism. The legend focuses on Onkelos, who was a famous ancient Jewish sage. He is known as "the proselyte." It is said that after visiting Jerusalem, Onkelos decided to become a Jew. He studied under Rabbi Eliezer ben Hyrcanus and Rabbi Joshua ben Chananiah. This experience led to his conversion. He learned the Torah and faithfully followed Judaism. This would have been odd enough, given the poor conditions that Jews suffered under the Roman occupation during the reign of Emperor Hadrian. The situation was even more incredible because Onkelos was a close relative of Hadrian.

The story goes that after Emperor Hadrian realized the dilemma posed by his nephew's conversion, he sent soldiers from Rome to bring Onkelos back from Palestine. After his conversion to Judaism, he stayed in Palestine studying the Holy Writings of Judaism. He apparently learned some wonderful truths about the God of the Jews. When the soldiers that had been sent from Hadrian reached Onkelos to remove him with force, Onkelos said, "Let me tell you one thing: among people it is customary that the one of lessor rank lights the way for those of higher rank, but my God is the greatest and still he lights the way that people may see where to go."[42] It is said that the soldiers were converted after hearing of Onkelos' wondrous God. Hadrian sent more soldiers to complete the job of bringing Onkelos back to Rome. This time, the emperor warned the soldiers not to talk to Onkelos. They reached their destination and proceeded to capture their prize for the journey home.

> As they were emerging from the house with him, he placed his hand on the *mezuzah*[43] and said to them: "See the difference between a human ruler and the great God of Israel. A human ruler stays within his house and his guards stay at the gate, but here the people stay inside the house, while the king stays at the door to guard them." Hearing this these soldiers also were converted and the emperor sent no more soldiers to bring Onkelos back.[44]

Like those soldiers, Gentile Christians should be stricken with the beauty and love of God portrayed within Judaism. Conversion to Judaism is not the issue; tolerance is. Gentile Christians must learn to find the hatred of Jewish people to be an insult to God. God most certainly does! Agreement is not a requirement; but love is mandatory.

Jewish Christians were alienated from Judaism after the time of Hadrian. It was during this Second Jewish Revolt that the followers of Jesus were alienated from those who eventually followed Bar Cochba. The revolt was a complete disaster. It brought the total destruction of Jerusalem sending the Jews who survived into the Diaspora. Gentile Christians continued to thrive in the Church and Jewish Christianity soon lost favor among the Gentile believers as well.

Replacement Theology

Conditions deteriorated between Jews and Christians until the Church led the world into the anti-Semitic excesses of the era known as the Dark Ages. It is worth remembering that the Dark Ages of the Gentile world revealed a renaissance of Jewish literature and philosophy. While the Gentile world floundered in illiteracy, the Jewish world gave rise to the birth of talmudic writings and rabbinic literature that might best be described as an era of Jewish Enlightenment. Yet the Christian world seethed with hatred against everything Jewish. And it was during these

Dark Ages that conditions further deteriorated for Jews. The history of the Church was marred by abominable medieval Christian atrocities against Jews.

The Church, as the "new Israel," attacked the original children of Israel with an unholy vengeance. Christian theologians boldly revealed their propensity to interpret the promises of God as having been shifted from Israel to the Church. In their view, Christianity got the blessings and the Jews retained the curses of God. As the theology of the Church solidified, their perspective on Jews and Judaism decomposed. The Church's premier thinkers inadvertently became the Jew's worst nightmare.

Aurelius Augustinus, the bishop of Hippo (354 - 430), better known as Saint Augustine, was a leader of the Church during the fourth and fifth centuries CE. Under his guidance, Christianity slid deeply into the error of anti-Semitism. It can be deduced from the teachings of Augustine that the Church came to a view that the Jews were a lost race without hope of redemption. The Church determined that Israel had forfeited her covenants by rejecting Christ. Augustinian theology provided for a dramatic shift in Catholic politics, worldviews, and eschatology. The leaders of the Church of Rome began to teach that all the future messianic promises of natural Israel were transferred to the new spiritual Israel—the Church.

The Roman Catholic Church appropriated the system of interpretation first developed by Origen in the early 2nd century. This permitted Church leaders to develop their own symbolic interpretations of the Bible. As the theology of Augustine became popularized, the Church soon began teaching that God had chosen the Church to receive all of the promises previously granted to Israel as a divine right of Christianity. To the detriment of the Jewish people, this dangerous system of thought continued to expand throughout the region touched by Church authority. That authority did expand to include as much political control as the Church could gain in the world. During portions of the Middle Ages, the Church was in a position of power that covered most of the continent of Europe. Unfortunately, the beliefs and practices of the Church that ruled Europe did not reflect the original orthodox views of the earlier leaders of the Church in Israel. It is clear from the accounts of history that when the Church was dominant in both religion and politics, it led to some of the most oppressive periods of Christianity. Sadly, it must also be admitted that the negative effects of power were felt by both Christians and those outside of the Church.

Augustine's teaching did not lose impact after his death. His views prevailed and furthered the depreciation of the Jewish people. Any system of Christian thought that presents the Church as having spiritually taken the place of Israel, such as Replacement Theology, or Dominion Theology,[45] is heavily dependent on the system of early Catholic biblical interpretation developed by Origen and Augustine.

This perverted heresy worked its way deep into the beliefs of the Roman Church. The effects have been felt in many Christian circles since the early fifth century when it became embedded in the spiritual DNA of many Christians. Soon the Church espoused the view that it had become heir to the covenant promises of God previously granted to Israel. This also included the Church's right to the Holyland. Some within the Catholic Church still hold the hope of a spiritual claim to Israel. I believe it is one of the reasons they refused to recognize the nation of Israel until recently. Instead of leaving Jerusalem under the control of Jews, Some Catholics would have preferred that the Vatican be granted control over the Holyland and the holy sites.

Modern history is closely connected to ancient history. In a sense, the Jews were in the way of the Church then. The Jews remain in the way now. The difference is that at that earlier time, the Church used its new-found political power to move the Jews out of their way. They did so by enacting and enforcing terrible anti-Jewish legislation. This wicked practice was one of the sad legacies of the era of Christian political dominion. As is well known by Jewish people, the Church was the primary source of problems throughout the Middle Ages. It must be remembered that the Church used terror and violence to control the Jews. And they used brute force to convert Jews to Christianity. It was common for Christians to exert political oppression and every form of cruelty to dominate Jews or kill them when it suited the oppressors.

Beginning in the Dark Ages and continuing throughout the Middle Ages, anti-Semitism came to the world from the Church. Jewish people were permitted to live in Christian controlled areas. However, this was not due to any beneficent attitudes. Rather, it was to prove the veracity of the Old Testament prophecies. Christian leaders, such as Augustine, presumed that Scriptures predicted that the Jews would be rejected and dispersed. Therefore, when Jews were found to be living below the standards of Christians, even if under horrifying circumstances, it revealed divine punishment and prophetic fulfillment. Jewish suffering proved God's will according to the perverse view of some Christians in that age. (For more information about the history of Christian anti-Semitism, please see the book titled, _Does Jacob's Trouble Wear a Cross?_ By Randy Weiss, published by Excellence in Christian Books and in electronic form through Logos Research Systems, Inc.)

God Has Not Disowned His Firstborn

Wrong views about God's love for Israel did not disappear with the further spread of Christianity. William G. MacDonald exhibits one other very dangerous assumption that has been widely believed and misapplied.

> Therefore, though the church in a metaphorical sense can be called "the Israel of God" (Gal. 6:16) because believers all have the faith of Abraham, it could no longer be said that nominal Israel remained God's special people of favor. They are "loved on account of the patriarchs" (Rom. 11:28), but not justified apart from faith in Jesus (Gal. 2:15-16). Since they rejected God's *chosen Servant* (Matt. 12:18), even his *chosen Son* (Luke 9:35), they could not spurn "the Seed to whom the promise [to Abraham] referred" (Gal. 3:19) and still maintain their historical Abrahamic status. For God has indicated, beginning with Jesus' anointing beside the Jordan River, the one "seed"—not "seeds"—that he had chosen (Gal. 3:16). They could no longer be associated with Abraham legitimately if they rejected Christ; any subsequent participation in Abrahamic election would be valid only "if they do not persist in unbelief" in Jesus (Rom. 11:23).[46]

This view, carried to its logical conclusion, has been abused by Christian anti-Semites for many centuries. This does not suggest that either Pinnock or those authors included in the book he edited, such as MacDonald, are anti-Semitic. Actually, they are all outstanding Christian theologians. However, similar conclusions have been drawn by anti-Semites and used to the detriment of the Jewish people. There is an implication that by rejecting Jesus, the Jews opted out of remaining God's chosen people. This notion must be discarded to make room for a clearer understanding. "Nominal Israel" has *not* been disposed by God! "Nominal Israel" has an unbroken "historical Abrahamic status" and is forever "associated with Abraham legitimately" apart from good beliefs, bad beliefs, or unbelief! It will not be disputed that Jews will not be "justified apart from faith in Jesus" (Gal. 2:15-16). Neither will it be ignored that "there is none other name under heaven given among men, whereby we must be saved"

(Acts 4:12b KJV). However, these issues should not be reduced to a discussion of Christian soteriology. The children of Israel are "loved on account of the patriarchs." The Church should forever settle this issue and also love Israel.

One clear example from Scripture may clarify this difficult premise. God chose to remind Moses and his desert wanderers of their history of rebellious behavior prior to leading them over the River Jordan. He wanted to make sure that they all understood that His actions were not in any way based on their virtues. God told Moses, "Know therefore that it is not for thy righteousness that the LORD thy God giveth thee this good land to possess it; for thou art a stiffnecked people" (Deut. 9:4-6). God chose to bless the children of Israel in spite of themselves. He did it because He had a covenant with their forefathers and God wanted to perform what was promised in that agreement "that He may establish the word which He swore to Abraham, to Isaac, and to Jacob" (Deuteronomy 9:5b). It is exactly as Paul explained in Romans 11:28: God blessed the children because He was in relationship with their fathers.

The behavior of a child cannot change a promise made by the father, unless it was conditioned on the behavior of the child. If God had been predisposed to make a promise to Abraham that he might choose to take away from later generations, that fact would have been disclosed to Abraham. Nowhere does the Hebrew Bible imply that the link will ever be broken between God and the children of Israel. Plagues, punishments, exile, enslavement, suffering may occur, but the Jews will remain the chosen people throughout time because God chose them.

A Jew is a child of Abraham if he is actually descended from Abraham. His faith is not directly related to his blood. The following logic might explain this as follows: If a father has legal title to a promissory note that is assignable to his heirs, upon the father's death, his estate would include that note as an asset of the estate. The heirs would then be entitled to the value of the note unless it was conditioned to the contrary. The heir might believe in Jehovah, he might believe in Jesus, he might believe in the Tooth Fairy, regardless of his belief system, if he is an heir, the content of the estate passes according to the will.

So as not to confuse anyone, I must explain that in my view, Christian salvation and Jewish choseness are *not* equivalents. Nonetheless, the love of God is secure. Some do propose that God changed His mind about the promises granted to the Jews. This is usually loosely based upon a view that the promises to the people were lost when certain particular Jews joined in the effort to have Jesus crucified. To those who submit to that odd view, I must ask if God changed His mind once, how do you know He won't change His mind again? If God turned His back on the Jews, how can you be sure He won't turn His back on you? If God rejected the Jewish people due to the wrong actions of certain Jews, what if certain Christians participate in wrong actions? Will you be judged for their behavior?

It has been established that the Church is responsible for creating anti-Semitism with its accompanying accusations of deicide. As the Church shifted toward Roman leadership, the gulf between Jews and Christians widened. Eventually, Jewish hatred was rampant in the Church and churchmen were capable of actions such as the Crusades and the Spanish Inquisition.

Information dispels the power of hatred. Will the sins of the fathers be visited upon, and reenacted, by the children of future generations? Perhaps a clearer view toward ancient errors will help insure correct behavior. When identified, these errors are easy to recognize. When understood, they are easier to avoid. The Church must look back if it is to protect the future. In an effort to understand modern expressions of Christian anti-Semitism, it will be helpful to identify several medieval examples of these distortions to consider their effects then and now. The errors in the pattern of the passion play grew out of the twisted interpretations of Church leaders from that era of darkness. The problem will be more carefully evaluated in the following chapter.

---

41 Bruce, 390.

42 Gershom Bader, translated by Solomon Katz, *The Encyclopedia of Talmudic Sages*, (Northvale, New Jersey: Jason Aronson, Inc., 1988), 223.

43 A *Mezuzah* is a decorative Jewish object containing certain portions of the Old Testament on a small scroll attached to the entry doorposts of Jewish homes.

44 Bader, 224. Taken from *Avodah Zarah* 11a.

45 Dominion Theology is a system of thought that also presumes that the Church has replaced Israel. An interesting text that deals with that topic in depth is Hal Lindsey's, *The Road To Holocaust*.

46 Pinnock, 218.

Chapter IV

Passion Plays & Other Examples of Medieval Anti-Semitism

During the Middle Ages, the Church had so much political power that it was able to legislate the Jews into near oblivion. The Jews of England were expelled in 1290. This was long before much of the greatest medieval English literature was produced. Geoffrey Chaucer's *Prioress's Tale*, of the famous *Canterbury Tales*, John Gower's *Confessio Amantis*, and William Langland's *The Vision of Piers Plowman* were all written nearly a century after the Jews were removed from the homeland of these authors. Since the Jews did not resettle in England until 1656, even Shakespeare's writings came during an era when England's Jews were in exile. Shakespeare promoted a distorted view of his Jewish characters in spite of the fact that he had probably never seen a Jewish person during his lifetime.

> The figure of the Jew was therefore almost certainly not drawn from life, but rather from imagination and popular tradition, the latter a mixture of prejudice and idealization. This approach is not untypical of medieval writing generally, which often used stereotypes and symbols and gave them concrete shape . . . The stage Jew down to the Elizabethan period looked rather like the Devil in the old mystery plays, and was very often dressed in a similar costume.[47]

Shakespeare and Classical Anti-Semitism

One of the most famous literary examples of a terrible Jewish stereotype comes from the work of William Shakespeare. He provides a dramatic description of how the character of Jewish people were distorted by Gentile writers to Gentile audiences. In his *Merchant of Venice* (c. 1596), Shylock (a money-lender) says to his audience about Antonio (the borrower's guarantor), "I hate him for he is a Christian! But more, for that, in low simplicity, he lends out money gratis, and brings down the rate of usance . . . He hates our sacred nation . . . Cursed be my tribe, if I forgive him!"[48] Within the same Act I, Scene III, of the play, further degrading dialogue presents Shylock mocking Christianity and accusing Jesus of having conjured up the devil. Before the scene concludes, Shylock insists that the Christian's promissory note contain the famous penalty permitting Shylock the literal right to personally cut off a pound of the borrower's flesh in case of a default. Shakespeare intentionally reduces the Jewish character to an inhumane, mean-spirited, legalistic enemy of the Christian. The "eye for an eye" harshness of the Jewish Mosaic code is symbolically contrasted with the more refined, elevated, Christian religion of love. Shylock, the Jewish character, is further depreciated by Antonio saying, "The devil can cite Scripture for his purpose. An evil soul, producing holy witness, is like a villain with a smiling cheek; a goodly apple rotten at the heart."[49] The Jew is represented as a bloodthirsty villain who would enjoy the painful death of a Christian. Two scenes later in the play, Launcelot Gobbo, the clown servant of Shylock, denigrates the Jewish character to the lowest level possible. Gobbo calls Shylock "a kind of devil; and, to run away from the Jew, I should be ruled by the fiend, who, saving your reverence, is the devil himself. Certainly the Jew is very devil incarnal."[50]

Medieval Passions and the Passion Play

The problem of perverting the image of Jews was not exclusively limited to English stage presentations. Anti-Semitism is an ancient Christian phenomenon that has a long history with many tracks to follow. Christian authors have characterized the Jews as evil for many centuries. Shakespeare was certainly not the first to characterize a Jew as the devil.

> The evil stereotype of the Jew is clearly based on the Christian account of the crucifixion of Jesus, including his betrayal by Judas (identified with the Jews in general) and his

often-stated enmity toward the Jewish scribes and Pharisees. This provided the basis for the image of the Jew in the early mystery or "miracle" plays, current from the 13th century, which presented the Bible records in dramatic form. [51]

English literature was not alone in promoting certain anti-Semitic allegations. German literature and drama also created an atmosphere to devalue the Jewish people.

> The medieval miracle or mystery plays, in Germany as in England and France, dramatized Old Testament themes and treated the Hebrew patriarchs with reverence, but the "passion plays" based upon the New Testament made the post-biblical Jew a demonic ally of the Devil. For special historical reasons, this latter portrayal came to have serious popular repercussions."[52]

Dangerous anti-Semitic messages communicated through various forms of medieval expression contaminated generations of Christian audiences with perverted views toward Jews and Judaism. In an insightful article about the passion play, Robert Gorham Davis points out that the presentation

> combines some of the worst of medieval and modern prejudices. The sinister character given the Jew in popular literature of the Middle Ages so encouraged superstitious fears that at times of social disaster, as during the Black Death, whole communities of Jews were burned alive. Pogroms[53] were especially likely to occur during Holy Week as a result of the emotions aroused by Good Friday sermons.[54]

Traditionally, the passion play dramas are enacted during the most sacred time, Christendom's Easter season. Perhaps the poignancy of the Good Friday message dealing with the death of Jesus magnifies the bitter sentiment that is elicited from the passion play audience. Clearly the emotional peaks and valleys associated with an undeserved execution, followed by an unexpected resurrection, present scriptwriters with ample fodder to manipulate the feelings of their audience. Wrongly, this form of manipulation has been an error that has blemished the chronicles of the Church for centuries. The stage crews of modern Christianity continue to erect an ugly wall of anti-Semitic hatred that is hidden behind a thin curtain within the Church. As often presented, the passion play can be an unhealthy drama capable of damaging tenuous Jewish-Christian relations.

Drama and Art as Educational Tools

During the eleventh century, the average Christian layperson was unable to read the Bible or the meaningful texts of Church history. Reading was a rare skill among an uneducated populace. The great Christian classics of medieval paintings, sculptures, and frescoes presented many Christian men and women with much of their understanding of the Bible. Teaching from the pulpit often provided the balance of their limited religious training. Church sermons were some of the most stimulating and educational experiences available to medieval Christians.

It is important to remember that among an illiterate laity, the ministry of the Church was urgently needed to help them understand the Bible. They did not have radio or television to occupy their time. Neither did they carry "walkman" CD players or listen to Scripture tapes as they plowed the fields of the wealthy land barons. They depended on preaching to understand the Bible. They depended on the Church to inspire their faith. "The sermon, especially if preached with eloquence, was the most exciting event of the week and must have had a powerful emotional effect.[55]

The agenda of the leaders of the Church was promoted with intensity during the sermonizing. Medieval Christianity also brought drama to the people as a means of expressing the beliefs and doctrines of the Church. The passion play presentation developed and grew against this backdrop. Stirring renditions of the death of Christ were presented in the hopes of stimulating Christian worship and practice. However, they were accompanied by an undercurrent of Christian anti-Semitism. The Jewish people were blamed for Christ's suffering.

The liturgical dramatic presentations became an important method for churchmen to educate the unschooled Christian laity of the Middle Ages. The passion of Jesus and His violent sacrificial death was presented with all the poignancy that could be mustered on stage. The Jews were presented as the scoundrels who were responsible for the death of Christ. "The Jew, the villain of the piece, was usually depicted in contemporary dress, with moneybags hanging from his belt, wearing the yellow Jewish hat, and sometimes with red hair, . . . a symbol of evil to the audience." This method of working up the emotions of the audience was extremely effective. It served to help them relate to the sufferings of Jesus. Unfortunately, the closer they related and were impacted by the pain and torment of Jesus, "the more they hated those who were supposed to have caused the suffering." This led to the dramatic stage form whereby "in a collective form, the Jewish people appeared in the character of Synagogue, portrayed as blindfolded, with broken banner, and grasping a goat's head, a symbol of Old Testament sacrifices and of Jewish stubbornness and unchastity.[56]

The Legend of Oberammergau

The error of the passion play is not new. This error remains. One such production has been performed in nearly every decade since 1634. "Of all the pageants that dramatize the Crucifixion story, the most famous undoubtedly is the Passion Play performed every ten years at Oberammergau, in the solidly Roman Catholic region of Upper Bavaria, in West Germany."[57]

The world famous production in Oberammergau began after the Thirty Years' War (1618-1648). Popular legend suggests that when a horrible plague struck Bavaria, that village enacted a strict quarantine. They hoped to stop the transmission of the disease from other communities. A worker named Caspar Schuchler carried the illness back from a neighboring village during a secret visit to see his wife. Within thirty-three days, more than eighty-four townspeople died. The colorful history of the production at Oberammergau was allegedly built upon that tragedy. As a result of that tragic event, the residents cried out to God. They jointly declared in a solemn vow that if God would spare their village from more sickness and death in that plague, "they and their descendants would perform a passion play every ten years. Once the vow was taken, according to the story, all those ill of the plague in Oberammergau recovered, and no one else contracted it."[58]

The Passion of Oberammergau

Many unfortunate representations of Jewish characters are a standard part of the Oberammergau production. For example, "Judas has always been very much the stereotyped Jew in appearance, dark-visaged with 'poison-yellow garb' and moneybag."[59] Interestingly, the actors portraying Jesus and the Virgin Mary have normally been cast with conspicuously Nordic features.

The Oberammergau villagers were not the first to present such a production. Actually, during the early 1600's Bavaria could boast of more than sixty other similar passion play productions. Oberammergau's rendition is merely the oldest functioning pageant. In 1970, 500,000 people were expected to watch the production in Bavaria showing the Jews sending Jesus to his death. Although the script for the production had undergone several revisions between 1660 and 1860, during that two hundred year period, monastery-trained priests took responsibility for the textual content. The 1860 version of the script was written by a priest named Joseph Alois Daisenberger. Since then, except for short periods, the script has remained fairly constant allowing mainly for changes related to acting methods and production enhancements. The basic scheme remained the same. One constant current throughout the tradition of passion play presentations seems to be the mass of bloodthirsty Jews calling for the execution of Christianity's gentle Son of God. The sensational wicked behavior of the Jews has become a significant component of the pronounced anti-Semitic aspect of typical passion play presentations. The monstrous consequence of these dramatic re-enactments is that it transfers the guilt and shame from the individual Jewish participants involved in the arrest and trial of Jesus, onto the Jewish people in general. It is normative, sometimes unwittingly, for passion plays to include "a strong anti-Jewish component, focused not only on Jesus' individual Jewish antagonists, but—by implication or explicit statement—on the Jewish people as a whole."

This conclusion about the Oberammergau Passion Play was reached after objective line-by-line review of the Oberammergau script by Mrs. Judith H. Banki, the Assistant Director of Interreligious Affairs for the American Jewish Committee, in conjunction with Dr. Gerald S. Strober, a Presbyterian educator. Their findings were made available to German government leaders, church leaders, the German press, the Catholic hierarchy, as well as to a distinguished group of Catholic and Protestant theologians. Their conclusions suggested that the script was free of "19th- and 20th-century-style racism; but it abounds with anti-Jewish religious prejudices and misstatements long established in popular tradition."[60] It is these commonly believed misconceptions that passion play errors convey from generation to generation.

Undoubtedly, this anti-Semitic message was successfully communicated to countless millions of medieval and modern spectators. One such visitor was so moved that he decreed, "It is vital that the Passion Play be continued at Oberammergau; for never has the menace of Jewry been so convincingly portrayed."[61] This forceful endorsement came directly from Adolf Hitler!

Hitler was one of the play's most ardent fans. This should not be surprising. After personally reviewing and studying the passion play, he believed that it supported and promoted his plans for Aryan domination. More delightful to Hitler was the fact that it cast the Jews as the wicked servants of evil as he wanted the world to identify. "Under the Nazi government, the Oberammergau Passion Play was classified as a 'racially important cultural document,' and on the occasion of the pageant's tercentennial, in 1934, a Nazified special performance represented Jesus and his disciples as Aryan heroes."[62] This fact should not be astonishing. Georg Johann Lang the director of the play from 1922 until after the war was one of the first men in Oberammergau to become a Nazi and "in 1946 was arrested by the occupation authorities because of his work for Goebbels' propaganda ministry."[63] Contrariwise, what should be very surprising is the fact that Lang was *again* placed in charge of the entire production in 1950! Could any reader be so naïve as to think that a Nazi would present an unbiased view of the Jews in the Passion of Jesus? Yet that was the condition that existed from 1922 continuing throughout the war years. Then the same Nazi was put in charge again in 1950. Perhaps that is why no memorial marks the site of the Oberammergau passion play to acknowledge that less than ten years before Lang was reinstated to coordinate that Christian drama, "bulldozers were literally covering with hills of earth the mass graves of Jewish women and children."[64]

Christian Century reported on December 4, 1946, in an article by Willard A. Heaps, that 151 members of the cast of the play were members of the Nazi party. The list included the actors who portrayed Jesus Christ and the Virgin Mary. Further, of the ten leading actors, nine were Nazis. Only the actor who portrayed Judas Iscariot remained anti-Nazi among the leading roles. These facts most certainly carried serious implications. The anti-Semitic leanings of the Church, the cast, and the community have undoubtedly facilitated the furtherance of anti-Semitic slurs contained within the play. Apparently, worldwide Christian audiences heartily approve. This can only be adjudged by 360 years of endurance with continued financial success.

Addressing the Problem of Oberammergau

Several Jewish and Christian scholars have objected to the manner in which the Jewish people have been represented in the Oberammergau production. Even the Declaration on Non-Christian Religions of 1965 which came out of the Second Vatican Council's recommendations did not accomplish a meaningful change in the content of that famous Christian drama. Father Stephan Schaller, a respected scholar and the headmaster of a school attached to a nearby monastery, was asked to draft a revised version of the script for the 1970 production. His version, though more accurate and less inflammatory, was rejected by Mr. Preisinger, the play's producer. Father Schaller, who had honestly endeavored to defuse some of the more provocative anti-Semitic flaws in the script, commented about the gauge for accurately evaluating the script as seen by those involved in the community.[65] "The locals believe they have one irrefutable argument to prove they are right – enormous financial profit at the end of the season, making them the richest village in Bavaria."[66] In 1969, it was estimated that box office sales were to reach at least $2,880,000 for the 1970 production. Beyond that, the town expected to reap an additional $3,600,000 from the tourists who were to visit the area to enjoy the spectacle. I am pleased to report that in 2000, the line from Matthew's gospel, "His blood be on us, and on our children," was removed from the script after inciting audiences for more than 350 years.

Separating Passion Fiction From New Testament Fact

There is a remarkable discrepancy between the drama portrayed in the passion play and the actual New Testament account of the arrest, trial, conviction, and execution of Jesus. This discrepancy presents its own condemning proof of Christian anti-Semitism. One such discrepancy is evidenced by the horrifying characterization of the Jews as violent turncoats who, to their own universal condemnation, rejected Jesus and had Him killed. The specific charge of deicide, as associated with Christianity's invention of anti-Semitism, has clung to Jews since the third century. According to Father Edward H. Flannery, since that early point in Church history, the Jews have been presented as "a people punished for their deicide who can never hope to escape their misfortunes." The perverse attitude that is widely held presumes that Jewish suffering is the will of God because of the Crucifixion. Father Flannery expressed his view stating that, "This thesis formed the first seeds of an attitude that would greatly dominate Christian thinking in the fourth century and greatly contribute thereafter to the course of anti-Semitism."[67] Personally, I find it horrifying that the depiction of the event that set sinners free is used by anti-Semites to bind guilt to my people.

The Church will be severely handicapped if it attempts to correct the excesses and errors associated with Christian anti-Semitism if it is unwilling to remove obvious anti-Semitic characterizations from other influential Christian expression. When religious errors are retained for centuries, they become ingrained in the nature of the religion. As in many long-established religions, the traditions often replace the basis of original beliefs. It would be correct to say that this has always been one of the standard accusations against the religion of the Jews made by Christians. The same consideration herein applies to the passion play, so beloved within Christendom. The distorted presentation of Jews as it relates to the arrest, trial, and execution of Jesus "derives from a tradition which had its beginnings in the preaching and teaching of the Christian Church in its early days, and which became solidified between 250 and 450 A.D."[68]

With no intention of denigrating the severity of Christ's suffering or misinterpreting the sanctity of the event, one writer has suggested that Jesus "got off His cross after but a few hours; but, *for two thousand years now, generation after generation, Jews have been nailed afresh to theirs. Why?*"[69] Perhaps the answer to "Why?" lies buried beneath nearly eighteen centuries of misguided interpretation. The actual circumstances surrounding the death of Jesus cannot be perfectly recreated. There is simply not enough information or documented facts to insure the fullest understanding. However, the New Testament provides sufficient information to argue against the most popular understanding of what occurred on the night before the death of Jesus. *Like Jesus, the Jewish people may have been convicted of a crime they did not commit.*

---

47 *Encyclopedia Judaica*, 1978 ed., S.v. "English Literature."

48 William Shakespeare, *The Works of William Shakespeare*, (London: Studio Editions Ltd., 1993), 391.

49 Ibid., 392.

50 Ibid., 394.

51 *Encyclopedia Judaica*, 1978 ed., s.v. "English Literature."

52 *Encyclopedia Judaica*, 1978 ed., s.v. "German Literature."

53 Pogroms were organized beatings, attacks, and/or massacres of Jews. Generally, these were sanctioned by the government.

54 Robert Gorham Davis, 199.

55 Nicholls, 252.
56 Ibid., 252.
57 Judith Banki and George S. Strober, *Oberammergau 1960 and 1970: A Study in Religious Anti-Semitism*, by the American Jewish Committee, (Institute of Human Relations of the American Jewish Committee, New York, NY, 1970), 3.
58 Davis, 201.
59 Ibid., 200.
60 Banki and Strober, 3.
61 Ibid.
62 Ibid.
63 Davis, 198.
64 Ibid., 199.
65 Liel Leibovitz, *The Jerusalem Report*, "Putting 'The Passion' in Perspective," (March 22, 2004), 41.
66 "Passion at Oberammergau," *Institute of Jewish Affairs* in association with the World Jewish Congress, Background Paper No. 15, (December 1969), 1.
67 Banki and Strober, 18-19.
68 Ibid.
69 Jeffrey L. Seif, *Origin of the Christian Faith*, (Dallas, TX: JSM Publishing, 1992), 112.

Chapter V

The Passion Error

With continued malice, the Jewish race has been presented as a mob of violent, vicious, angry, treacherous, bitter malcontents, who are blamed for the crucifixion. The New Testament provides an interesting contrast about the Jewish people and their alleged hatred of their kinsman, Jesus of Nazareth. There is an especially expressive scene that portrays the triumphant entry of Jesus into Jerusalem. Jesus received a welcome party that might be compared to a modern ticker-tape parade. He was a hero of the people. The news had rapidly spread that Jesus was healing sick folk and casting out demons. Some believed he was their long-awaited Messiah sent to deliver the Jewish people from Rome's oppressive domination. No evidence suggests that these same Jews loved him on Palm Sunday and hated him on Good Friday. No text within the New Testament offers any hint that His Jewish admirers did a complete and violent turn-about (other than Judas) to demand his arrest or execution. A few accounts reveal that His message was not always received by all hearers. Perhaps that merely shows the honesty of a realistic report. No public speaker pleases everyone, everywhere, every time; not even Jesus. With respect to the inherently critical slant of the Bible, it is correct to consider that the Jewish writers have historically been unashamedly willing to display their own mistakes. Unfortunately, Gentile readers have abused and misused their openness.

Both the Old and the New Testament contain many passages harshly critical of the Jewish people. What was and often still is disregarded is that these strictures were uttered by persons—Jesus being one of them—who were themselves Jews. In all periods, the Jews have been strongly given to self-criticism; perhaps no other people have so candidly recorded its failings in its official history. But only too often Christians have used these Biblical passages as a stick to beat the Jews with, while claiming Biblical blessings and promises for themselves as successors to the covenant.[70]

Most readers admit that Jesus was opposed by an angry faction within a segment of Jerusalem's Jewish leadership. That fact must not be expanded into a view that Jesus was hated by all Jews, or all Jewish leaders of the era. "In many passages of the Gospel of John translators should now know that the appropriate rendering of *Ioudaioi*[71] is not 'Jews,' but 'Judaean leaders'."[72] It should not be presumed that a consensus existed against Jesus among the broad spectrum of Jews during the time of Jesus. This subject has already been addressed but it is imperative to understand that first century Judaism was not homogenous or uniform. Sectarian groups with diverse practices existed within Israel and the broader scope of world Jewry. These sects ranged from varying theological, political, and sociological views to actually having different beliefs about what was to be included in their sacred writings. In light of the diversity within Judaism, different sects would have responded to Jesus in different ways. Yet, as a result of the stereotyped casting of the Jewish participants in the passion play drama, it is possible that some visitors leave the spectacle convinced that the entire Jewish nation hated and rejected Jesus. This is a misrepresentation at best; and, it is a malicious attempt to promote religious hatred at worst.

The Messiah and Public Opinion

The Gospel of Matthew reports the following about the enthusiastic welcome of Jesus:

> A very great multitude spread their clothes on the road; others cut down branches from the trees and spread them on the road. Then the multitudes who went before and those who followed cried out, saying:
> "Hosanna to the Son of David! 'Blessed is He who comes in the name of the LORD!' Hosanna in the highest!" And when He had come into Jerusalem, all the city was moved (Matthew 21:8-10).

The entrance of Jesus into Jerusalem was a major event. The New English Bible suggests of the same reference that "Crowds of people carpeted the road with their cloaks . . . went wild with excitement."[73] J. B. Phillips' version says, "And as he entered Jerusalem a shock ran through the whole city."[74] It is unrealistic to suggest that Jesus suffered an overnight reversal in the opinion of the general public. Rather, the report pictures a hero's welcome for an expected, well-received dignitary. The Jews of the region were inclined to love Jesus and hate the Romans. Jesus fed the multitudes; the Romans taxed them. Rome sent domineering soldiers into Israel. Rome backed heavy-handed local politicians. Rome installed an oppressive style of government. Rome was despised by large segments of the Jewish citizenry. Jesus brought the people a reason to have hope.

Jesus arrived at an opportune time in Israel's history. Messianic expectations were abundant in that land of promise. More than once, false messiahs had raised the hopes of the hopeless. Judaism carried the promise of a Savior.[75] To many, Jesus appeared to be more effective than prior "messiahs" who preceded him. So, therefore, some of the Jewish followers of Jesus may have been upset that he was not an overnight socio-economic or political savior. Certainly, many Jews, including several of his disciples, misunderstood his reticence to actively and aggressively pursue his perceived "rightful" position as the promised Jewish deliverer. Although many impatient Jewish followers were disappointed, no implication suggests that they waited a few days after the Palm Sunday parade and decided to kill Jesus on Good Friday. It did not happen like that. The Jews were simply not prone or empowered to killing criminals.

Rabbi Tarphon, an early opponent of nascent Christianity was one of the most vehement antagonists of the Jewish Christians during the era. Nonetheless, he declared the specific tendency among Jews of his day to disdain execution for any reason. He states "that despite his angry disposition he nevertheless said that if he were a member of the Sanhedrin at the time when it had the right to condemn people to death, there would not have been a single death sentence passed."[76] It is unlikely that Rabbi Tarphon was alone in that sentiment. Jewish people had suffered greatly over many centuries at the hands of many political oppressors. Therefore, some would have been averse to a call for execution due only to religious differences. Jews were very accustomed to tolerating varied viewpoints. From that vantage point, the execution of Jesus would not have been tolerated by the mainstream of Jewish people had they been aware of it.

Though Jewish law permitted certain punishments, sensible men were normally responsible in the issuing of those most severe judgments. In spite of everything else, crucifixion was only an option for Rome. Neither the Temple police, nor the Sanhedrin had the authority to crucify Jesus. No Jew could make that decision reserved exclusively for Rome.

The Church: God's Avenger for the "Blood Curse"?

Christian anti-Semitism is birthed in misguided religious convictions. It is as if some form of mysterious "common knowledge" existed in the minds of some Christians who implied that Israel had rejected her Messiah and the Church had the duty to right that wrong. The Jewish author of a major portion of Christianity's sacred texts is credited with this reference from Deuteronomy 32:35: "Vengeance is mine; I will repay, saith the Lord." (Romans 12:19). Paul never added any commentary instructing Gentile Christians to act as God's avenger. This religious bigotry is a form of arrogance that presumes that only the Church had the spiritual insight to see what the "blind leaders of the blind" within first century Judaism could not see. More mysteriously, this view suggests that the Jews of the first century committed an unpardonable sin which destroyed all hope for all Jews of all times.

As a result of biblically near-sighted Christian teaching, Jews in general have been presented as a condemned race. When that Christian argument is based on the commonly held view that the first century Jews rejected Jesus, they patently ignore the fact that the early Christian Church was predominantly a Jewish organization. Therefore, Christian anti-Semites should be cautious when wielding their sword of Holy Writ invoking Matthew 27:25. They are quick to quote the Jewish detractors of Jesus who answered Pilate, saying, "His blood be on us and on our children." Rarely do they acknowledge that neither Mark, Luke, nor John recount such detail as described in that singular Matthean phrase.[77] Coincidentally, it is commonly ignored that in the Acts of the Apostles (probably written by the Gentile gospel writer of Luke), the Jewish leadership was particularly sensitive to that exact form of accusation. The Sadducean high priest publicly criticized the apostles in front of the Sanhedrin. It is apparent from the dialogue that they were particularly concerned about the Christians trying to "bring this Man's blood on us!" (Acts 5:28). More important to this investigation is the fact when that verse is quoted within the passion play, it suggests beyond any doubt that a giant angry mob of Jews were demanding the violent death of Jesus, while willingly bringing that horrible "blood curse" on all Jews of all times. With regard to the continual and apparently intentional misrepresentation of the "angry Jewish mob scene," several relevant concerns about the accuracy of that depiction will be considered.

The court area of Pilate could not have contained the enormous crowds often pictured. It is common for passion presentations to create the illusion that all the Jews of Jerusalem were jammed into the area to condemn Jesus. It is also the norm to cast them as an unruly mob on the verge of an uncontrollable riot. Pilate would not have permitted an unruly Jewish mob to demonstrate or react uncontrollably without violent Roman intervention. Without doubt, the Jewish leaders knew that fact better than anyone. They were committed to avoiding a confrontation with Roman authority at that time for fear of reprisals (such as occurred later in 70 CE and again in 132 CE).

Most significant, it is often overlooked that Pilate had already issued his sentence over Jesus of Nazareth by sunrise. John reports on the time of Pilate's judgment that it was "about the sixth hour" (John 19:14). Robertson's, *A Harmony of the Gospels* says concerning the matter of timing:

> It appears that John, who wrote in Asia Minor, long after the destruction of Jerusalem, makes the day begin at midnight, as the Greeks and Romans did. We seem compelled so to understand him . . . and in no passage of his Gospel is that view unsuitable. Here then we understand that Pilate passed the sentence about sunrise, which at Passover, near the vernal equinox, would be 6 o'clock.[78]

Therefore, it is highly unlikely that enormous crowds of angry Jews would have gathered at Pilate's before sunrise to hear judicial matters.

Most important to any investigation of this type, no group of Jews carried with them the consensus to represent all Jews of first century Judaism. Since Moses, no Jews at anytime have been empowered to represent all Jews of all times.

A serious error exists within the passion play presentation. It is imperative that modern Christian audiences recognize the intentional overemphasis that some passion plays infuse on the "blood curse" portion of the presentation. This particular Scripture may have been abused more by Christian anti-Semites than any other.

In popular anti-Jewish ideology, God's alleged rejection is usually assumed to extend to all present and future generations of Jews. This belief derives mainly from the Gospel report according to which the people themselves invited the responsibility for Jesus' execution by shouting: "His blood be upon us and our children."

The "blood curse" episode rests on a narrow Scriptural foundation . . . Nevertheless, the Passion Play—like countless anti-Jewish screeds through the centuries—makes much of it.[79]

The Oberammergau script of 1960 amplified the perception of universal Jewish guilt by inserting seven dramatically inflammatory references to the "blood curse" on the Jewish people. This "miraculous" multiplication of one phrase into seven suggests that *truth and Christian drama do not always share the same stage*. Jesus was famous for nourishing his audience by multiplying the "loaves and fishes." The passion play has provided poison multiplying hatred and condemnation.

Anti-Semitism and the Money-Changers

Anti-Semitism leaves a broad trail. Its identifying marks have been spread from the simplest Sunday school lessons to myths about Jewish wealth and greed. The tracks of anti-Semitism can be followed back to pulpits and passion play stages around the world. One such track will suggest that it is appropriate to reprocess information about the Jewish money-changers encountered by Jesus at the Temple. They have been understood to be greedy, archetypal Jewish villains. According to common Christian perception, they are classed among the most avaricious Jews involved in the gospel drama.

This errant view is harshly promoted in the Oberammergau production. For example, the moneychangers are given a place of much greater significance on stage than was ever granted in the Gospels. The New Testament writers only briefly mention that they were driven from the Temple by Jesus. Yet in the presentation at Oberammergau, they were "transmuted into a gang of traders and usurers who play a major role in Jesus' arrest. Bent on reimbursement and revenge for the losses they sustained when Jesus drove them from the Temple, they serve as intermediaries who induce Judas to betray Jesus."[80]

The moneychangers have generally been understood to be little more than religious mercenaries who were satiated through price-gouging the naive pilgrims who had come to worship and offer sacrifices. More than a few Sunday sermon topics have been preached about "righteous indignation" from that particular New Testament account which showed a stern side to Jesus. That "righteous indignation" allegedly displayed by Jesus is usually then contrasted with the greedy side of the Jewish moneychangers. Often inadvertently, "the greed of Jews" in general is promoted. The moneychangers were more than parasitic vermin of the Temple who robbed God in His own house. It is sad that this is how they are often portrayed to the depreciation of Jews, Judaism, the Jewish Scriptures, and the sacrificial system they served. That rendering, if not bigoted, is one-sided and unsophisticated.

It must be remembered that Jews were required to travel from distant lands. Pilgrimage festivals brought them on long, tedious, and dangerous journeys to Jerusalem. This question must therefore be asked and answered: "How could a visitor to the Temple hope to get doves, bulls or lambs, etc. across the mountains, valleys, deserts or oceans alive?" Another less obvious question should also be asked. "If the animal lived, and made it to the holiday season, how could it be kept from being bruised or blemished on the journey?" God demanded and deserved perfect sacrifices. An animal damaged in transit would have been rendered "unclean" for a holy sacrifice. The questions continue, "If bruised, what could be done with an angry, sacrificially worthless bull?" "If the animal could have been successfully transported, what would it have been fed and who would have followed behind it to clean up?"

These thoughts may appear odd or petty, but to a first century Jewish pilgrim, they would have been realistic concerns. The sacrificial system was quite explicit and particular. The pilgrims of Jesus' time would have gone to the dove sellers right after they had visited the moneychangers. It was the only practical method allowable to satisfy the sacrificial laws to which the pilgrims submitted.

The moneychangers served an important religious purpose. It must be remembered that a picture was embossed on most Roman coinage containing the image of Rome's famous emperor. Caesar was viewed by the pagans as their self-proclaimed god. The Jewish people were forbidden to worship other gods, or have idols, or images of those gods. Certainly, they used common currency in many of their common dealings outside of the holy city; however, their pilgrimage to Jerusalem was by no means common.

Observant Jews would not bring profane money directly for their sacrificial purchase, or the Temple tax. Actually, the half-shekel Temple tax normally required a special coin. "The coinage most acceptable for this purpose was the silver tetradrachm of Tyre, equivalent in value to a shekel; two Jews normally combined to pay their contributions with this coin." [81] When the Gospels are carefully analyzed, this coin was the type referenced by Jesus (Matthew 17:24-27) when he instructed Peter to give the coin to the tax collectors "for me and for yourself."

Greedy Moneychangers or Other Sins?

As has been shown, the sin of the moneychangers was not inherent to the jobs they were doing. Mark's rendering of the episode says,

> Jesus went into the temple, and began to cast out them that sold and bought in the temple, and overthrew the tables of the moneychangers, and the seats of them that sold doves; And would not suffer that any man should carry any vessel through the temple. And he taught, saying unto them, Is it not written, My house shall be called of all nations the house of prayer? but ye have made it a den of thieves (Mark 11:15-17 KJV).

Jesus raised the issue of "thieves," in the Temple, but readers must still be cautious not to stereotype Jews in general. I believe Jesus also had other concerns about the activities within the Temple. J. B. Phillips' version of the event is even more expressive; "he would not allow anyone to make a short cut through the Temple when carrying such things as water-pots."[82] It could be understood that different sins were emphasized by Mark. One possible alternative view could be that the physical carrying of merchandise through the Temple was the activity that angered Jesus. Many festivals and every Sabbath has a prohibition against certain types of labor. It is entirely possible that these folk were profaning the Temple by carrying their water-pots in the Temple area. If so, Jesus may have been responding to their behavior, not their prices or their profession. Yet another alternative focus of the anger of Jesus may be identified in his words. Jesus said, "My house shall be called of all nations the house of prayer?" Potentially, the court where the Gentiles were permitted to enter was being blocked up with commercial activity. Perhaps, Jesus was reacting to the problem caused by the commerce. The people of "all nations" may have been hindered from entering God's house. It is possible that the Gentiles were being robbed of access to God. According to any of these interpretations, it is not as simple as portrayed in the passion play, which simply parrots centuries of misinformation. It is true that Jesus likened them to a "den of thieves," but it is erroneous to suggest that no further explanation exists. Neither the moneychangers nor the Jews can be unconditionally presumed greedy as implied in the passion play. Bible students who ignore the *Sitz im Leben* (setting in life) of the people addressed in a biblical text ignore the truth of the text. As has been shown, and will be further detailed, one might erroneously presume greed by ignoring other possibilities of interpretation. The most basic system of hermeneutics requires examination of the context. The system of Temple sacrifices was a biblical mandate, as was the basic practice of the money changing and purchasing sacrificial animals and grain. From the earliest inception of the tithe, the concept of exchanging money for the animals and grains to be used for the tithe was a normative practice among the Jewish people. To ignore this is to deny the context of the practice. It was not a despicable pharisaic inclusion; it was a correct biblical mandate, which dated back to the time of Moses and was ordained by God.

> Thou shalt truly tithe all the increase of thy seed, that the field bringeth forth year by year. And thou shalt eat before the Lord thy God, in the place which he shall choose to place his name there, the tithe of thy corn, of thy wine, and of thine oil, and of thy flocks; that thou mayest learn to fear the Lord thy God always. *And if the way be too long for thee, so that thou art not able to carry it;* or if the place be too far from thee, which the Lord thy God shall choose to set his name there, when the Lord thy God hath blessed thee: *Then shalt thou turn it into money in thine hand,* and shalt go unto the place which the Lord thy God shall choose: And thou shalt bestow that money for whatsoever thy soul lusteth after, for oxen, or for whatsoever thy soul desireth: and thou shalt eat there before the Lord thy God, and thou halt rejoice, thou, and thine household [emphasis mine] (Deuteronomy 14: 22-26 KJV).

It is possible that this omission of information has deepened the conviction that Jesus was literally accusing the Jewish moneychangers of greed, thereby opening the floodgates of anti-Semitism to accuse Jews in general of greed.

Barring divine revelation, modern readers may never know the full meaning of the accusations leveled by Jesus against the moneychangers. However, it is wrong to suppose that Jews are greedy. Unfortunately, this is a rather normative accusation leveled against the general population of Jewish people as a stereotypical character trait. This study is not intended to confront the spiritual errors of first century Jews. Rather, it is focused on the spiritual errors of medieval and modern Gentile Christian anti-Semites. It is for this reason that the assumptions and accusations of "Jewish greed" commonly promoted in reference to the moneychangers is addressed and held up to scrutiny. It would be wise to evaluate other rational considerations prior to blindly accepting the presumption of "Jewish greed." Jesus did relate them to a "den of thieves." However, the serious student of Scripture might ask, "Why?" It is likely that a broader criticism than greed existed.

In addition to examining the culture and practices of the people to which Jesus spoke, the origin of the text itself must be examined to reach a more correct analysis of the exchange between Jesus and the moneychangers. It is an erroneous interpretation of New Testament Scripture that ignores the Hebrew Bible text from which it is quoted. All too often, this occurs with reference to the "den of thieves" accusation. Those words of Jesus were not original in the sense that Jesus quoted Jeremiah. New Testament readers would therefore do well to consult the context of the original quote in Jeremiah 7:11. In the case of the Temple conflict, it is entirely likely that Jesus drew on the more general spiritual malaise of the Jewish nation during the time of Jeremiah. It would be kind to reduce the charges of Jeremiah to mere greed. In fact, the problem of 600 BCE Jerusalem was much deeper because their list of offenses included murder, adultery, and idolatry. The choice of that specific quote from Jeremiah might imply that thievery and greed were not the issues that angered Jesus. I believe Jesus was relating a more serious condition of spiritual dishonesty. Symbolically, Jesus may have been comparing members of first century Jewish leadership to the more perverse and wicked situation encountered by Jeremiah.

The commotion at the Temple created a heightened public awareness about Jesus. Luke informs his readers that as the ministry of Jesus developed, support continued to grow among the Jewish people: "And He was teaching daily in the temple. But the chief priests, the scribes, and the leaders of the people sought to destroy Him, and were unable to do anything; for all the people were very attentive to hear Him" (Luke 19:47-48). The leaders were faced with a dilemma as their own base of support appeared to erode. "The Pharisees therefore said among themselves, 'You see that you are accomplishing nothing, Look, the world has gone after Him!'" (John 12:19-20). Their influence may have been jeopardized at home and abroad. "And there were certain Greeks among them that came up to worship at the feast . . . and desired him, saying 'Sir, we would see Jesus'" (John 12:20-21 KJV). Even among the religious faithful, the Pharisees were discovering growing numbers who had chosen to consider the claims of Jesus. According to the Gospels, the impact of Jesus even reached to the highest levels influencing some within Jewish leadership, "among the rulers many believed in Him" (John 12:42).

Packed Palestine and the Passover Pilgrims

Another important fact impacting the death of Jesus revolves around the social, economic, and political atmosphere of Jerusalem in that era. Herod was in power and he was a great builder. He constructed the elaborate Jewish Temple, his most famous national monument in Jerusalem. This brought him the money and prestige of ruling the greatest tourist area in that part of the world. Herod wanted to protect his control, and he enjoyed the fruits of that control with the blessings of Rome. The sacrificial system with its husbandmen, priests, Levites, moneychangers, dove sellers and inn-keepers helped make Jerusalem a thriving metropolis compared to other ancient towns in the area.

Scholars and rabbis seem to differ as to the population of Jerusalem during the great festivals. Likewise, they seem unable to reach a consensus about the general population of Palestine during the first century. The rabbis present a reasonable argument for estimating the count of pilgrims by calculating the quantity of lambs sacrificed at Passover. One rabbinic source (Talmud *Pesachim* 64b) reported that during the reign (41-44 ce.) of Jewish King Agrippa, 600,000 lambs were slaughtered during one Passover celebration. In all likelihood, that is a gross exaggeration.[83]

Another more famous overstatement was recorded by Josephus. He alleged that the report of the Jewish priests who had tallied the number of paschal sacrifices during the last Passover prior to when Rome destroyed Jerusalem during the First Jewish Revolt, equaled 256,500. According to his calculations in light of biblical requirements, each lamb would have served a Jewish family gathering of approximately ten persons. Then after reducing his estimate to account for those who were ritually impure, and increasing his estimate to account for those groups that were larger than the ten person minimum, the great Jewish historian of the Roman Empire estimated the Passover population in Jerusalem to be precisely "two million seven hundred thousand and two hundred persons that were pure and holy."[84] Other scholars suggest far smaller normal population counts. Some as few as 30,000 residents with that number tripling during pilgrimage festivals. Since the range of residents and pilgrims varies dramatically, I personally appreciate the comment of a great New Testament scholar who is most informative. F.F. Bruce rightly proposes that "to estimate the size of populations in antiquity is a hazardous exercise; contemporary writers, even when they appear to give precise figures, are not always reliable."[85] In this case, the exact number is not relevant. Even if the rabbis and Josephus were a bit exuberant in their census calculations, it is an unquestionable fact that the Passover festival brought an enormous influx of pilgrims. Jerusalem was a spiritual hub and business activity greatly increased to meet the spiritual and material needs of all who arrived for the event.

In April of 30 CE, Jerusalem was gorged with people as they commemorated the end of 430 years of slavery in Egypt and celebrated the annual Passover festival. That celebration was always one of the most important events of the year as Jews continued the tradition of describing God's redemptive hand of deliverance. The Exodus account was retold annually amidst the slaying of the Passover lamb. That special pilgrimage festival brought multitudes to the city. The population swelled from the tourist trade. Jerusalem was heavily dependent on the pilgrims. The city had no seaport for shipping income. The city's location did not inherently lend itself to popular trade routes for growth. The natural resources of the area were limited. Farming was not easy or always prosperous in the region. Without the pilgrims, the city could not thrive. The Temple trade assured Herod and Rome that perpetual wealth would flow to and from Jerusalem. The city was prescribed by the Mosaic Law as the only place in the world where observant Jews could offer sacrifices. The only acceptable location for the altar was in the Temple. The Temple brought the pilgrims. The Temple brought the Temple tax. The pilgrims brought the money. The city flourished because of that tourist trade focused on Herod's Temple. Each of these historical and social considerations is relevant to understand the true setting of the drama described in the passion of Jesus. The event did not happen in a quiet, quaint village far away from public scrutiny. As described in the New Testament account, this was one of the primary problems faced by the religious leaders as their world was impacted by masses of Jewish pilgrims who had flooded into Jerusalem.

70 Banki and Strober, 19.
71 Or *Ioudaios*-pronounced ee-oo-dah'-yos
72 James H. Charlesworth, Ibid., 2.
73 Curtis Vaughan, *The Bible From 26 Translations*, (Grand Rapids, MI: Baker Book House, 1988), 1920.
74 Ibid., 1921.
75 Judaism had many forms in the first century and many Jewish sects expected a Messiah. Certainly exceptions existed then among Jews, as exceptions exist currently among so-called Christians.
76 Bader, 250.
77 I do not question Matthew's accuracy nor his reasons for including the passage. What is herein addressed is the emphasis given to the phrase and in its abuse by anti-Semites. Bible scholars would not attempt to build a doctrine from one verse, yet, Christian anti-Semites have tended to amplify that text and often remove it from its context in an effort to depreciate Jews.
78 A. T. Robertson, *A Harmony of the Gospels*,(San Francisco: Harper, 1950), 161.
79 Banki and Strober, 14.
80 Ibid., 7.
81 Bruce, 140. Actually, for normal commerce, different coinage bearing the images of various rulers were used at different times and places. Within Jewish territory, some coinage was available without sacrilegious images. These would not have been commonly available to pilgrims coming from the outlying regions.
82 J. B. Phillips, *The New Testament in Modern English*, (New York: Macmillan Publishing Co., Inc., 1977), 92.
83 Jeffrey M. Cohen, *1,001 Questions and Answers on Pesach*, Northvale: Jason Aronson Inc., 1996, 16.
84 Josephus, Flavius, Edited by William Whiston, *The Works of Josephus, War of the Jews*, Peabody, Massachusetts Hendrickson Publishers, 1983, Book 6, Chapter 9.
85 Bruce, 38.

Chapter VI

Conspiracy:
The Deicide Alternative

The passion play freely blames the Jewish people for deicide. This is abhorrent! It ignores the relevant fact that the Jewish people of the first century lived in a very broad geographical area around the world. Many Jews outside Judea would have been completely uninformed about the charges brought against Jesus. The ancient world lacked telephones, fax machines, and e-mail. How could the Jews outside of Israel have been notified before daybreak about the actions of the judge, jury, and executioners? During His brief ministry, Jesus did not personally engage Jews in conversation in the wider area outside of Israel. It is highly unlikely that He would have impacted those Jews in the outlying nations who lived in a predominantly Gentile environment. It is even more unlikely that Jesus or His disciples would have internationally broadcast the charges of blasphemy raised against Him by His enemies. Therefore, those Jewish people from afar would have not known about the circumstances to condemn Him. Furthermore, as has already been affirmed according to the New Testament, Jesus had a large following of Jewish supporters in Israel. He was loved by the average Jewish citizen suffering under Roman domination. They yearned for a deliverer. They would never have approved of His arrest had they known of the plan. *Unless all justice is abandoned, no injustice can be blamed on any Jewish person who was not directly involved with the crime.* The idea that any race can be blamed for the action of any member or group of members is ludicrous. That form of confusion is the material upon which stereotypes are built.

Christian anti-Semitism feeds on a "wandering Jew" syndrome to justify Jewish suffering and to support the perverse forms of Replacement Theology that grew out of the dark ages. If the curses of Scripture can be laid on the Jews, Christianity can lay claim to the promises which remain unclaimed by the supposedly unwilling, ungrateful, unholy, unworthy Jews. It is wrong to accuse the Jewish people of rejecting Christendom's Messiah. There would be no Church if many Jews had not believed and followed Jesus. Though Christianity has often chosen to ascribe guilt and condemnation to the Jews as a result of rejecting Jesus, a debt still remains. I submit that Christianity owes a debt of gratitude to those Jews who carried the Christian religion to the Gentiles of the first century.

A Per Capita Consideration

Some people insist on blaming the Jews for the death of Jesus. Yet few seem willing to inquire as to which Jews in particular were responsible. How many Jews were alive during the time of Jesus? As previously discussed, it is difficult to be certain. Estimates vary quite a lot as to the Jewish population of Jerusalem and Palestine. In the broader scope, it is believed that approximately 4,500,000 Jews lived throughout the world at the time when Jesus Christ died. (By the time of the Reformation, after the Crusades and part of the Inquisition had been completed, the Jewish population was reduced to approximately 1,500,000 in 1500. This number had grown to 16,000,000 just prior to Hitler.)[86] More Gentiles than Jews existed in the world at the time of Jesus. Proportionately, many more Jews than Gentiles accepted Christ in the early days of Christianity. Therefore, on a per capita basis it was the Gentiles, not the Jews, who rejected Jesus in the early first century church movement. This is certain based upon the New Testament accounts that report the sensationalism and shock attached to the conversion of Cornelius and the other early Gentile believers to the Christian faith.

> Now the apostles and brethren who were in Judea heard that the Gentiles had also received the word of God. And when Peter came up to Jerusalem, those of the circumcision (Peter was referring to the early Jewish Christians living in Jerusalem probably engaged in regular Temple worship) contended with him, saying, "You went in to uncircumcised men and ate with them!" (Acts 11: 1-3).

Peter was strongly reprimanded by the Jerusalem Jewish Christians for going so far as to eat with Gentiles. The concept of permitting Gentiles into the "church" was unheard of and unthinkable! It took a series of supernatural events to convince Peter and the Jewish Christians to allow Gentiles into the fold. After the miraculous occurrences were described by Peter, the Jerusalem Jewish Christians finally acknowledged, "When they heard these things they became silent; and they glorified God, saying, 'Then God has also granted to the Gentiles repentance to life' " (Acts 11: 18). From this account and others it is obvious that Christianity was exclusively a Jewish institution in its infancy.

Unquestionably, the New Testament does portray a Jewish involvement in the death of Jesus. This investigation does not pretend to ignore that fact of the Gospel accounts. Instead, adherents to the New Testament message are asked to delve into how deeply that involvement spread among the Jewish people not specified by writers of the gospels. Specifically, who was involved in the arrest, trial, and execution of Jesus? Guilt by association is the only way the Jewish people can be blamed universally. It is obvious that 4,500,000 Jews did not get together to discuss the death of Christ. This investigation will now seek to determine the more probable extent of Jewish involvement.

The Alternative Theory

My theory suggests that the conspiracy to kill Jesus was masterminded and implemented by a very, very small group of Jewish leaders. However, because of the anti-Semitic twist of popular Gentile Christian interpretations of the New Testament, this more obvious understanding has been ignored. It is clear who the conspirators were, as identified in the Gospels.

> Then assembled together the chief priests, and the scribes, and the elders of the people, unto the palace of the high priest, who was called Caiaphas, And consulted that they might take Jesus by subtlety, and kill him. But they said not on the feast, lest there be an uproar among the people (Matthew 26: 3-5 KJV).

The group consisted of Caiaphas, the high priest, and probably selected leaders of the Sanhedrin. Luke's account also seems to reduce the size of the group. "And the chief priests and the scribes sought how they might kill Him, for they feared the people" (Luke 22:2). This suggests that some segment of the Jewish leaders were willing to take action in the conspiracy in spite of the immense popularity enjoyed by Jesus. Their behavior appears to have been motivated by fear. Returning to the narrative, the last group of individuals involved is described by Luke. "Then Satan entered Judas, surnamed Iscariot, who was numbered among the twelve. So he went his way and conferred with the chief priests and captains, how he might betray Him to them" (Luke 22:3-4). The Lukan account shows that Judas committed to keep the enterprise a private affair. This was of the greatest importance to the conspirators. "And they were glad, and agreed to give him money. So he promised and sought opportunity to betray him to them in the absence of the multitude" (Luke 22:5-6).

The conspirators obviously did not want anyone outside their inner circle to know their plan. They rightly assumed that their scheme would not have been approved by the full council. They were also convinced that a significant potential for a revolt existed. The city was filled with supporters of Jesus. The conspirators were very concerned that their actions could be met with a public outcry prohibiting their action if the masses learned of their violent designs against Jesus. I believe the plan of the wicked Jewish leaders was intended to be enacted before the Jerusalem citizenry knew of their action.

"Then Judas, having received a detachment of troops, and officers from the chief priests and Pharisees, came there with lanterns, torches, and weapons" (John 18:3). The translation given by E. V. Rieu[87] details that they were "taking a party of soldiers as well as some police." The Centenary Translation by Helen Barrett Montgomery[88] gives even more clarification explaining that they were specifically the Temple police. Referring once again to F. F. Bruce, this expert on New Testament issues offers an extremely pertinent insight. "The Johannine account, according to which the officers of the Sanhedrin were accompanied by a *speira* (John 18:3, 12), has been taken to mean that Roman soldiers were also present, members of the cohort on duty in the Antonia fortress."[89] What has been presented by the other translators and Bruce is that the conspirators within the Sanhedrin met with the Roman officials in advance of the arrest. *The deal had been prearranged*. Then the conspirators sent their delegation with Judas, along with some of the Temple guard, under the authority of Roman soldiers, with their own captain. The closer one gets to the historical facts, the less it appears that the Jewish masses turned on Jesus and the more Rome is connected to the crime in cahoots with a very small group of Jewish leaders.

Passover in the Last Supper

On Thursday night of the passion week, Jesus, with his disciples, celebrated a Passover *Seder*.[90] Jesus was a Jew participating in a traditional Jewish ceremony, with his closest Jewish friends. Everything from the wine to the *matzah* was part of the Jewish liturgy. Jesus was an observant Jew fulfilling His Jewish duty. He was obeying the words of Scripture that deemed several festivals, including the Passover celebration, to be conducted as a "statute for ever throughout your generations in all your dwellings" (Lev. 23:14). Jesus, along with his Jewish disciples, and the other ancient Jewish followers honored these words of Moses. Accordingly, they regularly celebrated the appropriate festivals. Modern followers of Jesus do not honor the festivals that he honored in the way he honored them. Jesus never stopped being a Jew. He never told His friends to discontinue Judaic practices. He certainly never instructed his followers to disdain the Jewish people. Yet many passion play presentations seem scripted to diminish the obvious Jewish attributes of Jesus.

When Christians allow the presentation of Jesus to depart from his Jewish persona, that departure obscures the truth. It is my view that this error remains one of the most heinous crimes of the normative passion play. The Jewishness of Jesus should never be erased, yet this is a typical deficiency in most presentations. In so doing, the relationship between Judaism and Christianity is strained, crushed, and then broken. Referring again to Oberammergau, it was reported that, "In both the old and the new version of the play, Jesus is represented as renouncing Judaism: 'The Old Covenant which my Father made with Abraham, Isaac, and Jacob has reached its end' . . . There is no basis whatsoever for such a statement in the Gospel accounts."[91] This is an abomination. It is a vicious misquote. It rips the truth from the pages of the Gospels, which clearly leaves no room to doubt that Jesus was committed and dedicated to the Jewish Scriptures. It is certain that Jesus never abdicated the position to which He was born—Jesus was an observant Jew.

Mystery and the Upper Room

A significant factor, often ignored, relates to the manner in which the location for the *Seder* was chosen. Consider Mark's account of the way in which the house for the *Seder* was selected.

> And the first day of unleavened bread when they killed the passover, his disciples said unto him, Where wilt thou that we go and prepare that thou mayest eat the passover? And he sendeth forth two of his disciples, and saith unto them, Go ye into the city, and there shall meet you a man bearing a pitcher of water: follow him. And wheresoever he shall go in, say ye to the goodman of the house, The Master saith, Where is the guestchamber, where I shall eat the passover with my disciples? And he will shew you a large upper room furnished and prepared: there make ready for us. And his disciples went forth, and came into the city, and found as he had said unto them: and they made ready the passover. And in the evening he cometh with the twelve (Mark 14:12-17 KJV).

This passage about the "upper room" is an important verse in analyzing the account of the last days of the life of Jesus. Many questions exist about the New Testament description of the specific site selection. The apparent secrecy incorporated by Jesus may have been intended to suppress public knowledge about the location of the Passover *Seder*. Perhaps an important purpose existed in surrounding the setting for this last gathering with the disciples in a mystery. Matthew and Mark give identical renditions of the scenario. Luke's account adds information. He identifies the two disciples that went on this secret mission as Peter and John. Jesus gave the "keys of the kingdom" to Peter, and John was known as "the beloved," yet Jesus waited until the last moment to let His closest friends know the location of their Passover service. The code used by the householder to identify himself was exactly as Jesus had predetermined. It is quite likely that nobody was to know the location until the last possible moment.

Jesus knew that if any accidental disclosure had taken place a crowd might have come to His side. The basic doctrines of Christianity proclaim that the death of Jesus was purposeful, necessary, and central to the divine plan for salvation. Therefore, any prohibition of His death would have been counter-productive and disastrous. From a Christian worldview it would seem that Jesus could not afford to have permitted a crowd of Jewish supporters marching to set Him free from his captors. His purposes could only be fulfilled by allowing the conspirators to successfully accomplish their ends as prophesied according to the Hebrew Bible.

The Passover *Seder* would have started after sundown and could have lasted for several hours. Then they enjoyed their Passover meal together as Jesus ministered to His friends. The service apparently continued until its logical, traditional conclusion because the Scripture suggests,

> And he took bread, gave thanks and broke it, and gave it to them, saying, "This is My body which is given for you; do this in remembrance of Me." Likewise He also took the cup after supper, saying, "This cup is the new covenant in My blood, which is shed for you" (Luke 22:19-20).

These famous words are detailing an ancient Jewish tradition. *Matzah*, the unleavened bread used during this specific festival, would have been the only "bread" shared at the table. They literally "broke bread" together as Jesus divided the *matzah*, and broke it into pieces to distribute among the participants. Then He poured another cup of wine after dinner as was the custom. The tradition described in the New Testament is that of the sharing of four cups of wine among participants at the Passover celebration. Two cups would be shared before the Passover meal and two cups after the meal. Each is believed to have biblical symbolism attached relating to the Exodus from Egypt as well as to the future deliverance promised by God. It is widely believed by many scholars that the fourth cup was not concluded during the Last Supper. This suggests added symbolism and implies a future prophetic fulfillment at the return of Jesus. Nonetheless, whether three or four cups were enjoyed by Jesus and the disciples, the final cup of wine poured during that *Seder* was not dispensed until very late in the evening.

It could easily have been ten o'clock at night before the *Seder* was completed. The intensely serious nature of the fellowship could have delayed it even longer. This, however, was not the end of the story. After the *Seder*, Jesus took a long walk over to the Mount of Olives. The night was growing late. The walk was long, and the garden prayer vigil was intense. Jesus was in anguish. "And being in an agony, He prayed more earnestly" (Luke 22:44). This episode probably continued for an extended period. It is plain that Jesus was deeply involved in prayer. He prayed late into the night. His closest friends fell asleep even though Jesus had asked them to remain with him in prayer. The disciples were not weak, tired, spineless failures. These men were rugged fisherman, accustomed to the demanding regimen of their trade. They fell asleep because the evening's activities lasted into the middle of the night.

Arrested in Darkness—IT WAS A CONSPIRACY!

Coming up the hill, Jesus saw the band of men led by Judas, accompanied by Roman soldiers. They were carrying torches. The reason for the torches is obvious; it was still dark. These men came to arrest Jesus in the dark while Jerusalem slept into the late night hours of that emerging Good Friday morning. Jesus understood what was happening. He asked them "When I was with you daily in the temple, you did not try to seize Me. But this is your hour, and the power of darkness" (Luke 22: 53).

It has been made obvious in numerous places in the Gospel accounts that the chief priests were afraid that the Jewish people of Jerusalem would find out about their plan. This was the reason for their need to act in darkness. Many of the Jewish people of Jerusalem would never have tolerated the calculated behavior of the conspirators. "His popularity with the crowds was such that they dared not take overt action against him."[92]

I believe that support for Jesus went beyond the crowds and the common people. The people in the streets readily hailed Jesus as a popular hero. His popularity did not end with them. I am certain that even some within the Sanhedrin would have attempted to prohibit the arrest had they been aware of it. Jesus had made an amazing impression on most of the people who had met Him. Some would later choose to die rather than deny His deity. A similar impact appears to have been made on at least two of the Jewish leaders.

Jesus touched the lives of both Nicodemus and Joseph of Arimathea. Both became involved in the final hours of the life of Jesus in kind and gracious ways. Both risked their reputation and well-being in so doing. As is well known, according to Matthew 27:57-60, Joseph, a wealthy Jewish man, went directly to Pilate and requested permission to give Jesus a proper Jewish burial. It is also known from Luke's Gospel that this same Jewish man was a "counselor." Yet more relevant, Joseph was "a council member, a good and just man. He had not consented to their decision and deed. *He was* from Arimathea" (Luke 23:50-51). It is unknown if Joseph was actually present at the mock trial held before the quorum of the Sanhedrin. It is just as likely that he had "not consented to their decision" because he had not been invited. His sentiments were well known among the other Jewish leaders. Likewise, Nicodemus was also a friend to Jesus. Perhaps his kind gesture was belated, but nevertheless, he put his beliefs on the line with his reputation when he went to help prepare the body of Jesus for burial according to religious Jewish standards (see John 19:38-42).

Jews of every generation since the Dark Ages have been blamed for the death of Jesus, yet how many Jews were actually involved in this conspiracy? I propose that the group consisted of a small majority of the Sanhedrin, Caiaphas, Annas (his father-in-law), and several hired false witnesses, Judas, a small contingency from the Temple guard, and a small group of Roman soldiers. The ringleaders were probably the powerbrokers of the Sanhedrin. They certainly had the motivation to coordinate the arrest. But this was a very small group. The Sanhedrin was the ruling authority for all important matters. They were "the council" often referred to in the New Testament. Yet the entire Sanhedrin only consisted of a total of seventy men (in addition to the high priest). If the dominant players could have won support of forty or fifty members, it would have been sufficient. It is also likely that others within the Sanhedrin would have objected to a conspiracy intended to lead to the death of Jesus. Certainly Joseph of Arimathea and Nicodemus would have encouraged their friends within the council to reject such a wicked plan. Caiaphas and Annas knew they needed a small, controllable quorum to protect their religious power base. Jesus was a serious threat.

Yet some within the Church continue to blame the general population of Jewish people for an act of betrayal perpetrated by a small handful of men. Since the night of Jesus' arrest, that passion lie has been festering. It is clear that the conspirators would have wanted the smallest group possible involved. For the reasons stated above, I believe that it is entirely probable that less than seventy Jewish men knew anything about the plot to have Jesus destroyed.

Once arrested, they scurried Jesus off to their first stop at the influential home of Annas, the father-in-law of Caiaphas. He had in earlier years been the high priest himself. He knew the most effective methods of getting things done. The most expedient manner of concluding the problem promptly was to take Jesus before the cooperative portion of the Sanhedrin in an unofficial fashion with Caiaphas. Immediately thereafter they would go see Pilate so that Rome could conclude their part in the plan. "If a case against him was to be presented to Pilate, it would carry official weight if the high priest in office presented it on behalf of the supreme court."[93] Caiaphas and Annas probably had everything planned in advance.

The Sound of Dawn

The other reason the arrest needed to be made in the middle of the night was so that they could have a quiet confrontation in front of the

Sanhedrin completed by the early morning hours. While Peter was out mingling by the fire outside the house of the high priest, a servant girl spotted him. His famous denials by that fire are easily recalled. That fire offered light and heat in the cool, dark night before "the cock crow . . ." (Matthew 26:75 KJV). The normal time for a rooster to crow is also a relevant fact. Most of the events of the evening had already transpired before daybreak. Daybreak, when the world rests between daytime and darkness was the time chosen for the trial of Jesus. It is likely that those present at the Sanhedrin hearing were specifically invited by Caiaphas. It is possible that those members of the Sanhedrin who were friendly to Jesus, such as Nicodemus, were allowed to sleep late and miss the event. The conspirators started early so that they could be prepared for Roman justice. It is quite conceivable that Jesus was judged in an unfair trial in front of only a portion of the Sanhedrin.

> Haste was imperative, because Passover was due to be celebrated the following evening, and it was desirable to have the whole affair concluded before that. Moreover, people in Pilate's position transacted business early in the day and concluded it by noon. A night session of the court—or at least of a quorum—was therefore held.[94]

The passion play is not required to justify the action of the Jewish leaders; nonetheless, no reason exists to add to the hideousness of the wrongdoing. The characterization of the Jewish leadership within the passion play has often been most inflammatory. Caiaphas and Annas have been portrayed as screaming,

> Death to this criminal! This corrupter of Israel! . . . With this stammering tongue will I cry for the life and blood of this malefactor and then descend into the tomb of my fathers when I have seen this evil-doer die upon the cross . . . It would delight mine eyes to see his body torn by wild beasts.[95]

No healthy purpose can exist for this typification of Jewish religious leaders. No evidence suggests that these words were uttered. No positive enhancement to the Gospel story is brought by these erroneous embellishments.

> It remains a slur on the Jewish leaders of Jesus' time, whose true nature is amply documented in contemporary

sources. Furthermore, it is calculated to encourage an unwarranted sanctimoniousness in the audience. The priests (and other enemies of Jesus) are so caricatured that the spectator cannot identify with them—which is precisely what he ought to do, because according to Christian teaching all men, by their sins, contribute to Jesus' suffering.[96]

The Conspiracy Ignored by the Passion Play

Jesus was arrested, indicted, beaten, judged, and crucified *before nine o'clock in the morning*. How can anyone blame the general population of Jewish people for a crime that was hidden from their view? They did not have access to cell phones and CNN. There were no Internet warriors spamming the countryside warning about the conspiracy at hand. The dastardly deed was concocted behind closed doors and done in secrecy. Most Jews of Jerusalem could not have known. They were innocent of the crime. Jesus was dying before anyone could intervene. When the New Testament records "Then answered all the people, and said, His blood be on us, and on our children," it does not refer to all Jews in all places at all times. It may never be known how large or small the contingency was that actually insisted on the arrest of Jesus. What is certain, however, is this; it was not the voice of world Jewry!

Caiaphas was probably first on the docket of Pilate's court seeking Roman justice on that early Friday morning. "He had first stood before Pilate (about half-past six)."[97] Mark's Gospel suggests it was "straightway in the morning" (Mark 15:1). And injustice was swift. The conspirators acted with clarity of mind and purpose of heart. They wanted to rid the world of Jesus before anyone could stop them.

The views of Father Ralph Gorman present a correct analysis of the passion play's erroneous and damaging depiction of the Jewish involvement in the death of Jesus. He suggests that Christian spectators should contritely see themselves as the crucifiers of Jesus "instead of sanctimoniously condemning the Jews." [98] His understanding is profoundly Christlike and consistent with the true and noble goals of the Christian faith.

> The true Christian identifies himself with those who schemed against Christ, clamoured for his death, and crucified Him on Calvary. Looking for the guilty, the true Christian strikes his own breast and acknowledges that it was because of his sins

that Christ died . . . No man can harbor hatred of the Jews in his heart and be a Christian.[99]

I must conclude this discussion about problems in the Passion Play of Oberammergau. It appears obvious that serious errors in judgment have impacted the ability of those Christians responsible for the presentation. They have not been fair and accurate in their presentation of the drama depicting the most important period in the life of Christ—His last days on earth. Christian anti-Semites have characterized the birth of Christianity as the death of that which was good and noble within Judaism. The blessings of the Jewish birthright have not been exchanged for eternal condemnation as a result of a perceived brutality against Jesus. Jesus did not permit His followers to fight or prohibit His arrest. Rather, He informed them that He could have prayed to summon legions of angels if resistance was His intention. Jesus reminded them of God's sovereign purpose in the midst of the conflict by asking, "how then shall the scriptures be fulfilled, that thus it must be?" (Matthew 26:54). If the claims of Christian doctrine are accurate, the death of Jesus brought to fruition His purposeful suffering. His victory over death should never be tainted by a reductionist view presenting the living sacrifice as a helpless victim of Jewish assailants. Jesus was not "killed" by the Jews or Romans, He willingly gave His a life a ransom for sinners.

---

86 Basil Matthews, *The Jew and the World Ferment*, (New York: Friendship Press, 1935), 173.

87 Vaughan, *The Bible from 26 Translations*, 2110.

88 Ibid.

89 Bruce, 195.

90 The Passover *Seder* is the Hebrew term for the actual celebration. It literally means "order." Each Passover is remembered through a specific "order" of events. The liturgy known as the *hagaddah* is precisely followed to help each generation of Jewish people remember our miraculous deliverance from bondage to slavery. It is on the occasion of Passover that we celebrate our Exodus from Egypt.

91 Banki and Strober, 11.

92 Bruce, 187.

93 Ibid., 196.

94 Ibid.

95 Banki and Strober, 7.

96 Ibid.

97 Alfred Edersheim, *The Life and Times of Jesus the Messiah: New Updated Edition*, (Hendrickson Publishers, Inc., 2000), 875.

98 Banki and Strober, 19.

99 Banki and Strober, 19, citing Ralph Gorman, "Again the Jews," *The Sign*, May 1960, 6.

Chapter VII

Sin in the Superstar

Some American Christians may feel comfortably distant from the errors reported at Oberammergau because anti-Semitic behavior may appear less offensive coming out of Germany, a nation with a long history of anti-Semitism. Europe may be so far removed from the thoughts of American Christians that they sense no common heritage or spiritual link to their German brethren. However, a link exists which cannot be broken by a mere desire to disassociate. The results of this investigation should not be ignored by America Christians because the problems have not been limited exclusively to the error of Europeans. Insensitivity, inaccuracy, and even blatant Christian anti-Semitism can be discerned in various forms of Christian expression. Sometimes the error is subtle, often it is pronounced as a modern outgrowth of ancient misinformation.

One such outcropping may exist in the well-known presentation of *Jesus Christ Superstar*. This rock album / stage play / box office film presentation gathered enormous publicity and popularity. The film critics were quite vocal about the material. James R. Huffman commented,

> The very first fact that the critic must deal with—rationally, not in righteous indignation—is the tremendous popularity of *Jesus Christ Superstar* . . . Like the Beatles, though without apology, *Superstar* is probably more popular than Christ himself.[100]

The enormous success of this pop-media version of the passion play had a unique opportunity to impact millions of people in a relatively short time. In his *New York Times'* review of the film, Clive Barnes reminded his readers of the huge success of the soundtrack. "Nothing could convince me that any show that has sold two-and-one-half million copies of its album before the opening night is anything like all bad."[101] Dan Morgenstern's critical review offered a rhetorical question, "Can a work so monstrously successful be all bad? The answer, sadly, is yes . . . the theological conception of the Passion of Christ [is] a travesty."[102]

The American Jewish Committee published a report analyzing the message presented within the famous "rock opera" by Andrew Lloyd Webber and Tim Rice. In the foreword to the report, Rabbi Marc H. Tanenbaum discussed his view of the playwrighters' intent, as well as the scope of the committee's analysis.

> Seeking to bring the Christian religious heritage to youth in youth's own terms, Webber's and Rice's play translates the record of Jesus' last week on earth into the popular musical idiom of our time . . . What this study is concerned with is the possible impact of Jesus Christ Superstar on the relation between Christians and Jews.[103]

The report was actually written by a Presbyterian educator who readily acknowledged that the New Testament was the only reliable source of data for making a comparison about the life of Jesus to the content of the play. He reviewed the printed text from the script and attended previews of the play during the New York production. His finding revealed that many, though not all of the same errors found in the Oberammergau passion play were in this one as well. Of the priests' characterization he says, "The priests are portrayed as hideously inhuman and satanically evil: contemptuous, callous and blood-thirsty. There is no warrant in the New Testament either for the attribution of primary guilt or for the caricatured characterization."[104] Strober correctly points to another distortion about the circumstances surrounding Judas:

> Similarly, in the scene "Judas' Death," an unnamed priest coldly tells the contrite Judas:
> "Cut the confessions forget the excuses
> I don't understand why you're filled with remorse
> All that you've said has come true with a vengeance
> The mob turned against him—you backed the right horse"

> There is no antecedent for either of these utterances in the gospels.[105]

The scene continues with the priests inviting Judas to enjoy the view of Christ's suffering. The bloodthirsty attributions are boldly presented by the priest. "Judas thank you for the victim—stay awhile and you'll see it bleed!"[106] The Jewish view of Jesus is reduced to an "it," a subhuman in the priest's brief discourse. Good and evil are starkly contrasted. Issues are made to appear black or white. The Jews obviously represent evil. Webber and Rice portrayed Judas more compassionately than many passion play renditions. Additionally, seen as a disillusioned friend of Jesus, instead of a heartless greedy traitor, Judas was more human than generally typified, yet, several critics commented that the producers seemed specific in their decision to cast Judas as a black actor.

The Apostle's Greed

One of the troublesome features in the film presentation of *Jesus Christ Superstar* relates to another representation of Judas. He was portrayed as the greedy disciple who wanted to profit from the sale of the costly perfume wasted by the foolish woman with the alabaster box. Before multi-media presentations, it was common to relate this story of Judas in simple Sunday School lessons. The Bible recounts,

> Then took Mary a pound of ointment of spikenard, very costly, and anointed the feet of Jesus, and wiped his feet with her hair: and the house was filled with the odour of the ointment. Then saith one of his disciples, Judas Iscariot, Simon's son, which should betray him, Why was not this ointment sold for three hundred pence, and given to the poor?" (John 12: 3-6 KJV)

It is normally presumed that since Judas was a thief, he probably wanted to keep the money for himself. The margin note of the popular *Thompson Chain Reference Bible* calls this event "The Murmuring of Judas,"[107] yet, Judas was <u>not</u> alone. "But when his disciples saw it, they had indignation, saying, To what purpose is this waste? For this ointment might have been sold for much, and given to the poor" (Matthew 26: 8, 9 KJV). It is common to focus on Judas, the greedy Jew, but Matthew clearly indicts them in plural. The Markan version also assures that several of the disciples were involved.

And there were *some* that had indignation within *themselves*, and said Why was this waste of the ointment made? For it might have been sold for more than three hundred pence, and have been given to the poor. And *they* murmured against her [emphasis mine] (Mark 14:4-5 KJV).

Judas the betrayer has often been associated with Jews in general by those who have accused the Jewish people of being greedy, deceptive, or disloyal. The same perceived Jewish character flaws have been promoted by individuals who have also focused exaggerated attention on Judas as a Jew. At issue, is neither a defect exclusive to Judas nor a character flaw limited to Jews. If greed was the motive for prohibiting the anointing with costly ointment, Judas was not the only "greedy" disciple; yet, few would broadly accuse the other disciples of greed. If Judas is to be blamed, the blame must also be shared with the larger group of disciples who were also disturbed. Neither the merits of the "good" disciples or the flaws of the "bad" disciple reflect the character of a people group. There are both good and bad traits among all people. It is a dangerous error to promote the image of Judas to reinforce despicable stereotypes about Jews. When Christians limit their focus to the actual greed of Judas, it becomes easier to shift their concern to the perceived greed of the Jews. Then, it seems unnecessary to concentrate their focus on the more serious human problem of greed in general. I believe that is the only reasonable stereotype to be gleaned from the Gospel account. Jeremiah's description of the human condition should speak to all Jews and all Christians because it is an accurate understanding of humanity, "The heart is deceitful above all things, and desperately wicked: who can know it?" (Jeremiah. 17:9 KJV). Though it should be obvious, it is often overlooked that the depravity of mankind was the reason for the death of Jesus. Fortunately, at least one person at the scene understood the situation and chose to tangibly show her gratitude. It cost her the great price of an alabaster box filled with valuable ointment.

Judas: a Scripted Anti-Hero

Only a few verses later in Matthew's account, Judas fulfilled a role that was predetermined by God. "The Son of man goeth as it is written of him: but woe unto that man by whom the Son of man is betrayed!" (Matthew 26: 24). The entire event was God's idea.[108] If one is predisposed to believe the prophetic writings, the inescapable conclusion is that God called forth a Messiah who would suffer and become an atonement for sin. The Bible makes clear that God had a plan for the salvation of man that included the betrayal of Jesus by Judas. Jesus warned His listeners, "Have not I chosen twelve, and one of you is a devil?" (John 6:70). God's intentions were carefully planned and precisely implemented. "Him, being delivered by the determinate counsel and foreknowledge of God" (Acts 2:23). The fact that Judas was Jewish should only be incidental to the truth of God's higher purpose. Wrongly, that fact has often been exaggerated and over emphasized. Judas was Jewish. That fact is true. That fact need not be promoted separate from the fact that Jesus was also Jewish. They were all Jewish! Some have handled the betrayal by Judas as a reason for distrusting Jewish people. The error of Judas has been a focus of anti-Semitic emotions too often in Church history. The initial problem was a sin problem, not a Jewish problem.

Judas has been a very specific infamous Jewish example used to further the cause of anti-Semitism. The dramatic characterizations of Judas have been disparagingly stereotypical of Jewish people. As a result, Judas is often identified more as a Jew than as a legitimate disciple chosen by Jesus. Although Judas was the betrayer, he was nevertheless undoubtedly an Apostle. This can best be seen by reviewing the New Testament text surrounding the issues of replacing Judas as an Apostle after his conspiratorial actions and subsequent death.

> The question as to who was to take the place of Judas had to be settled. Note that the genuineness of Judas' ministry was not in doubt. Peter said he "had obtained a part of this ministry." In other words, Judas had preached that Jesus was the Messiah, and in His name had healed the sick and cast out devils.[109]

Within the history of Christianity, Judas has been more readily identified as a Jew, instead of being primarily represented as a sinner. Guilt by association has transferred from Judas to the Jewish people. The betrayal of Jesus by Judas was neither a mistake nor a surprise, and it was definitely not a Jewish invention. Jesus was fully aware of the entire situation. "For Jesus knew from the beginning who they were that believed not, and who, should betray him" (John 6:64).

Judas did betray Jesus, but this fact does not present the whole explanation of responsibility. The New Testament informs that Satan had already given Judas a sinful, conspiratorial idea. "And supper being ended, the devil having now put into the heart of Judas Iscariot, Simon's son, to betray him" (John 13:2). One might suggest that after Satan had used his influence, he went back to his normal *modus operandi*. First he used influence from the outside; then he used the power to control from the inside. "And after the sop Satan entered into him" (John 13:27). It would certainly seem that Judas was not working independently after that moment. At the prompting of Jesus, Judas left the group and went to betray Jesus to the Jewish leaders. E.V. Rieu's version of the Gospels interprets the text to suggest that Jesus told Judas, "The quicker you act the better"[110] (John 13:27). This act of horrific betrayal resulted in the death of Christ, but it also led to His glorification. "So, when he had gone out, Jesus said, 'Now the Son of man is glorified'" (John 13:31).

Satan may have been artfully manipulated by God Himself. It is possible that Satan was moved by God to influence Judas to accomplish God's desired end. This view conforms to a high view of the sovereignty of God. God has been highly exalted over His enemies. When it suited His purposes, He used them for His unseen eternal purposes. By bringing Jesus to the only circumstance whereby He could be assured of a true curse-breaking, atoning death on the cross, God won His predetermined final victory over sin and death. If some in the Church are angry over the treatment of Jesus, the Jews should not be the prime targets for blame. It could be successfully argued from a Reformed position that although Judas betrayed Jesus at the behest of Satan, this was done at the foreordination of God Almighty. No Christian would suggest that God acted in error or that a blunder occurred in Jerusalem. His will was effectively applied. His purposes successfully achieved. To thinking Christians, the truth of Easter Sunday, proves the purpose of Good Friday!

The film version of *Jesus Christ Superstar* made an unfortunate mistake in the scene preceding "Hosanna Heysanna." This song introduced Jesus' triumphant entry into Jerusalem. Completely contrary to the biblical information, the film presented the priests as responsible for the death of John the Baptist. Caiaphas sang, "We must crush him completely so like John before him this Jesus must die."[111] That chorus was repeated intensely as the arrogant priests towered over the commoners from fabricated scaffolding. The Gospel account is clear that Herod gave the order for John the Baptist to be beheaded. "So he sent and had John beheaded in prison. And his head was brought on a platter and given to the girl, and she brought it to her mother" (Matthew 14:10-11). The priests had no guilt in the crime attributed Herod. The film's portrayal is a complete invention that could only be considered as disparaging to the priests. Herod's characterization was more absurd, though less anti-Semitic. He was played as a fat, stupid, arrogant clown who was surrounded by obviously gay men. He wanted Jesus to prove himself by walking across the "swimming pool."

Pilate: Pawn or Prefect?

Jesus Christ Superstar also committed another common mistake. In the rendering of the Gospel account the producers presented Pilate in a favorable light. The obvious danger is that by portraying the Jews as the true enemies of God, Pilate appears to be a helpless pawn in the hands of the Jews. This all-too-common recreation of the character of Pilate is an offense to the Jews, as well as to the memory of Pilate who was a cruel, brutal, calculated, and domineering ruler. Nonetheless, the producers traveled the same deluded path that tends to exonerate Pilate.

> In what follows, Pilate repeatedly demonstrates his liking for Jesus. At one point in the scene "Trial before Pilate," as currently staged, he falls to his knees and sympathetically puts his arms around Jesus in an effort to make him respond. In the same scene he underlines that the other side, not he, is responsible for any mistreatment of Jesus: "You have been brought here—manacled, beaten by your own people—do you have the first idea why you deserve it?" This entire portrait of Pilate, designed to minimize his role in Jesus' scourging, trial and death and thereby maximize that of Jesus' Jewish antagonists, is wildly unscriptural and unhistorical. Roman and other sources leave no doubt that Pilate was an exceptionally harsh governor even by the far from lenient standards of Roman occupation government. While in Jesus' case he did not see any compelling reason to carry out a death penalty, he was nevertheless notorious for his arbitrary executions. He was eventually recalled to Rome and tried for oppression.[112]

From these descriptions it can be seen that the "rock opera" presentation of the passion carries many erroneous interpretations. There can be no comfort in the thought that "Broadway" is not the theological equivalent of Oberammergau. Though the specific presentation of the German passion play presumes a closer tie to biblical accuracy, American culture has been impacted by the world of mass media. It can be expected that this film will gain new relevance and new viewers due to the success of Mr. Gibson's recent film success. I can only hope that new viewers who rent "Superstar" at their local video store will view it with a more critical eye as a result of the information in this research. One critic accurately made this comparison:

> There is one thing more in which the film also maintains a stubborn consistency, and that is its anti-Semitism: having this film in general release is a bit like having a performance of a with-it version of the Oberammergau Passion Play . . . Not only is all culpability in Christ's death passed on to a malignant Jewish priesthood and blood-thirsty Jewish mob; the priests are also portrayed in a way that is clearly indebted to classically vilifying stereotypes.[113]

Another Look at Ben Hur

Untold millions of American adults have seen the fifteen-million-dollar box office epic, *Ben Hur*. The production reportedly cost an enormous $15,000,000.00 in 1950's pre-inflation money. It was based upon the book by General Lew Wallace. Interestingly, *Ben Hur* was subtitled *A Tale of the Christ*. The film was a financial, technical, and artistic success, however, that famous Hollywood extravaganza passionately informed a generation of Americans that huge crowds of angry Jews turned on Christ. The producers successfully avoided some of the most egregious errors often included within presentations depicting the passion week. Had they avoided trying to present every scene as a grandiose display, they might have overcome the need to employ thousands of "extras." More importantly, they might have achieved even more realism. Pilate's trial of Jesus was held in broad daylight in front of what appeared to be "all" the Jews of Jerusalem. The trial should have been portrayed at sunrise. The court scene of Pilate was bigger than a football stadium and certainly much larger than the actual area would have been. The staging suggests that "all" the Jews in Jerusalem were the enemies of Jesus encouraging his death. The small group of his followers seemed to have identities, whereas the masses of nameless Jews in the crowd scene served to convince the viewer that Jesus had few Jewish friends in a predominantly hostile Jewish environment.

The film was sensitive to the sense of patriotism, national identity, and zealous religious hope in which the Jewish people believed. These positive attributes of Judaism were shared with enthusiasm and care by the producers. Therefore, it was disappointing to see the manner in which Pilate's guilt was reduced to a symbolic hand washing. He never uttered a word against Jesus. In the film the Romans were not wicked crucifiers as much as they were controlling the Jewish mob. These contradictions in the presentation and the attending fundamental errors did nothing to prohibit the film from earning a record-breaking eleven Academy Awards.[114]

The message of Jewish guilt has been transmitted from coast to coast in the "theology" of Broadway and Hollywood. Both *Jesus Christ Superstar* and *Ben Hur* were spectacular successes attended by many American Christians. The problems of anti-Semitic influence in the Gospel presentation are not limited to Hollywood's cinema or Broadway's stage presentations. *America now has its own Mount Oberammergau*!

---

100 Sharin R. Gunton, Editor, *Contemporary Literary Criticism* Volume 21, (Detroit, Michigan: Gale Research Company Book Tower, 1982) 427, citing James R. Huffman, *"Holy Boredom: The Jesus Christ Superstar Film,"* in Melody Maker , (IPC Business Press Ltd.) June 16, 1973, 3.

101 Gunton, 425, citing Clive Barnes, *"Theater: Christ's Passion Transported to the Stage in Guise of Serious Pop,"* in The New York Times, October 13, 1971.

102 Gunton, 427, citing Dan Morgenstern, *"'Superstar': Beyond Redemption!"* in Down Beat, Volume 38, No. 21, December 9, 1971, 1, 13.

103 Gerald S. Strober, *"Jesus Christ Superstar": The "Rock Opera" and Christian-Jewish Relations*, The American Jewish Committee, Institute on Human Relations, 1971, foreword.

104 Ibid., 3.

105 Ibid., 4.

106 Ibid.

107 Frank Charles Thompson, *The Thompson Chain-Reference Bible*, (Indianapolis, IN: B. B. Kirkbridge Bible Co., Inc., 1988), King James Version, 1137.

108 This is reminiscent of the words of King David. "Yea mine own familiar friend, in whom I trusted, which did eat of my bread" (Psalms 41:9), and again, later to Psalm 55:12-14. David probably was relating his feelings about the broken relationship with his friend and counselor, Ahithophel. Speaking prophetically, the verses allude to the future person of Judas. This is clarified by the New Testament explanation given by Peter in Acts, "Men and bretheren, this scripture must needs have been fulfilled, which the Holy Ghost by the mouth of David spake before concerning Judas, which was guide

to them that took Jesus. For he was numbered with us, and had obtained part of this ministry" (Acts 1:16,17).

109 Gordon Lindsay, *Acts in Action Volume I*, (Dallas, TX: Christ For The Nations, Inc., 1985), 8.

110 Curtis Vaughan, 2101.

111 *Jesus Christ Superstar*, book by Tim Rice, screenplay by Melvyn Bragg and Norman Jewison, music by Andrew Lloyd Webber, lyrics by Tim Rice. Universal an MCA company.

112 Stober, *Jesus Christ Superstar*, 6-7.

113 Gunton, 430.

114 The National Board of Review of Motion Pictures, Inc., *500 Best American Films to Buy, Rent or Videotape*, (Simon & Schuster Pocket Books, 1985), 42.

Section 2

Christian Bigots & the Passion

Chapter VIII

The Passion of Eureka Springs, Arkansas

In the hollow between Magnetic Mountain and Mount Oberammergau (as named by the past head of the Elna M. Smith Foundation), a 4,100-seat amphitheater is the "profit center" for a six hundred acre Ozark mountain non-profit religious entertainment complex. Spectators come from around the world to see the presentation of America's own version of *The Great Passion Play* in Eureka Springs, Arkansas. Their brochure advertising the 1994 season proudly proclaimed that they were in their twenty-seventh year of the presentation.[115] Prominently erected on the mountain stands their impressive seven-story statue of Jesus known as "Christ of the Ozarks." The monument can be seen from four states. It accents an enormous complex that boasts the following attractions: the Church in the Grove, the Sacred Arts Center, the Bible Museum, a recreated ten foot section of the Berlin Wall, a full-scale reproduction of the Tabernacle in the Wilderness, two gift shops, and a buffet restaurant. Pre-play performances of gospel music concerts and the *Parables of the Potter* add to the experience, plus tickets for their daily tours of The New Holyland are also available.

I personally toured portions of the facility in 1994 and also viewed their videotape from the 1992 edition of the performance. After completing the research for my doctoral dissertation that became the basis for this book, I visited with the gentleman who was running *The Great Passion Play* in Eureka Springs at that time. Through the invitation (and in the presence) of one of their major supporters, I explained my grave concerns for the tenor of the play. I also described what I believed to be unnecessary anti-Semitic aspects to their presentation. Finally I attempted to suggest some simple modifications that would have rendered the drama much less inflammatory. Before I could finish my comments, the conversation was abruptly ended. The elder gentleman informed me in the clearest of terms that when I produced my own Passion Play I could change the script any way that I wished. He made it known that he was not at all interested in my comments or any concerns I might have about anti-Semitic aspects to the script in use.

It is my hope that others will be interested in these issues and additional future modifications will be made to passion play presentations. It is also my opinion that since my "meeting" with the gentleman in charge, some changes may have been incorporated. However, for the purposes of this review, their videotaped rendition of the drama from that most recent 1992 production was all that was available for evaluation when this report was completed. The review was not concerned with acting ability, production quality, or stage presentation. It was merely focused on any anti-Semitic inclusions or blatant errors that were presented to the masses. Their videotape boasts the following in their introductory titling:

> What you are about to see is America's number one outdoor drama in attendance, seen to date by more than five million visitors. We believe you will enjoy and be blessed by this video presentation, but there can be no true substitute for the unforgettable spiritual experience of witnessing this unique Christian presentation[116] in person with your family and friends.[117]

The claims of success will not be debated; however, one might disagree with some of the other claims. The video soundtrack includes the same prerecorded voices heard by the live audiences while they watch the actors lip-synch the script. Therefore, a fairly accurate "substitute" exists making it unnecessary to travel the winding mountain roads to Eureka Springs to hear a comparable taped script. Similar passion plays are presented in many parts of Europe and a myriad of elaborate presentations can be seen in America. Some of the larger churches in America also include an impressive array of live sheep, horses, camels etc. I attended one such presentation that even included an awesome full-grown tiger staged as a Roman pet! Therefore, "unique" may be an exaggeration. The claims of offering enjoyment, blessings, and a spiritual experience will be disputed on the basis of errant presuppositions similar to the problems contained in the Oberammergau production.

The video begins by depicting Jesus and his disciples. Then the villains of the story are presented. The Jews discuss the miracles of Jesus, and an angry Jewish leader announces, with marked Arkansas drawl, "We must let it be known among all the Jews and Gentiles that we are most anxious to have this Jesus." Caiaphas, dressed remarkably like a Klu Klux Klansman, publicly read a prepared scroll saying, "I Caiaphas, chief priest of the Sanhedrin, now decree, any man who knows where Jesus of Nazareth may be found, and provides us with this information so that we might arrest him, that man shall be well rewarded." The New Testament offered no information that would suggest such a scroll existed, nor did it give details from which a stage could be set to suggest that Caiaphas announced to all of Jerusalem, as though angry bounty hunters were waiting among the passing Jews and Romans, or that the entire Sanhedrin was out to get Jesus.

An Unfair Portrayal

As Jesus went about healing people in full view of the Sanhedrin, instead of marveling at the miracles they said, "This Jesus is a crafty one, far brighter than we anticipated." Then they attempted to trick Jesus with questions. The stage presentation ignores that the Jewish leaders were correct in testing Jesus. It was a method to know the content of Jesus' teaching. "It was very common to test a Rabbi with hard questions. . . . The Sanhedrin was within their rights in challenging the ecclesiastical and scholastic (scribal) standing of Jesus. He did not dodge in his answer."[118] According to the text of Matthew 22:16, the event did not take place at the Sanhedrin headquarters. Actually, they sent out a small group acting as though they were genuinely interested in his comments. The Arkansas portrayal showed Jesus addressing the Jewish audience like the captain of the cheerleaders holding up a Roman coin, "Who's head is on this?" The crowd shouted back in unison, "Caesar's!" Jesus then asked, "Who's inscription?" The dutiful crowd responded, "Caesar's!" Jesus then instructed the Sanhedrin to pay Caesar what belonged to Caesar and give God His due. The New Testament described the event as follows: the Sanhedrin "sent spies who pretended to be righteous, that they might seize on His words, in order to deliver Him to the power and the authority of the governor" (Luke 20:20). The question of the spies had meaningful implications that were ignored by the surface level treatment of the passion drama. To Jews under Roman domination the issue was quite serious. It was a "dilemma about paying tribute to Caesar, a live question in current politics and theology. They offered Jesus the alternative of popular disfavor or of disloyalty to the Roman government."[119] This might also have shown the concerns that the Jewish leaders felt about trying to harm Jesus. They would have preferred that Rome respond to Jesus. Coincidentally, neither the account from Luke 20:20 nor that of Matthew 20:16 gave any indication that Jesus addressed a large Jewish crowd with the question of the coin. It is apparent from both sources that Jesus asked his famous questions about the coins to the rabbinic "spies," not the Jewish spectators.

Wickedness Personified

The next outrageous excess concerns Herod. The Jewish king was presented as the personification of wickedness. He mockingly threw change into the street which permitted Salome the pleasure of watching the beggars grovel for the money. He laughed satanically and reveled in his machinations to kill Jesus as he had killed John the Baptist. This completely ignored Scripture and was a departure from the fact that Herod was greatly disturbed about being tricked into executing John. Matthew reports that after Salome asked Herod for John's head as her promised reward, "the king was sorry; nevertheless, because of the oaths and because of those who sat with him, he commanded it to be given her. So he sent and had John beheaded" (Matthew 14:9).

The next grievous assumption is reflected in Judas' betrayal. After his deal was settled with the Sanhedrin, one of the Jewish leaders gave this order, "Take the guards and go into the street, gather a crowd, stir the people up, and take that Judas with you." Judas walked off with the Jewish Temple guards (no Roman soldiers appear to be involved) then the scene turned back to the Jewish leaders gloating about their soon-coming vengeance. The Sanhedrin ended their meeting proudly announcing, "He shall die!" That line became the cue for the actors to begin running like lions to the kill. They screamed throughout the streets of Jerusalem. Judas cried out, "Awake, awake, the high priests [sic] call on the people of Jerusalem!" Then Jewish soldiers echoed, "Awake, awake, everyone proceed to the council!" Soon it appeared that the Jewish community was headed after Jesus as an angry lynch mob. Judas began to regret his action as he told the soldiers, "Just listen to these people; there is blood in their eyes." The soldiers comforted Judas assuring him that the behavior was normal. "It is only the nature of crowds to be a bit rowdy. Do not concern yourself; we have an agreement." The New Testament is quite clear in detailing that the Sanhedrin would never have permitted Judas or the soldiers to run through town waking the followers of Jesus. The presentation was absolutely contrary to the message presented in the New Testament. Sadly, it was consistent with other inflammatory anti-Semitic presentations that suggest that the Jewish nation rose up against Jesus. In this regard, this play, along with others, depart from the description given by the Gospel writers. Unfortunately, the angry mob portion of the video presentation was quite difficult to see. Presumably, it was filmed in poor conditions without proper lighting, or the cameras were of insufficient quality. Regardless, the scene portraying the mob hunting Jesus with sticks and torches deteriorated until all that was evident were men and women repeatedly screaming "Kill the traitor! Kill him!"

The arrest led Jesus to a Jewish "kangaroo court." At the close of the mock trial before the Sanhedrin, Annas offered the completely unfounded pronouncement that Jesus was found guilty, and sentenced him to death by a unanimous decision; and Pilate would have no choice but to likewise condemn him. The priests thereby hoped to shift blame to Roman authority. Pilate was presented as a kind and reasonable advocate of Jesus. He seemed constrained to perform according to the plan of manipulative Jewish conspirators. Pilate was presented as astounded by the Jewish insistence for the death penalty. He refused to handle the uncomfortable business at hand and sent them to Herod.

Herod mocked and ridiculed Jesus. He called him John the Baptist, reminding the audience of the murder of John. As he arose from his throne to further taunt Jesus the scene revealed an enormous Jewish star on his throne. The Star of David prominently displayed on Herod's throne served to convey Jewish guilt. However, in truth, Herod was only half Jewish. This fact was a constant source of frustration to Herod. Some circles of Jewish leaders resented Herod and refused to accept him because of his impure bloodline. This probably led to his unstable behavior during his reign. In the presentation, Herod was cast as a horribly bloodthirsty Jewish villain. "Thank you for bringing him to us! We are greatly pleased to meet him at long last." It was apparent that he desired to kill Jesus. Herod's extra-biblical antics elicited animosity against the Jewish political ruler. Herod toyed with the notion of releasing Jesus. Then the scene generated more resentment against the Jewish religious leadership as the priests were enraged at the thought of release. Ultimately, Jesus was sent back to Pilate.

Pilate & Claudius as Friends of Jesus

The Sanhedrin met and informed the audience that Pilate wanted to release Jesus. They determined to find a manner in which to force Pilate to condemn Jesus. The drama also inserted Joseph of Arimathea and Nicodemus into their meeting. It cannot be known from the Gospels if they were present during the hearing. However, if they were in attendance, it is likely they would have objected and attempted to stop the travesty of justice that was being planned. Pilate was again presented as sensitive and friendly toward Jesus. He seemed to be a pawn in the hands of the Jews. Claudius, the beautiful Gentile wife of Pilate, warned her husband to not be involved. Pilate humbly presented Jesus to the angry Jewish mob desiring to set the innocent Jesus free. The vengeful Jews refused to permit Pilate's mercy. After Jesus was beaten, Pilate begged the unforgiving Jews, "Behold your king! He has been flogged, beaten, ridiculed, spit upon, what more can you want?" The Jewish crowd insisted that Jesus be crucified. Pilate begged them, "Do I not have your consent to release this man?" The Jewish crowd unmercifully demanded the death of Jesus. The crowd howled for the release of Barabbas in juxtaposition with the crucifixion of Jesus. They resorted to accusing Pilate of being a traitor to Caesar. It is apparent that this presentation seeks to place primary guilt on the Jews, while alleviating the weight of Roman responsibility.

One cannot overlook the fact that Pilate and his wife are so sympathetic to Jesus in this drama that after the Resurrection, Claudius is shown going off to follow Jesus along with a penitent Roman soldier. The script makes it clear that the Jewish people insisted on the death of Jesus. It is as if the Jews on stage showed complete disregard for the humane desires of Pilate. The death scene removed any doubts that might have remained as to the character of the Jews. That scene presented the Jewish leaders mercilessly taunting Jesus. After he was pronounced dead, the Gentile Roman soldiers told the audience, "Beyond all doubt, this man was innocent." The next soldier proclaimed, "Truly this man was the Son of God!" Then they knelt down and worshipped the body of Jesus on the cross.

An Angel Beyond Imagination

The climax introducing the Resurrection scene showed the angel speaking to Mary at the tomb of Jesus. Their choice of a female angel was extremely creative since the Gospels make it clear that the angel was not female. Matthew, Mark, and Luke clearly assigned masculine attributes to the angel. The angel's dialogue went far beyond creative and became inventive. She said, "You have nothing to fear. You are looking for Jesus who was crucified, who died and descended into Hell. Do not fear for him for he has struggled valiantly in the very bowels of the earth. He has battled with Satan retrieving the keys to Hell and to the grave." This exchange suggests that the playwright took excessive liberties. The Gospels suggest nothing about the angels commenting that Jesus had descended into Hell, or that while there, he engaged in battles with Satan. That imagery may be similar to later versions of the Apostle's Creed;[120] nonetheless, like much of the script, the angel scene carries with it many mistaken presumptuous views.[121]

As in the version of Oberammergau, *The Great Passion Play* was intensely slanted to portray untrue characterizations about the Jewish people. It indelibly scars the Jewish image and insures that the charge of deicide follows Jews into future generations. Some of these false interpretations of the New Testament are preposterous; yet, some Christian audiences accept the presentation with enthusiasm. If things do not change, Eureka Springs will continue spreading anti-Semitic myths to pervert future generations. One must wonder how an American presentation of such magnitude could be so full of such obvious Christian anti-Semitism. The answer to that inquiry will be addressed in great detail as the founder of *The Great Passion Play* is investigated.

As previously mentioned, I traveled to Eureka Springs in connection with this research. After visiting nearly every business establishment in the city's quaint downtown, contacting the local Chamber of Commerce, visiting the local Christian bookstore, surveying the secular bookstores, and asking numerous people around town, it became apparent that nobody wished to discuss the pageant's founder. This was most apparent when seeking information directly from the Smith Foundation. Several phone calls were made, and it became clear that issues surrounding the founder would not be addressed by the organization. They were unwilling to openly discuss the man who birthed the cash cow of this tourist destination. It was as if they were hiding the truth.

Upon visiting the premises, one senses that Jesus himself watched over the founders. This is because the couple who developed the enterprise are buried directly across the walkway a few yards away from the giant statue of Jesus. Elna M. Smith, for whom the foundation was named, is entombed next to her late husband, Gerald L. K. Smith.

Organizations often carry the torches that have been lit by their founders. Certainly, men of vision can only pursue their goals while they have their strength and personal drive. These same men often channel their energies into drawing followers behind them to help carry on the battles in which they are engaged. Gerald L. K. Smith was just such a man. He was a fighter. He had a "call" on his life. The culmination of that "call" is represented in the drama that has been going on for more than three decades since his death.

---

115 Brochure, The Elna M. Smith Foundation, Eureka Springs, Arkansas

116 The claim of this being a "Christian presentation" is one underlying question that this study circumvents. It is readily acknowledged that Christians have been attending passion play dramas for many centuries. Whether the presentations are truly "Christian" in nature, or merely an appeal to Christian audiences is more difficult to ascertain.

117 Unless otherwise noted, all quotes from this play will be from *The Great Passion Play*, Kent Tallakson, Executive producer (also listed Robert C. Foster and Ken Smith as Executive Producers), Elna M. Smith Foundation, videotaped by Venture for Christ International, Fayetteville, Arkansas, 1992.

118 Robertson, 160.

119 Ibid, 164.

120 The Old Roman Form of the Apostles' Creed (c. 390 CE) does not include the later addition found in The Received Form, "He descended into Hell (Hades);" which was added after the seventh century, probably from the Aquilejan Creed. This information from Philip Schaff's, *The Creeds of Christendom*, Volume I, (Grand Rapids, MI: Baker Books, 1993), 21.

121 With regards to the angelic decree of Jesus having visited Hell, Smith's scriptwriter joined himself to a distinguished company of expositors. Though equally curious, even Pope John Paul II recently espoused the same assumption that Jesus was in Hell. His Holiness John Paul II, *Crossing The Threshold Of Hope*, (New York: Alfred A. Knopf, 1994), 46

Chapter IX

Legacy of Hate: Gerald L. K. Smith & Famous Friends

Gerald Lyman Kenneth Smith (1898-1976) was raised in a solid Christian home. His lineage can be traced back to English pioneers. Smith's roots in the Christian faith are well known. He was proud to have come from "four generations of rock-ribbed Republicans and three generations of fire-and-brimstone, circuit-riding, fundamentalist preachers."[122] His heritage is admirable. His commitment to Jesus was central to his upbringing. "Gerald accepted Christ at the age of seven and was baptized in his father's church in Richland Center. Five years later he decided to become a minister and never seriously considered any other profession,"[123] although his career crossed several occupational lines.

Smith was educated at a small Midwestern school, Valparaiso University, originally organized to help indigent students. The Reverend Claude Hill, pastor of Valparaiso's First Christian Church helped Smith begin his ministerial career while Smith was yet a student. Smith's time in northwest Indiana was productive. In addition to completing his studies, he was the regular preacher at a church in Deep River, as well as a church in nearby Gary, Indiana. After graduation, in the fall of 1918, Smith applied to several graduate schools. This would seem out of character for a man who apparently disdained education. He declared that he had come from a long line of country preachers. Many would heartily agree with Smith's views on vocational Christian compensation and preparation. He considered himself to be a working preacher, "the kind that earned an honest living in the week and preached on Sunday and didn't sit around and do nothing but eat chicken dinners."[124] He disparaged vocational ministers comparing them to prostitutes saying, "A man who took money for serving God was like a woman who took money for making love."[125] He apparently did not trust professional clergy suggesting, "The most dangerous thing we have in this country is paid preachers."[126] He also showed disdain for ministers who needed advanced university degrees. "Christianity is as simple as a Western Union telegram," he said. "Suppose you inherited a hundred thousand dollars. It wouldn't take an intellectual to bring a telegram to your door. Jesus said everything that needed to be said about Christianity."[127]

In 1919, after a bout with "nephritis, a serious kidney infection,"[128] Smith entered full-time ministry with tremendous dynamism. He was what seemed to be a never-ending stream of energetic evangelism and enthusiastic soul winning. These traits made him very popular with his growing congregation. He was known to spend his Saturdays visiting local pool halls seeking sinners. His antics included periodically jumping up on top of pool tables and preaching spontaneous sermons. His efforts were very effective and in the remarkably short period of a few months, Smith turned the struggling church into a very successful local congregation. But neither Smith nor fate was satisfied. In less than a year, Pastor Gerald L.K. Smith accepted a call to a larger church.

As a communicator, Smith did not stop with preaching. He was a prolific writer. He was known to have had twenty-five thousand subscribers to a magazine he published called *The Cross and the Flag*. Far beyond his subscribers, Smith's writings were widely read and available. He successfully produced many millions of pieces of his literature.

> Smith became one of the most prolific polemicists in America. He claimed to have written over five hundred books, tracts, and pamphlets, 90 percent of each issue of the *Cross and the Flag*, and collected works that surpassed in length the *Encyclopedia Britannica*. In sheer output, Smith ranked with Toynbee and the Durants.[129]

"The Voice of America"

His documents and speeches were sometimes inserted into America's *Congressional Record* by senators and congressmen. One senator called him "The voice of America."[130] Smith became involved in the political arena in 1934. That year he spoke to more than one million people as the national organizer for Huey P. Long, who was better known to Louisiana voters as the Kingfish. It is apparent that Gerald L. K. Smith was very influential long before producing *The Great Passion Play*.

During the tenuous days before America entered World War II, Smith was active and vocal about America's international affairs.

In July 1940, Senator Arthur H. Vandenberg presented to the Senate a Smith petition to outlaw Communism and to avoid American entry into the war. Smith claimed that his petition contained more than a million names. Vandenberg praised Smith and his movement on the Senate floor, and Senator Robert R. Reynolds inserted the text of the petition in the *Congressional Record*.[131]

The Senate called upon Smith later that same year to offer his opinions on foreign policy. The Senate Foreign Relations Committee invited Smith (as one of only ten witnesses) to speak on the issue of Lend-Lease. That subject was very troubling to the government at the time. It was believed that Smith's opinions were valuable because he represented a very large constituency. Congressman Roy Woodruff of Michigan "inserted a letter from Smith in the *Congressional Record*, terming him a 'great leader,' and the following year he inserted the featured editorial from the first issue of Smith's *The Cross and the Flag*."[132]

The magnitude of his influence is difficult to measure. While still in Christian service, as a young pastor in Indianapolis, Indiana, Smith was responsible for gaining sixteen hundred new converts to Christ in a single year. He could not rest in that accomplishment. He went on to pastor larger and more influential churches in various states.

Smith began a media movement with which most American Christians have become familiar. The distasteful schemes of "bleeding the sheep" did not begin with the excesses of 1980's televangelists. Gerald L. K. Smith had a significant head start at incessantly begging sheep-like followers for contributions to pay broadcast expenses, regardless of whether or not the flock had enough money for their own food and housing. He learned to carefully work the audiences of his radio "ministry."

When it came to mixing religion and politics, Smith was not an innovator. He had a famous relationship with another promoter of religious

Radio Priest or Renegade Religious Bigot?

Father Charles E. Coughlin was a very dynamic young Catholic priest from the Detroit diocese. He rose to national prominence after he entered the medium of radio preaching in October 1931. His message was political and it was informed by his own quest for power as well as his flavor of anti-Semitism. Early in his radio career, as an ardent supporter of President Franklin Roosevelt, Coughlin coined the political slogan, "Roosevelt or Ruin." But in his later years, he turned against FDR with a vengeance. In 1936 he coined a new slogan in his effort to see FDR defeated declaring, "Roosevelt and Ruin." Coughlin liberally borrowed from the words of Jesus to demean FDR suggesting that the "money changers have not been driven from the temple." He wanted his radio flock to presume that the influence of the wicked moneychangers was guiding the White House.

Father Coughlin's fame spread across America and his influence was both feared and respected. Some believed that Coughlin had the single largest following of any person in the United States of America! The enormous level of response from his audience demanded employing fifty-two secretaries to deal with the volume of mail that was reported to reach a flow of 250,000 letters per day![133] (Although one report suggested about half the number of secretaries handling 200,000 letters per week.) In any case, he was an extremely powerful man. His enormous organization was known as the National Union for Social Justice. Students of history, politics, business, and religion should find it interesting that Father Coughlin's sixteen-point program for social justice was unveiled at the Ford Motor Company in 1937. Significantly, all non-Christians were excluded from membership! This was absolutely aimed directly at the Jews and represented Coughlin's clear answer to the CIO's efforts to organize autoworkers.[134]

Many, including Gerald L.K. Smith, shared Coughlin's growing hatred of President Roosevelt and the Jews. At one point, Smith announced a political alliance with Father Coughlin. Many believed their formation of a third political party was the answer to the quagmire confounding America. Smith also mimicked Father Coughlin's successful efforts to mobilize supporters through the creative use of radio preaching. In 1937 Smith entered the radio ministry in Cleveland. Later he moved to Detroit where his success grew exponentially.

> He took over the forty-eight-station network that had carried Father Coughlin's program. . . . Within months Smith had 250,000 names in his files . . . Smith organized his own activities into four areas: direct mail, radio, book distribution, and personal appearances . . . In January 1942, Smith created an elite group of especially generous contributors, which he called the Inner Circle . . . Smith continually warned that unless his most trusted supporters responded with money, he would be compelled to cease his broadcasts. . . By 1942 he claimed three million members . . . and boasted that he was adding between three and six thousand per week . . . His radio speeches, broadcast to a population area of 30 to 40 million potential listeners."[135]

Although Gerald L.K. Smith's name was never a household word, even in his later years, "Thousands of small, anonymous donors contributed from $1.00 to $10.00 two or three times a year. A few of them tithed 10 percent of their income to Smith because they believed he was doing the 'Lord's work.' "[136] It was said by his biographer that nobody "could match the man himself in lungpower, stamina, and organizational skill. During the latter half of the 1940's, Smith spoke to more and larger audiences than any other American of that time."[137]

Preacher, Politician, Man of Passion

Smith was driven by a sense of divine purpose. In addition to running in political campaigns for the U.S. Senate, he also contended in the presidential campaigns of 1944 and 1948 as he carried the fight against evil around the nation. He wanted to protect America from the White House by being in the White House. "He provided material for textbooks and for church seminars and study groups. He told his supporters to pray, read patriotic literature, and contribute money to the Christian Nationalist Crusade."[138]

The preacher living inside of Gerald Smith had a habit of rising up to meet any political occasion. During his unsuccessful 1942 Senate race he spoke in terms quite reminiscent of sermon enhancements that churchgoers still hear today. He told one audience the following:

Now I know some of you folks out there don't like what I've been saying. We'll stop right here for just a minute to let you go home if you don't like it, because I warn you, it's going to get hotter as I go along." The audience chuckled. Then turning to the press table: "All right, you fellows get out your asbestos paper now because I want you to get this down. It's going to be hot stuff. . . . I am perfectly willing to burn that the bonfire of my bones may light the way for future generations." Crouching at the microphone, grinning slyly, he whispered, "They say I am insane." Then, rising to his full height, he shouted: "Maybe I am insane, and I will continue to be insane—insane enough to believe in the Bible and America First."[139]

Passion to Save America

His message was particularly appealing to religious fundamentalists, but what indeed was his message? What was his "call?" Perhaps Smith's 1948 presidential campaign platform can describe the inner beliefs of the man who founded *The Great Passion Play*.

What did the "insane" man who believed in the Bible hope to accomplish as president in 1948? Smith was convinced that his Christian Nationalist Party was going to take over America. Smith's representative, Don Lohbeck, was the chairman of the party's 1948 national convention. Lohbeck explained to the delegates that they had created the party "to save America from Christ-hating Jews and their Communist pawns."[140] Smith was the keynote speaker, and with all the intensity of a pulpit-thumping preacher he announced the sordid details of the Christian Nationalist platform in a fashion that appears to be regularly duplicated by speakers skilled in the art of audience manipulation. The following example is worth remembering the next time a religious leader pushes his listeners into the "amen-corner." Smith apparently used his religious experience to his greatest advantage.

> After stating each plank he asked the audience to applaud if they approved. They responded enthusiastically, and when Smith called for a standing vote to endorse the entire platform the delegates rose. The platform advocated the deportation of blacks and Zionist Jews. Ghettoes would be constructed for Jews remaining in the United States, and the housing shortage would be resolved by giving the homes of deported Jews to veterans.[141]

According to the famous editor and critic H. L. Mencken (1880-1956), who himself has been compared to modern media moguls Ted Turner and Norman Lear,[142] Gerald L. K. Smith was highly regarded and uniquely qualified to excite an audience. Mencken was known to have believed Smith to be

> superior to William Jennings Bryan, describing Smith as "the greatest rabble-rouser seen on earth since the Apostolic times." Smith himself believed he was the third most powerful person in the nation, just behind Roosevelt (F. D. R.) and Long (Huey P.) He boasted to a reporter in 1935 that he might enflame the entire country and "duplicate the feat of Adolph [sic] Hitler in Germany."[143]

The issue must be considered as to how Smith justified his depth of bigotry as a so-called Christian.

> Smith rationalized his hatred of the Jewish people by claiming that they had crucified the Son of God. The Jews, not Pilate or the Romans, were solely responsible for the Crucifixion . . . Jews lied when they claimed to be the "chosen people" of God, Smith charged. "The crucifiers of Christ were not God's chosen people," he wrote. "They were a throng of devil-possessed agents of the anti-Christ." Nor were Israelites, the chosen people, necessarily Jews, Smith argued. A tract he published claimed that the present-day Jews were descendants of "pagan phallic worshippers" . . . "I warn you in studying the Bible not to confuse the Israel of the Old Testament with the people we now call Jews," he wrote.[144]

Smith was obviously a deluded, bitter, confused man. He was deceived, yet certain of his own accuracy and perpetually innocent in his own view. He was convinced of the error of the world around him, yet oblivious to his own spiritual shortcomings. He actively promoted and was drawn to every hoax that might implicate wrongdoing on the part of Jews. His logic prohibited him from conceiving of the true Jewishness of the early Church.

> It was difficult for Smith to believe that Jesus was a Jew, so he blithely changed history to suit his fancy. Jesus was not a Jew, he claimed, but a blue-eyed blond with a golden beard.[145] Smith said that modern Jews did not look anything like Jesus

and offered pictures to his readers as proof. "It is a matter of common knowledge," he wrote, "that the physical Jesus was fair and blond . . . and bore no resemblance whatsoever to the modern hook nose shop keeper, money changer, brothel owner, and whiskey peddler." . . . Christ's disciples were not Jews either; they were "Galileans"—except for Judas Iscariot, who was a Jew.[146]

The zeal with which Smith hated the Jewish people is monumental. Referred to as a "gutter bigot" by one author, Smith, and his Christian Nationalist Crusade were recognized for their true nature.

He now argued for the complete and absolute social and political segregation of the Black and White races, and insisted the American people were held in slavery by the Jews. Smith proved to be a transparent fraud, constantly pleading poverty. Although highly successful with his followers, Smith's religious enterprises were a pseudopolitical racket carried on by a very professional Protestant Fundamentalist. Smith was the earliest of the genre that had discovered sham-religious bigotry to be a lucrative operation. Whipping up his supporters in "tent" meetings, he built a national organization with tens of thousands of followers. Three decades of raucous hate-mongering made his crackpot Christian Nationalist Crusade a fixture on the American scene.[147]

The Divine "Call" of Hatred

In 1933, "Smith had experienced an emotional 'call' which revealed to him that Jews were an evil force."[148] He spent much of the rest of his life pursuing that hatred. He hated the Jews with such intensity that he believed and promoted the idea that

Jews worshipped the Devil; they worshipped snakes and goats; they participated in sexual orgies, infanticide, and cannibalism as part of their religious ceremonies. Jewish physicians murdered Christian patients. Jews manipulated Stalin and Roosevelt. The Holocaust was invented or staged by Jews to elicit sympathy.

Smith published and distributed a classic hoax, *The*

> *Protocols of the Learned Elders of Zion*, describing a meeting of Jewish elders at Basel, Switzerland, in 1897, where they outlined plans to undermine Gentile civilization and make themselves rulers of the world. Actually, *Protocols* originated in an obscure French novel that attacked Napoleon III. It was later plagiarized by a Russian cleric who made Jews into villains in order to justify pogroms in czarist Russia. . . . *Protocols* was smuggled to America . . . Historians branded the book a forgery and ninety-three leading Americans, including President Woodrow Wilson, issued a statement repudiating it. American and British newspapers discredited it, and courts of law in Switzerland and South America pronounced it false. . . . this did not stop anti-Semites from peddling it. Smith insisted that it had to be true, regardless of its origins.[149]

In Smith's spiritual and political metamorphosis, the media presence of "Reverend Gerald L. K. Smith emerged from a secondary role in the 1930s to become the most prominent American spokesman of anti-semitism . . . and through the early 1970s ranked among the nation's most vituperative bigots."[150]

The man invested decades trying to convince the world that Jews were responsible for Communism, poverty, and the assassinations of Abraham Lincoln, John F. Kennedy, and Jesus, in addition to continual attempts to control the world economy.

Smith had an unhealthy admiration for the German madman who tried to conquer the world. This made him even more despicable to reasonable people. He was deluded and felt that he and Hitler were both great men who were misunderstood and persecuted by the Jews.

> During the waning days of World War II, Gerald Smith continued to identify and sympathize with Adolf Hitler. . . . He saw Hitler as the innocent victim of a Jewish conspiracy to destroy the German race. As "evidence" he stated, "Hitler's servants speak of him with the deepest regard." The Jews hated Hitler, Smith argued, because Hitler was a Bible-believing Christian.[151]

Was the Preacher an Early Holocaust Denier?

Gerald Smith was possibly one of the first Holocaust deniers to reign among modern anti-Semites. His views are still promoted by racists and ignorant fringe fanatics in many nations.

> Smith believed the charge that Hitler had killed six million Jews to be preposterous. The Jews had not been slaughtered, he said, but illegally admitted to the United States to keep Roosevelt in power. He claimed that there were more Jews after the war than before. "Most of the dead Jews whom 'Hitler killed' are now walking the streets of American cities" . . . When, many years later, Jewish Nazi-hunters captured and tried Adolf Eichmann for his role in the Holocaust, Smith concluded that his arrest was a clever ploy to gain sympathy and money for Israel. "Eichmann looks like a Jew to me," he wrote; "I wouldn't be a bit surprised to find out that the whole thing was a Jewish conspiracy with Eichmann's collaboration."[152]

Smith's hatred and intense desire to cure the "Jewish problem" seemed to endure and grow with age. Not content with poisoning the minds of his followers, Smith wanted to insure that America would be free from his fancifully perceived Jewish domination. He continually linked Zionism with Communism and "sent a copy of *The Protocols of the Elders of Zion* to every member of Congress in 1947."[153] Later in his life, Smith continued to breed hatred and "he sold copies of 'The International Jew' in bulk in 1964, and then serialized it in *The Cross and the Flag* in 1966."[154]

"Smith liked to cite from the New Testament the Jewish mob's reply to Pilate's statement that he found Jesus Innocent: "His blood be on us and on our children"[155] This attitude has been reflected in Smith's presentation of *The Great Passion Play* with malicious intent. His life was committed to breeding hatred. It is ludicrous to consider gaining spiritual insights from a Christian drama presentation founded and funded by a man of such intense hatred. Few Americans have ever plumbed the depths of bigotry as has Gerald L. K. Smith. His incessantly hateful behavior was so embarrassing that *he was refused membership in the John Birch Society* by Robert Welch.[156] Could it be that the John Birch Society has higher standards than segments of American Christianity? Consider the excellent warning given by Saint John in his first letter to the church at large:

> Beloved, believe not every spirit, but try the spirits whether they are of God: because many false prophets are gone out into the world . . . Hereby know we the spirit of truth, and

the spirit of error. Beloved, let us love one another: for love is of God; and every one that loveth is born of God, and knoweth God. He that loveth not knoweth not God; for God is love. (1 John 4:1, 6b-8 KJV)

It may never be known if Smith was a "true" but terribly misguided Christian, or merely an unpleasant Gentile. Though he was "saved" as a child, as an adult, his behavior certainly deteriorated. It seems more likely that he was little more than a hateful, loud, religious profiteer who became an unsuccessful politician. Additionally, Smith was better known for thumping his Bible than he was for reading it. "He was not much of a student of the Bible: he lacked the patience to read it regularly, and most of his biblical quotes were acquired secondhand."[157] Although the status of his salvation cannot be known with any certainty, it has been wisely suggested by various religionists that a person cannot call himself a Christian and hate the Jews (or any other people groups).

Memories are short and apparently the sins of successful Christian entrepreneurs are easily forgiven. Eureka Springs is an example of just such forgiveness. Many Christians have chosen to overlook the lifetime of bigotry that was exhibited by Gerald L. K. Smith. It is my opinion that the life and core beliefs of the man behind the religious drama are too hate-filled to be quietly tolerated.

> An Esquire writer who interviewed him in 1968 termed him "a kindly old hatesmith," a friendly man who greeted children and handicapped persons at the entrance to the Passion Play . . . This superficial geniality was deceptive. Beneath the surface still boiled his hatred of Jews. He never shed this hatred.[158]

Facts explode myths and love overcomes hate; unfortunately, only Christian love can undo the damage done by Christian anti-Semitism. Only confession and repentance can erase the sin that lurks in the background of *The Great Passion Play* of Eureka Springs, Arkansas.

Faithful Christians should not give a voice to a monster that desired to deport Jewish Zionists and blacks away from the shores of the United States of America. Followers of our Jewish Messiah should trust no one who wanted to force Jews into ghettoes so that their homes could be stolen. Nobody who taught that the Jews worship the devil should be entrusted with a Christian ministry to millions of unsuspecting believers unless first there was clear evidence of confession and true repentance for the grievous sin of blatant anti-Semitism. Christians should not place their confidence in anyone who promoted *The Protocols of the Elders of Zion*. Yet the heart of such a bigot is responsible for presenting *The Great Passion Play* during five decades to millions of Americans who are probably unaware of the intense hatred toward Jews harbored by the founder. Is the passion play anti-Semitic? It doesn't have to be. But without love for the Jews it is highly probable.

    122 Glen Jeansonne, *Gerald L. K. Smith: minister of hate*, (New Haven: Yale University Press, 1988), 11.
    123 Ibid., 14.
    124 Ibid.
    125 Ibid.
    126 Ibid.
    127 Ibid.
    128 Ibid., 19.
    129 Ibid., 135.
    130 Ibid., 87.
    131 Ibid., 81.
    132 Ibid., 88.
    133 Charles J. Tull, *Father Coughlin & The New Deal*, (New York: Syracuse University Press, 1965), 14.
    134 Ibid., 177.
    135 Jeansonne, 68-69.
    136 Ibid., 149.
    137 Ibid., 97.
    138 Ibid., 118.
    139 Ibid., 78.
    140 Ibid., 158.
    141 Ibid., 158-159.
    142 Don Feder, *A Jewish Conservative Looks at Pagan America*, (Lafayette, Louisiana: Huntington House Publishers, 1993), 134.
    143 Jeansonne, 39.
    144 Ibid., 102-103.
    145 Smith's view of the appearance of Jesus though outrageous, is not unique. Consider the opinion of the University of British Columbia's founder of the Religious Studies Department, William Nicholls. He says, "Let us put the matter in more pictorial terms. In the western world, Christians generally imagine Jesus as tall, probably with blond hair and beard, blue eyes, and wearing a white robe and an other-worldly expres-

sion. Almost certainly, he was short by modern standards and dark-skinned. His black beard was long and untrimmed. He undoubtedly wore earlocks, the *peyot* that are displayed today only by the ultra Orthodox but were once worn by all Jews as a matter of course. We know from the Gospels that he wore fringes on his garments like other Jews. Like other Jews, he wore *tefillin* (called 'phylacteries' in the Gospels) when he prayed formally." From William Nicholls text, 13.

146 Jeansonne, 103-104.
147 Arnold Forster, *Square One*, (New York: Donald I. Fine, Inc., 1988), 86.
148 Jeansonne, 105.
149 Ibid., 107.
150 Dinnerstein, 134.
151 Jeansonne, 89.
152 Ibid.
153 Dinnerstein, 163.
154 Ibid.
155 Ibid., 102.
156 Jeansonne, 119.
157 Jeansonne, 137.
158 Ibid., 208.

Chapter X

Ford & Hitler: Anti-Semites, Fanatics or Respected Leaders?

Gerald L. K. Smith was not an aberration. His form of Christianity did not exist in a vacuum. Jews cannot be safe precisely because Christians like Gerald L. K. Smith have proven to be forgettable. As his hatred for Jews has been hidden below the surface and forgotten, anti-Semitism also remains dormant. It will not disappear; it will only be forgotten. Anti-Semitism may not arise until it can come forth in a more respectable fashion. First, all the traces of its disrespectful past must fade. To some it would seem that those scars are no longer obvious and sensitive so the fading process may have begun.

As has been shown, men like Gerald L. K Smith were masters of manipulation. They knew how to apply "heat" to the emotions of the masses. Smith once explained his methodology. "In a moment of candor he revealed his basic approach: 'Religion and patriotism, keep going on that. It's the only way you can get them really *het up*.'"[159] Smith needed the turmoil caused by national problems to build his platforms of hatred. The Reverend Smith was a self-avowed teacher of hatred. Discontent was his greatest tool. He once remarked about his use of political turmoil:

> When the politicians overplay their hand, certain nerve centers of the population will begin to twitch. The people will start fomenting and fermenting and then a fellow like myself,

someone with courage enough to capture the people, will get on the radio, make three or four speeches, and have them in his hand, *I'll teach 'em how to hate* (emphasis mine).[160]

Hatred is bred in the darkness of men's hearts. It rarely grows by itself. The venomous emotions of Gerald L.K. Smith were not unique among the rich and powerful.

#1-Christ, #2-Napoleon, #3-Henry Ford?

Many Gentile Christian Americans may remember that in 1920, Henry Ford was the richest man in the world. America was in love with the genius behind movable assembly lines and the successful American industrial complex. Henry Ford was so beloved that

> A poll of college students in 1920 voted Ford the third greatest figure in recorded history, behind Jesus Christ and Napoleon. There was even a grassroots movement to promote him for president—and one observer believed that he was just a Dale Carnegie course away from political office.[161]

Henry Ford is still greatly admired. The Ford Foundation recently performed a promotional *coup d'état* of outstanding proportions. They sponsored the commercial-free television performance of *Schindler's List*. This film depicted the atrocities of the Nazi Holocaust against Jews. It is a cinematic monument to help us never forget. The movie shines a light on our obligation to insure that the Jews will NEVER AGAIN be without a place of refuge. The TV presentation undoubtedly brought great publicity to the Ford Foundation and created an aura of tolerance about the man for which the foundation is named. Yet was Henry Ford tolerant? Did his life suggest that he voiced the same concerns about the plight of the Jews? Did his personal efforts regarding the Jews mirror the sentiments of the film or the Ford Foundation? What can be ascertained with certainty about the man behind the motorcar? What can be learned about American sensibilities from studying his legacy?

The Henry Ford museum is located in Dearborn, Michigan. It is a monument to American ingenuity. If Gentile Christian America is capable of losing sight of the behavior of a public figure like Henry Ford, they are capable of selective memory to frightening degrees. If Henry Ford's volatile brand of anti-Semitism can be forgotten, history can diffuse any form of hatred into an idiosyncrasy. Henry Ford's beliefs were not eccentric, they were outrageous! It must therefore be asked whether the decision by the Ford Foundation to sponsor <u>Schindler's List</u> was for the benefit of TV viewers, or rather, was it an act of penance on behalf of the bigot that lived inside the man who also reinvented America's manufacturing process? If it was an act of repentance, it failed. Since no public confession followed the presentation, it must have simply been an expensive work of publicity.

Unlike the founder of America's *Great Passion Play*, Gerald L.K. Smith, Henry Ford did not run for president. He did, however, run for political office in 1918. Ford was a Democratic nominee for the U.S. Senate. He lost and attributed "almost everything that went wrong with his political fortunes to Jews and Jewish capitalism."[162] Gerald L. K. Smith "considered Henry Ford the best American representative of Christian faith, hard work, and patriotism."[163] American Christians should understand the reason that Smith was so enamored with Henry Ford (most Jews are already familiar with many of these facts about Ford). Sometimes it seems that the Church in America is unaware of the bitter legacy of Henry Ford.

Have You Been Driven By a Ford Lately?

Even Smith needed a mentor before he could teach others how to hate. He claimed that Henry Ford had been the one to teach him the relationship that existed between the Jews and the Communists. The two men met in 1937 at which time Smith claimed to have been less anti-Semitic than Ford. However, it is alleged that Ford had already gained a better understanding about the Jews and the problems they presented. Ford believed that Jewish people posed very real dangers to America.

> Smith claimed that Ford once asked him when he would recognize the real enemy of America. Smith asked Ford what he meant and Ford replied: "No one can understand the issues of this hour unless he understands the Jewish question." Smith then read *The International Jew* and concluded, "The day came when I embraced the research of Mr. Ford and his associates and became courageous enough and honest enough and informed enough to use the words: "Communism is Jewish."[164]

Though he tended to exaggerate the depth of his relationships with famous people, Smith was very outspoken of his admiration for Henry Ford.[165] Of course, as has been previously shown, Gerald L.K. Smith argued that "Hitler was a Bible-believing Christian" (see prior chapter). If Smith is not a qualified character-witness against his "teacher" of hatred, what can we learn from the leading anti-Semite of modern history—Adolf Hitler? (More on Ford's behavior later.)

Hitler's Church Connection

Henry Ford was known for his hatred of Jews. However, he lived in an era when Jew-hating was a popular theme in other cultures. The name "Hitler" has become synonymous with hatred and genocide. It is well known that Adolf Hitler highly admired Henry Ford. However there is much that is not widely known about the most despicable megalomaniac of the 20th century. For example, Adolf Hitler had his roots in the Church. He had been born into a Catholic family and he remained a connected into adulthood. His youth had been influenced by Church music and worship. His father desired to become the local pastor of their hometown. Young Adolf had even aspired to ascend to the position of abbot! In Hitler's own words,

> I received singing lessons in my spare time in the choir of the Lambach Convent, I repeatedly had an excellent opportunity of intoxicating myself with the solemn splendor of the magnificent church festivals. It was perfectly natural that the position of abbot appeared to me to be the highest ideal obtainable, just as that of being the village pastor had appealed to my father.[166]

There is no doubt that the Church had impacted Adolf Hitler. After studying his writing, I am convinced that he had a reasonable acquaintance with the Holy Bible. For example, while criticizing certain political gatherings in his book (that revealed both his political aspirations and his incredible plan to rid the world of Jews) Hitler gleaned a scripture verse from the parable of Jesus in Matthew 7:6 to help him make his point. He wrote, "To speak before such a 'forum' means really to cast pearls before certain well-known animals. This is really not worthwhile."[167] Hitler also exhibited a minimal command of biblical history and the Babylonian captivity experienced by the Jewish people. What I found to be quite astonishing was that Hitler had some limited connection to the ancient Hebrew language. He demonstrated this mastery by discussing, in very impressive terms, a relevant theological concept based on interpretations of the opening verses of the Bible in the original language of the Jewish Scriptures. He wrote eloquently about his hope for the dismantling and removal of the political system controlling Germany in the 1920's. Hitler explained that only the total collapse of the failing German government would make way for a new system to replace it and thereby save Germany from total ruin. In so doing, he also showed a rudimentary understanding of Jewish history contained in the Bible. It is quite extraordinary that he selected the same term used by the God of Israel in the first chapter of Genesis to describe the environment in which his proposed change would materialize. Using that powerful imagery of the Bible, he chose to refer to the well-known rabbinic concept of *tohu-vavohu* to make his point. The concept put forth in Scripture is that the earth was "without form and void" (Gen. 1:2). These few words are pregnant with relevance to Jewish and Christian scholars. As God created the world from nothing, Hitler proposed he would do the same from the chaos and confusion in the leadership vacuum he perceived in the governing body of 1920's Germany that he derided. Hitler was therefore extremely creative as he infused powerful new meaning into the application of the theological language he selected stating,

> I, therefore welcomed every development which in my opinion would lead to the breakdown of the State which had pronounced the death sentence on ten million German people. The more the linguistic *tohuwabohu* [Hebrew—Genesis 1:2—meaning chaos, confusion, hubbub] ate into and tore at the parliament, the sooner would come the hour of doom of this Babylonia realm, and with it, the day of freedom for my German-Austrian people.[168]

This example reveals Hitler's familiarity with the judgment of God on the Jews that resulted in the Exile from Israel. The Babylonian Captivity that followed the destruction of the Jewish Temple in the 6th century B.C.E. became an allegory for Hitler to suggest that only he could bring Germany's political deliverance. He intended to create a new world order from the boiling chaos that consumed Germany.

Hitler clearly had an early link to the Church but it would be wrong to blame the convent for Hitler's malevolence. He had an insatiable urge to despise Jews. His hatred transcended anything the Church could have proposed. Hitler actually believed that as he worked to rid the world of Jews, he was being a faithful servant of the Lord. In his book *Mein Kampf* which means "My Battle," which was first published in 1925, the Nazi fiend declared,

> If, with the help of the Marxian creed, the Jew conquers the nations of this world, his crown will become the funeral wreath of humanity, and once again this planet, empty of mankind, will move through the ether as it did thousands of years ago.
> ... Therefore, I believe today that I am acting in the sense of the Almighty Creator: *By warding off the Jews I am fighting for the Lord's work.*[169]

Yet remarkably, in the book he chose to present himself as tolerant of Jews early in his adult life. He wrote, "I had no idea at all that organized hostility against the Jews existed."[170] He even admits to considering the few Jews that he had known to be "human; yes, I even looked upon them as Germans."[171] But as only Hitler would confess, he then corrected that wrong view by declaring, "The nonsense of this notion was not clear to me."[172]

Quite surprisingly, Hitler even brought criticism to the Church for the treatment they hurled on the Jews during the Crusades. And he rebuked the press of Vienna for slurs printed against the Jewish people, but he also implied their views caused him to modify his own. He wrote, "I did not agree with its (*Volksblatt*—a local German newspaper) sharp anti-Semitic tone, but now and then I read explanations which made me stop and think."[173] Hitler took the opportunity to cast himself as a liberal-minded, caring individual.

> For reasons of human tolerance I continued to decline fighting on religious grounds. In my opinion, therefore, the language of the anti-Semitic Viennese press was unworthy of the cultural traditions of a great race. I was depressed by the memory of certain events in the Middle Ages which I did not wish to see repeated.[174]

Of course, soon thereafter, Adolf Hitler perpetrated crimes far worse than the Crusaders that he criticized. If he sought affirmation for his deviant behavior, Hitler found welcome assurance in the writings of Henry Ford. In fact, Ford's printed materials were highly respected in the company of the world's worst bigots.

The International Jew

Henry Ford is credited with being one of the first Americans to publish the lies contained in the infamous *Protocols of the Elder of Zion*. These writings were reproduced in Ford's own newspaper, *The Dearborn Independent*. Ford's paper ran the article on page one May 22, 1920. He accused the Jews, as his lead article was subtitled, of being at the root of "The World's Problems." *The International Jew* "inaugurated a series of attacks upon Jews that the newspaper ran for 91 consecutive weeks, and then intermittently until 1927."[175]

> The Dearborn *Independent's* first consideration of Jewish matters was titled THE INTERNATIONAL JEW: THE WORLD'S PROBLEM and announced, "There is a race, a part of humanity which has never yet been received as a welcome part." It went on from there, every issue without fail for years on end discussing Jewish evil. The Jews were responsible for short skirts and immorality among the young and the decline of wrestling as a sport. "Jewish Jazz—Moron Music" was a disgrace, as were the lyrics of Irving Berlin, which the *Independent* could not print: "The pages of this paper never yet have been defiled by obscenity." . . . Baseball had one trouble: "Too much Jew." These unscrupulous "Orientals" concocted "nigger gin, a peculiarly vile beverage compounded to act upon the Negro in a most vicious manner," producing "Negro outbursts" that led to rape . . . The Treaty of Versailles was Jew-inspired, and all wars were the Jews' harvest; they controlled financial markets and the price of gold and mercilessly exploited the farmer and craftsman.[176]

It would seem that thinking Americans would have recognized how abhorrent and untrue the articles were. But some Americans have trouble separating fact from fiction. The circulation of the *Dearborn Independent* might be an example of the power of the press to deceive.

> When the essays began, *The Dearborn Independent* had a circulation of about 72,000 copies a week. By 1922 that figure had increased to 300,000. It peaked in 1924 at 700,000, only 50,000 fewer than that of the largest daily paper in the United States at that time.[177]

It would appear that anti-Semitism sold newspapers. Ford lacked less than 7% in added distribution to have surpassed the highest circulation of the most successful daily newspaper in America! This was definitely an outstanding accomplishment from an unforgettable character. Yet is appears that his character has been forgotten. Henry Ford was a genius.

However, he was also a man given to hatred. In spite of his personal flaws, he had the "Midas touch." How many other newspapers could lay claim to Ford's 10-fold circulation increase in just a few years?

Mr. Ford was convinced that the nation's major newspapers were unwilling to publish the stories about the "Jewish problems." His delusion was fueled by views that the press was controlled by Jews. He seemed to perceive an obligation to proclaim that the Jews were the primary problem of Wall Street, big business, and the banking industry. Even though "no industry has been more antisemitic than commercial banking."[178]

Jews have never controlled the purse strings of America or Europe. Ford was compelled by his racist ideology to poison the minds of Americans against the Jews. He determined that his paper would be,

> The Chronicler of the Neglected Truth. He ordered that every purchaser of a Ford car should be sold a year's subscription. That meant a lot of potential readers, for the Ford Motor Company was on its way to turning out nearly 60 percent of all American cars and about half the cars produced elsewhere.[179]

He may have been the greatest American industrialist that ever lived, but he was also one of the most anti-Semitic men on earth. This is not an exaggeration. Ford was committed beyond reason to the goal of promoting his disparaging views of the Jewish people.

> Henry Ford had an obsession that began early and lasted all his life. He detested Jews. There was nothing he would not attribute to them. They had ruined one of his favorite candy bars; it didn't taste nearly as good as it used to. They had been behind Lincoln's assassination. They had put Benedict Arnold up to his evil deeds. These financiers and middlemen and moneylenders were dedicated to cheating and corrupting God-fearing, hardworking people. No one could tell him otherwise.[180]

However vocal Henry Ford was about his animosity toward Jews, he was obviously not alone in his generation. I have shown some of the connections that existed between these bigoted racists and the attitudes that influenced certain Passion play presentations. These attitudes ultimately were reflected in negative actions taken against Jews. Without doubt, the attitudes and actions of Adolf Hitler established the benchmark for the worst examples of racism and bigotry. Yet few realize the clear philosophical connections that existed between the leading hate mongers in America and the leading figure of Nazi hatred. To make this link clear we must consider a few final facts about Adolf Hitler.

Hitler's Helper?

Adolf Hitler was a great fan of the writings of Henry Ford. Hitler publicly declared his high esteem for Henry Ford in the infamous text of *Mein Kampf*. Incredible as it might seem to those unfamiliar with the anti-Semitic hatred of Henry Ford, he was the only American to be discussed in Hitler's book. The Nazi leader raved about an alleged Jewish conspiracy to oppress the world referring to so-called Jewish control of the monetary system. "Every year they manage to become increasingly the controlling masters of the labor power or a people of 120,000,000 souls; *one great man, Ford, to their exasperation still holds out independently even now*" (emphasis added).[181] Hitler was deceived, but he was obviously not alone. Henry Ford was filled with the same venomous hatred for Jews!

> Ford believed that Jewish moneylenders caused wars and manipulated the stock market and that Jewish intellectuals had created Communism. He thought Jews "lewd" and "erotic" and accused them of corrupting the morals of Gentiles by promoting chorus girls, liquor, and jazz.
>
> Ford's anti-Semitic publications even inspired Adolf Hitler. Hitler paraphrased Ford's anti-Jewish articles in *Mein Kampf*, hung a portrait of the automaker on his wall, and awarded Ford a medal which Ford unwisely accepted.[182]

In retrospect, many of Ford's ridiculous accusations against the Jews appear so farfetched that they might sound humorous. It is certain that he meant no levity in his depictions.

> Henry Ford never wavered in his beliefs. Months after Hitler's conquest of Poland and the commencement of the Second World War he told an acquaintance there really wasn't any war at all going on. "There hasn't been a shot fired. The whole thing has just been made up by the Jew bankers.[183]

Henry Ford may have performed a few outward efforts to soften a few of his most abhorrent anti-Semitic positions later in his life. Walter Winchell, the well known newscaster and columnist of the war years, read a letter to his vast radio audience in 1941 purporting that Henry Ford was "disavowing anti-Semitism and repudiating certain native anti-Semitic movements."[184] Though this might have helped improve Ford's image among car buyers. I doubt the genuineness of Ford's gesture. Unless the heart of man is first converted by love, hatred is bound to the soul. It may hide, but it will not disappear. After the war ended and information regarding the conditions discovered in the Nazi death camps was sent back to America, Ford was never to be the same.

> In the spring of 1945 soldiers . . . liberated Hitler's concentration camps. The founder of the Ford Motor Company sat with one of Ford's first woman executives, Josephine Comon, to view newsreels of what the soldiers discovered. When he saw the piles of corpses and the few walking skeletons of what would be called the Holocaust, he was then and there taken by one of several massive strokes he suffered. "He never recovered his mind or physical strength," she wrote, and in a little while Henry Ford was dead.[185]

When hatred is the focus of one's passion, even the richest people die in failure and despair. Sometimes they destroy multitudes in the wake of their hatred. No amount of denial will erase the pain caused by the Holocaust. When love embodies passion, passion enriches life. It is the passion of God for His people that provides life eternal. It is a particularly grievous sin for anyone to deny that love or to allow anti-Semitism to diminish God's intended expression of His passion.

---

159 Jeansonne, 58.
160 Ibid.
161 Ibid., 73.
162 Dinnerstein, 81.
163 Dinnerstein, 134.
164 Ibid., 75.
165 Ibid. Early in their relationship, Ford was known to have rashly commented, "that he wished Smith were president." He even made several sizable donations to Smith's work. Later in his life, Ford regretted being associated with Smith because Smith had become so controversial.
166 Adolf Hitler, *Mein Kampf*, (New York: Reynal & Hitchcock, 1940), 7.
167 Ibid., 134.

168 Ibid., 51.
169 Ibid., 84.
170 Ibid., 67.
171 Ibid.
172 Ibid., 68.
173 Ibid., 71.
174 Ibid., 68.
175 Jeansonne, 80-81.
176 Gene Smith, "American Characters," *American Heritage*, Vol 45, Number 7 (November 1994), 93-94.
177 Jeansonne, 81.
178 Dinnerstein, 238.
179 Gene Smith, 93.
180 Ibid.
181 Hitler, 930.
182 Dinnerstein, 74.
183 Gene Smith, 94.
184 Forster, 95.
185 Gene Smith, 94.

Chapter XI

Stumbling Blocks to Passion

Why are Jewish people often skeptical of the passion of Jesus and His Church? It is because some within His Church have often been stumbling blocks. Centuries of pain have scarred my people. We are skeptical because our experience with some "christians" has been painfully unpleasant. Bigotry is fueled by the myths and accusations of anti-Semites like Henry Ford, Father Coughlin, and Reverend Gerald L. K. Smith. Yet in spite of anti-Semites, American Jews have generally experienced more acceptance than Jews of other nations. Nevertheless, dangerous myths persist. They are difficult to dispel and they continue to perpetuate anti-Semitism in America and abroad. Common examples exist such as, "Jews run the banks and they are all rich." These are recurring lies that should be refuted to clear the path for the true passion God wants to shower on His people.

Jews Do Not Run the Banks

A survey of the 25 largest American banks was published by the American Jewish Committee. Their findings dispel any notion that the Jews control the banking industry. Of the 377 senior management positions operating the largest banks in the United States, only one Jew served in a senior management position! When the same investigation reviewed the 3,027 middle level managers, only 38 Jews were included among their ranks. There were a total of only 26 Jews among the 491 bank officers."[186]

Myths regarding Jewish wealth have also been broadly believed. The possibility of poor Jews living in America, or elsewhere for that matter, seemed almost unbelievable to anyone except those Jews who, in fact, were poor.

"All Jews Are Rich"—According to a Jewish source, the Jewish people constitute the third largest minority of poor people in New York City. 400,000 Jews there live near or below the poverty level, but are mostly passed over by the City's poverty programs.[187]

The United Jewish Communities (UJC) reported data from the National Jewish Population Survey 2000-01 that economic conditions among the 5.2 million American Jews was worse than many readers might have anticipated. "A fifth (19%) of all Jewish households are low income, defined as $25,000 or less per year, compared to 29% among all U.S. households."[188]

The economic plight of poor Jews is even worse in Israel. It was reported by a Tel Aviv based think tank that in 2001, more than 32% of all Israeli families lived in poverty. The condition among the young was even worse as more than 35% of Israeli children were stricken by poverty according to reliable data published by the Adva Center.[189] Rich or poor, money is rarely the biggest problem.

In my opinion, it is not the quest for money that drives Jewish people. Often, it is the hope for a future. The Holocaust denied millions of a future. Holocaust denial (this horrible phenomenon will be addressed in the next chapter) carries with it the hatred that launched the catastrophe. Those who deny that the Holocaust actually happened often declare that Israel exists today because the world granted land for a Jewish state in response to the so-called "lie of the Holocaust." They are wrong. Israel exists today for two reasons. God ordained that Israel be restored in these last days. And a strong nation of Israel is the hope of Jewish people worldwide. However, I believe some people overestimate the stability of that hope.

Israel: A State, Not a Savior

A pervasive false sense of security exists among many Jews. To them, Israel symbolizes future safety, and it generates national pride among Jews--even those who have never been to Israel. Israel is supported by Jews because they believe it to be the best insurance policy against another Holocaust. It is true that Israel offers refuge to Jews; however, Israel is unable to guarantee a future. Jews cannot be safe in the Middle East because the region is surrounded by enemies. Israel lacks true national security. The nation has been under enemy threats since its inception. That is why Israel must provide defense for its citizens, even if the world judges Israel harshly for being defensive.

Currently, many Evangelical Christians are extremely pro-Israel and pro-Jewish. Christian tourists continue to visit Israel when others consider the journey to be foolhardy. Devoted Christians see it as a pilgrimage. Jewish studies programs seem to be gaining importance in Christian higher education. Studies in and about Israel are becoming common. This is a very desirable trend. The philo-Semitism exhibited by segments of Christianity is a most encouraging example of correct behavior among Christians; however, Jewish-Christian relations have never been truly stable. They can only be gauged in current terms. The future is always tenuous. At some point, Middle East tensions may sway popular support away from Israel.

The media has often portrayed Israel as vicious and promoted the Jews as an uncontrollable, evil bully. Is it possible that under certain conditions Christians might accept these hateful depictions and turn against the Jews?

When the founder of *Al Queda*, Osama Bin Laden, is killed, captured, or found dead, America will celebrate the end of a known terrorist leader. It won't matter if his end comes in a coffin-sized hole in the ground like Saddam Hussein, in a mosque, or on a ferris wheel at Disneyland. Americans want this terrorist dead. On the other hand, when the founder of one of the worst terrorist organizations on earth was killed by the Israeli military, Jews were vilified. The press featured a poor, old, crippled spiritual leader brutally murdered outside an Islamic religious center. Israeli and American interests were loudly threatened by Palestinians. *Hamas* loyalists praised the terrorist leader and called for violence against Jewish civilian and American citizens. Still, many Americans seemed unable to see the obvious problem. It has become customary for the press to demonize Israel. This does not bode well for Jews. Hostilities from within Israel could lead to other forced infringements of human rights. Some within the Church might shift support from the Jewish nation if tragic errors take place. God forbid that we would ever be forced to send young Christians into combat to protect Jews or Palestinians in Israel. Any involvement of U.S. troops in Israel could be used by Israel's opponents to stimulate added resentment against Jews and Jewish issues at home and abroad. Yet greater than any future risk to Israel is the clear and present danger of the hatred perpetuated through the United Nations.

Israel's Most Powerful Enemy—The U.N.

Israel has been at the heart and soul of the Jewish world since 1948. Israel is a safe haven where most Jews believe they will always be welcome. The "Law of Return" assures the Jews of the world that there will always be a sanctuary. I believe that the anti-Semitic politics of the United Nations might be our greatest threat.

> The record plainly demonstrates the Jewish State is the primary target of an anti-Western coalition that virtually controls the international structure. . . . In the 1980 term exactly one-half of all resolutions adopted by the Security Council condemned Israel. Since then there have been more than one hundred resolutions of a similar character passed by the U.N. General Assembly.[190]

As early as 1975 a United Nations Resolution proclaimed, "Zionism is Racism." This view was supported by "a coalition of communist and Arab nations, the phrase became another weapon in the Arab propaganda arsenal."[191] Zionism is not racism! Racism presupposes a sense of ethnic superiority and generally deteriorates into ethnic hatred. Zionism is not an ethnic issue. Zionists welcome Jews of every ethnic origin. Zionism protects the rights of African Jews on an equal basis with Asian Jews. Under the goals of Zionism, black Jews receive the same protection as white Jews. Zionism assures that Jewish secular atheists are not denied access to citizenship in Israel and religious Orthodox Jews are not necessarily preferred because of their belief system.[192] Racists often hope to remove basic human rights from their "enemies." Zionists attempt to preserve basic human rights for all law-abiding citizens and punish law-breaking terrorists. Racists who hate Israel do not want Zionists to be successful in achieving their goals. Those racists deny that the Jews deserve a homeland in the land promised by God.

The United Nations tolerates horrific anti-Jewish prejudices. The enemies of Israel have lambasted Jews in the most insensitive ways.

> The late Saudi Arabian Ambassadour Jamil Barody once declared the Holocaust was simply fiction and Anne Frank's diary a forgery. . . . On December 8, 1980, the Jordanian ambas-

sadour, Hazem Nusseibeh, asserted in the General Assembly that the Arab world had long been "held in bondage and plundered" by the Jewish people's "cabal," which controls and manipulates and exploits the rest of humanity by controlling the money and the wealth of the world. During this "debate" Ambassadour Falilou Kane of Senegal added that news organizations are "dominated by Jews," a fabrication given currency by the Nazi propaganda machine almost fifty years ago. This provocative falsehood was also received without objection.[193]

The "Missed" Weapons of Mass Destruction

The recent war to liberate Iraq was proposed to remove the danger of Saddam Hussein's weapons of mass destruction. Prior to the invasion, the United Nations sent teams of arms inspectors to locate Iraq's cache of deadly biological, chemical, and nuclear weapons capabilities. Unfortunately, they missed a deadly virus that had already infected most of the United Nations Security Council and the entire Arab League. They are carriers of the "disease" described in the introduction to this book. They suffer from that form of "heart disease" known as anti-Semitism.

It is well known that most of the members of the United Nations (and the Arab League) hate Israel. They attack, discriminate, censure, and work to diminish or destroy Israel. This bias is not imagined. This diplomatic disaster is not exaggerated. The United Nations is one of the most anti-Semitic governing bodies in the world.

The United Nations has 189 member countries. How many of those 189 member countries of the United Nations are eligible to sit on the Security Council? Consider this fact: The most important key deliberating body within the United Nations, the UN Security Council, has 188 eligible member nations who can serve on this decisive board. Who is left out? Syria is known to support terrorism. Is Syria disqualified?

Syria supplied military aid to Iraq in their effort to defeat our coalition forces and propped up Saddam Hussein. Syrian terrorists fought against American and British troops sent to free Iraqi citizens from a dictator's reign of terror. Syria sends murderers to destroy Israeli citizens. But for some strange reason, Syria is eligible. In fact, Syria, a known sponsor of terrorism, was elected to a two-year term on the Security Council. Does this seem odd? Yet Syria was *not* disqualified from the Council. *In fact, Syria was elected to lead this influential body as Chair of the United Nations Security Council.*

Was Afghanistan excluded due to its support of Al Queda terrorism while under Taliban rule? No. Was Iraq restricted from membership due to its use of chemical or biological weapons on its own people under Saddam Hussein? No. Perhaps the restricted nation is one of the other axis of evil countries like North Korea, or Iran. Both now have potential nuclear capabilities and have been run by dictatorial lunatics. Are they excluded? No. Each of the renegade barbarian nations mentioned above are eligible and welcome to help decide the future of the world according to the United Nations.

In the entire world, only one member nation of the United Nations is forbidden from sitting on the Security Council. From 1948 until the moment of this publication, Israel is the only nation not eligible to serve on the United Nations Security Council. This is a travesty. This is proof of the hatred and "disease" resident among the nations of the world against Israel. The institutionalized anti-Semitism of the United Nations is the weapon of mass destruction that has been let loose right under the nose of the media. In fact, they have breathed lethal doses of this deadly toxin. This is the same virulent strain of hatred that brought the destruction of Haman in ancient Persia. It is the same man-made "disease" that destroyed Adolf Hitler and Nazi Germany. It is the spreading poison that empowered Yasser Arafat to send out Arab children who strap bombs to their bodies to kill Jewish mothers and their Jewish babies in suicidal mass murder. This uncontrollable infection turns normal sinners into monsters of destruction. And it is quite possible that this contagion will spread in light of the tensions following September 11, 2001.

Loyalties toward Jewish interests in the Middle East are fluid. Palestinian radicals hate the United States as much as they hate Israel. No one knows how mainstream Americans would respond to Jews if the U.S. were attacked by Palestinian terrorists in a direct response to the actions of Israel.

186 Dinnerstein, 233
187 Chira Kaplan, Editor, *Jewish Voice*, Volume 16, Number 11, November 1982, 8.
188 Carol Karol Editor, *Illiana News, The Newspaper of the Jewish Federation NWI*, December 2002, 7.

189 Friedman, Ina, *The Jerusalem Report*, "Talking about a Revolution (Again)," (November 17, 2003) 44
190 Forster, 366.
191 Ibid., 367.
192 One particularly offensive decision by the Israeli government does seem discriminatory, though not racist. It effects me quite personally. I was born to a Jewish mother and a Jewish father. I was raised in a Jewish home and became a Bar Mitzvah in a Traditional Jewish synagogue. I am currently a member of a Reform Jewish synagogue. Each of my four sons also became a Bar Mitzvah under the teaching of our Reform Jewish rabbi. I was educated in Jewish studies from my youth in Hebrew School. I completed a graduate studies degree at a well-respected Jewish institution of higher education, *nevertheless, in spite of these facts, I could legally be denied citizenship in Israel under the "Law of Return" merely because of my belief that Jesus is the Messiah!*
193 Forster, 369

Section 3

Holocaust Denial & the Passion

Chapter XII

Holocaust Denial

As in the American Revolution, the difference between a revolt and a revolution is determined by who won. The history books that record the victory are generally flavored by the appetites of the victors because the winners write history. Some may call this a "sweetened" version of the facts. Often it becomes revisionist history and the facts change and dramatically drift away from the truth. Sometimes, the losers rise up in response and write their own versions. At other times, liars have come out of the darkness to corrupt the truth of history. They promote a perverted view. When the past is forgotten, it can be rewritten to suit the fancies of those with a wicked agenda who are afraid of the past. *When the knowledge of a grievous past error is lost, the error is likely to be repeated.*

Did 6,000,000 Jews die in Nazi death factories? Some have labeled the Holocaust as nothing more than "group fantasies of martyrdom and heroics?" I believe this sentiment represents the worst form of anti-Semitism. Growing segments of fringe fanatics deny that the Nazi Holocaust actually occurred. As pseudohistorians, their premise is derived from their own revisionist view of history. These violent, modern, anti-Semites employ methods that have brought their ideas into the arena of consideration by mainstream intellectuals and naive college students. This is particularly disturbing because that arena should be reserved for thinkers who are removed from obvious infestations of hatred, arrogance, and ignorance. From my perspective, anyone capable of ignoring, or daring to deny the tragedy of the Holocaust, is not deserving of a hearing among civilized members of society.

Deborah Lipstadt, the author of *Denying the Holocaust*, dedicated her excellent work as follows: "To the victims and the survivors of the Holocaust and to those who preserve and tell their story. 'Remember the days of yore, Learn the lessons of the generation that came before you.' (Deuteronomy 32:7)."[194]

It is known that confused Christians have participated in a variety of non-Christian enterprises. This would explain how murderous Klu Klux Klan members have been included as part of the Christian fold. It could be argued that the beliefs of neo-Nazis and other radical racists should not be considered in an investigation of Christian anti-Semitism, for classing them alongside Christians might be considered outrageous. Indeed, it would seem outrageous to some orthodox Christians to be categorized with men in white sheets burning crosses. To a Jewish victim, violated with the passion of bigotry and hatred, it would be difficult to explain the difference. Too often, *the people who have painted the swastikas have also worn the cross.*

Guilt by association is inexcusable. Confusion by association is easier to understand. Clarity is unlikely as long as anti-Semitism is not loudly denounced. Some Jewish people will never take the Church seriously if it fails to distinctly separate itself from association with hate-mongers who wear crosses. Jewish victims do not distinguish the theological deficiencies of the perpetrators. They only remember the symbols. Some churches have dealt with these problems. I congratulate them! If one wears a cross, love must be exemplified. Errant strains of "christianity" have created dangerous examples of hatred.

The methods used by neo-Nazi revisionists are significant. This is due to their success in expanding their areas of influence. The historical fact of a horrible Holocaust which destroyed millions of Jewish lives during World War II is categorically unquestioned by reasonable people. Yet neo-Nazi revisionists continue to promote their books, newspapers, magazines, university courses, and lectures. They seek every method available to deny the facts of the Holocaust and promote anti-Semitism.

Eyewitnesses to the events abound among German troops and the victorious occupation forces who discovered the death camps. Holocaust survivors still live to insist upon the accuracy of the historicity of the tragedy. The problematic fact is that with each passing year, fewer first hand witnesses remain to tell the story. Someday, only history books will remind the world of the depth of mankind's bigoted depravity displayed by the Nazis.

Who will write tomorrow's history books? and If those writers are impacted by anti-Semitism against the Jews, how will the victims of Hitler's hatred be remembered? To most modern adults it would be unthinkable to print a new history book covering the Second World War and ignore the destruction of Jewish lives in Nazi death camps. Today, these books of hatred have gone beyond the stage of conception. These books of lies are being written, sold, read, and believed.

> Holocaust denial, as a serious enterprise, was founded by Willis Carto, founder of both the Liberty Lobby and the Institute for Historical Review (IHR), which publishes the Journal of Historical Review. Carto, a professional antisemite, has ties to the growing Neo-Nazi movement in the United States, in Europe and in Arab countries (where *Protocols* can be easily purchased in bookstores) . . . Given all the incontrovertible evidence—Nazi documents, the disclosures at the Nuremberg Trials, Nazi photos, survivor accounts, confession of Nazi leaders, memoirs, etc.—how is it possible that any intelligent being could possibly doubt the authenticity of the Shoah?[195]

Although the above-quoted question would seem to be rhetorical, many, otherwise intelligent people *have* rejected the historical facts about the Shoah (Holocaust). Equally foolish, one might question how guilty participants in the *Shoah* could be "forgiven" and permitted to rise to power in this generation. Incredibly, the Nazi Kurt Waldheim was honored by the Pope. Odder still, he was first elected to national office in a nation that had endured the Nazi violence during World War II.

At the outset of the 1986 campaign for the presidency, candidate Waldheim was well behind. Most pollsters agreed that he had only a slim chance of winning, perhaps none. But the expose` of the former U.N. secretary general's Nazi record radically changed the picture in the middle of the campaign. The wrong way; it put him in the lead.[196]

The world was notified that Kurt Waldheim had been a German army lieutenant in the Balkans. He was fully aware of Nazi atrocities, including the execution of captured Yugoslav partisans. Published reports proved Waldheim's involvement with the Fuehrer. His countrymen welcomed Waldheim as their leader after they learned of his wartime attitudes and actions. Time is said to heal; however, it is possible that time does not change everyone as much as some would prefer.

The hatred conceived in Nazi Germany did not occur overnight. Neither did it disappear the instant they surrendered in defeat to the Allied forces. "After World War II Germany expressed little remorse or guilt for the destruction of six million Jews. Instead most Germans continued to harbour anti-Semitic sentiments."[197] It is entirely possible that the exhibition of anti-Semitism in recent years is nothing more than the revelation that little has changed in the emotional makeup of some segment of that population.

> Such attitudes were also manifest in post-war Austria where a number of ex-Nazis were rehabilitated. More recently when Kurt Waldheim was criticized for his activities during the war years, many Austrians became contemptuous of the world Jewish community.[198]

Time passes; it does not heal all. Attitudes are not changed merely because time does what it does—pass. Attitudes are much more likely to change when people gain information and insight. Attitudes must change before the Jewish plight can truly be improved with any certainty. Many believed that the results of the Allied liberation should have protected the Jews from hatred forever. In fact, the revelation of Nazi atrocities brought little security to future generations of Jews.

> Crimes committed against Jews did not evoke remorse or guilt. Opinion polls undertaken in 1946-1947 revealed widespread indifference to the plight of the Jews. Thus in 1947 three-quarters of all Germans believed the Jews to belong to another race; in the following year 41 per cent of the population continued to approve of the Nazi seizure of power; in 1952, 88 per cent declared that they bore no responsibility for the mass exterminations.[199]

The phenomenon of Kurt Waldheim in Austria was not as farfetched as it might have appeared to Jews and Christians who followed his election in disbelief. One must only consider the facts surrounding the time frame immediately following World War II to reach the conclusion that anti-Semitism should be presupposed in the wake of the depth of bigotry that preceded the war.

> Post-war Austria has also witnessed the continuation of

anti-Semitic attitudes. By 1949 many Austrians ex-Nazis had been fully re-enfranchised, and from 1955 prominent National Socialists had been fully integrated into political life. The two dominant political parties—the Socialists and the Catholic conservatives—competed for the former Nazi vote.[200]

Time healed little. It may have provided salve for numbing the memories, but some wounds will never heal until truth can change the hearts of men. Austria's perverted political posture is proof for the need to overhaul the thought processes and attitudes of a culture in denial. Consider the backlash against Jews and Judaism after the Waldheim fiasco came into focus.

> Attitudes surfaced when the former Secretary General of the United Nations, Kurt Waldheim, was attacked for his activities during the war. The campaign against Waldheim provoked a backlash of anti-Semitism, and after 1986 it was widely believed that international Jews based on the East Coast of the USA manipulated the media to defame Waldheim's character. Thus in 1987 the former vice-mayor of Linz wrote to the President of the World Jewish Congress, drawing an analogy between the persecution of Waldheim and Jews handing Jesus over to the Romans. This was Hitler's legacy to the land of his birth.[201]

The fact that Waldheim was a Nazi and Jesus was a Jew was apparently overlooked by the Linz politician.

The anti-Semitic tendencies of Austrian politicians, and their measure of acceptance among many Austrian citizens should inform readers to the danger that exists for Jews of the region. Austria's far-right Freedom Party is currently led by a vicious anti-Semite. Joerg Haider "joined some 2,000 veterans of Adolf Hitler's army at an annual meeting . . . The Ulrichsberg gathering has been harshly criticized as a festival for old Nazis and a feeding ground for neo-Nazis."[202]

A New Breed of Nazi

The concern about rising numbers of neo-Nazis in Germany is a realistic concern. Their version of anti-Semitic hatred is infamous. They are a growing faction in Germany, and their influence is not limited to the hidden dens of darkness to which they were once confined. They have come out with a vengeance.

Hitler is dead, but his brand of hatred lives on. Germany is still a hotbed of fascist rhetoric and anti-Semitic behavior. Neo-Nazis have "graduated" from spray painting synagogues to breeding their spawn of bigotry electronically. "Computer games have been released in Germany, inviting the players to 'manage' a concentration camp and gain points by killing and torturing prisoners."[203] Hate has definitely moved into the modern era. New York's anti-Semites have established telephone "hot-lines" staffed by neo-Nazis. Various racist organizations support these programs intended to spread hatred against Jews, African-Americans, American Indians, immigrants, and homosexuals.

> Neo-Nazi groups provide callers with crude and often vitriolic recorded phone messages. . . The groups sponsoring the telephone lines include White Aryan Resistance, the Church of the Creator, the American Front, the National Alliance and the SS Action Group. The phone numbers are disseminated in leaflets and by word of mouth, as well as through white supremacist publications.[204]

One article titled "Bigots Go High-Tech" informed readers that anti-Semitism is not a child's game. Racism has entered the computer age with a vengeance.

> ARD television reported that large quantities of holocaust denial propaganda by German, Austrian and American neo-Nazis had recently been fed into the Internet computer network. Indeed, groups in Germany are reportedly trying to build a nationwide united front, using the most modern means of communication available, from computers and telefax machines to cellular phones for greater mobility.[205]

No reasonable person could consider this to be anything other than what it is—hate mongering. It is contemptible and yet motivational. This form of conduct has forced Jews around the world to reevaluate their loyalties.

The German government recognizes its responsibility to deal with the growing problem associated with anti-Semitism, violence, and organized racist hate groups. They have enacted laws to discourage racist extremism and Holocaust denial. These actions may help tomorrow but many scars have yet to heal from yesterday. "A recent opinion poll conducted by the Allensbach Research Institute showed that 42.9% of people polled thought

Jews were in great danger."[206] Many Jews now have a heightened sense of appreciation for the nation of Israel. This is not because of a deep love for the land of the Bible. No, instead it is often more practical than spiritual. Israel is viewed as a place of refuge. Because Israel exists, many Jews can say with some level of confidence, "Never again!"

With characteristic insight, the *Jerusalem Post* printed a story that keenly spoke what many Jews have often wondered. "Should We Start Packing? Jews in Germany are asking themselves if the latest wave of anti-semitism is a passing phase or not. It is heartbreaking that such a question has to be asked today. Have we truly forgotten the past?"[207] German Jews have much to be concerned over based upon current events in their nation. They are not alone.

> While it's true that much of the media coverage and attention has focused on Germany and other parts of Europe, anti-semitism is also quite evident in the U.S. According to a recent nationwide survey released by the Jewish Anti-Defamation League, 20% (nearly 40 million Americans) hold strong anti-semitic views.
>
> And while numbers and statistics on a survey are one thing, when they transfer into physical acts of violence, one can't help but take notice. In their first official study on the topic, the Federal Bureau of Investigation reported that of all "hate crimes" committed in the U.S. . . . Religious bias accounted for 19.3%, with the overwhelming percentage reported against Jews.[208]

Prophecy of General Eisenhower

Most veterans of the World War II Allied liberation could never have anticipated that the next generation could have forgotten the horrors that they discovered in 1945. Yet General Eisenhower was wise enough and exhibited sufficient foresight to understand that this was a very real danger. He appeared in several documentary films during the liberation of the concentration camps and rightly warned, "the day may come when people will dispatch the Nazi atrocities as propaganda."[209] He was a prophet. Revisionist historians promote that exact lie.

It would seem that the results of Hitler's "final solution" would have been indelibly etched on the minds of millions. It would also seem that the children or grandchildren of the European non-Jews would not forget the horror. The effect of the Holocaust should have brought protection to the remaining Jews of the region. It did not. In spite of the fact that Poland lost most of their entire Jewish population to the Nazi death camps, more horrific violence befell Jews in Poland within the short span of one year.

In 1946 a massive pogrom was carried out in Lielce, where forty Jews were killed and over seventy-five wounded. This pogrom, which was initiated by the ancient Christian blood libel charge, reflected the unstable atmosphere of the country. Right-wing activists as well as Catholic bishops viewed this massacre as the result of Jewish provocation.[210]

At some point, some Christians must carry some responsibility for the behavior of many adherents. Many Christians have acted on their beliefs, even when their beliefs were wrong and unfounded. Many Christians have placed Jesus in an awkward position. The Church must fundamentally change its teaching if it is to change the attitudes of anti-Semitism and hateful myths about the Jewish people. There is a foundation of ignorance and hatred that must be attacked from within the Church if it is to be removed. This foundation is based upon Christian hostility against Jews that has endured in varying degrees for centuries.

Many Polish peasants continued to believe in the medieval Christian blood libel; young Christians were still taught that all Jews killed Christ; and even university students tended to accept the validity of Jewish stereotypes. Such attitudes were reinforced by the pronouncements of the Primate of Poland. . . . Polish Christian anti-Semitism has thus persisted until the present, despite the absence of a Jewish population within the country.[211]

No generation should be allowed to forget what happened in Nazi Germany. No civilized society should permit such a lapse.

The defeat of Nazism did not universally discredit the belief in the Conspiracy Theory of History. A recent poll reveals that some twenty percent of the United States population is willing to believe that the Holocaust did not occur. President John F. Kennedy murder conspiracy theorists have created an industry, so it is no great surprise that holocaust deniers are finding fertile ground for their Conspiracy theory. That theory is guided by a belief in the authenticity of *The Protocols of the Elders of Zion*, despite the proof that it is a forgery. In this version of the Jewish conspiracy, deniers argue that the establishment of Israel needed the "Holocaust hoax" in order to win the sympathy of world opinion for the creation of the Jewish state.[212]

Jerry Adler questioned the results of that poll in the July 25, 1994 edition of *Newsweek* in his article "The Numbers Game." His concern was that the wording was confusing. Nevertheless, the Holocaust Memorial Museum in Washington reported that "One in five Americans doesn't know or isn't sure that Jews were killed in the Holocaust or that it happened in World War II . . . (However) 66% wanted to know more about the Holocaust."[213]

194 Lipstadt, IV.
195 Jack Fischel, *Jewish Spectator*, "Holocaust Denial and the History of the Conspiracy Theory," Fall 1994, Volume 59, Number 2, 9
196 Forster, 405.
197 Cohn-Sherbok, 210.
198 Ibid.
199 Ibid., 210-211.
200 Ibid., 212.
201 Ibid.
202 Evelyne Kayess, Editor, *Dateline: World Jewry*, (New York: World Jewish Congress October, 2000), 3.
203 Marlene Floyd, "The Rising Tide of Anti-Semitism," Editor, Andy Stebbins, *The Chosen People*, March, 1993, 6.
204 Rabbi Abraham Cooper, Editor, *Response*, "Telephonic Hate," Summer 1994, Vol 15, Number 2, 11.
205 Ibid., "Bigots Go High-Tech," 7.
206 Rabbi Abraham Cooper, Editor, *Response*, "Germany's Struggle Continues," Summer 1994, Vol 15, Number 2, 7.
207 Ibid.
208 Ibid., 8.
209 Larsson, Gore, *Fact or Fraud? The Protocols of the Elders of Zion*, (Jerusalem: AMI-Jerusalem Center for Biblical Studies and Research, 1994), 55.
210 Cohn-Sherbok, 217.
211 Ibid., 219.
212 Fischel, 9.
213 Evelyne Kayess, 4.

Chapter XIII

Politics of Hate

Unrepentant proponents of Holocaust denial have left the ranks of the fringe fanatics and are gaining an increasing amount of acceptance among mainstream Americans. They are writing their own historical accounts of Hitler's activities and they are being heard in forums that add to their credibility. Evidence to this exists in the knowledge that in the 1980's, David Duke, a former Imperial Wizard of the Klu Klux Klan, and a neo-Nazi Holocaust denier, won 40% of the votes in his bid to become the U.S. Senator from Louisiana. Duke had previously been elected to the state legislature and in his gubernatorial race of 1991 he garnered nearly seven hundred thousand votes. Many Americans have forgotten his presidential campaign in 1992, but it is important to realize that he gained many followers along the way. Duke supporters appear willing to ignore the fact of Duke's obvious anti-Semitic presuppositions, or worse, they agree with him.

> Duke, who celebrated Adolf Hitler's birthday until late in the 1980's, has been quite candid about his views on the Holocaust. In a letter accompanying the *Crusader*, the publication of the National Association for the Advancement of White People (NAAWP)—an organization Duke created—he not only described the Holocaust as a "historical hoax" but wrote the "greatest" Holocaust was "perpetrated on Christians by Jews . . . In 1986 Duke declared that Jews "deserve to go into the ashbin of history" and denied that the gas chambers were erected to murder Jews but rather were intended to kill the vermin infesting them."[214]

Hundreds of thousands of Duke supporters apparently were unaffected by the fact that Duke had sold "racist, anti-Semitic, and denial literature, including *The Hitler We Loved* and *The Holy Book of Adolf Hitler*."[215] Today, Duke travels around the world at the invitation of international anti-Semites. He lectures about his form of hatred and is considered a hero to the deceived followers who hate Jews.

David Duke, and others like him, should not be ignored. Their type of disease is contagious and deadly. There are a growing number of people who would have the world believe that the Holocaust never happened. Some of them seek the presidency. Duke was not alone.

Pat Buchanan—Holocaust Denier?

I believe that every candidate that runs to become the president of the United States must be held accountable for any anti-Semitic leanings they display. The heartfelt beliefs of Patrick Buchanan are frightening! Buchanan cannot be trusted and he should be castigated for his perfidious implications that the gas chambers at Treblinka did not kill Jews during the Holocaust.

> Patrick Buchanan, one of the foremost right-wing conservative columnists in the country, used his widely syndicated column to express views that come straight from the scripts of Holocaust deniers. He argued that it was physically impossible for the gas chamber at Treblinka to have functioned as a killing apparatus because the diesel engines that powered it could not produce enough carbon monoxide to be lethal.[216]

Those who died in the Treblinka gas chamber cannot stand to refute Buchanan's absurd remarks. Buchanan actually made these statements as part of the defense of John Demjanjuk, the retired autoworker from Cleveland, who had been accused of being the camp guard from Treblinka—Ivan the Terrible. It is known that Buchanan opposes the prosecution of Nazi war criminals. In fact, the magazine of Reform Judaism boldly declared in unmistakable capitalized headlines, "PATRICK J. BUCHANAN: MASTER HOLOCAUST DENIER."

The article reported what Christian conservatives should all know but seem to ignore. "Patrick Buchanan has introduced revisionist themes into mainstream media and, in so doing, has become the most effective Nazi war criminal apologist and Holocaust denier in America."[217] The former presidential candidate has been a great friend to aging Nazis and is no friend to the Jewish people. He has portrayed these Nazis as everything from American patriots to "innocent victims of 'revenge-obsessed' Nazi hunters."[218] The U.S. Justice Department's Office of Special Investigations former director, Neal Sher was quoted as saying, "Buchanan went to bat for every Nazi war criminal in America."[219] Perhaps that is why Buchanan received the overwhelming support of the Liberty Lobby, one of the most notorious anti-Semitic organizations in the United States.

Many of my readers may find it absurd that anyone would be so bold or so cold as to suggest that the Holocaust never happened. However, some have built careers trying to disprove the historicity of the event. One such man is David Irving. He is touted to be a serious historian. He has authored books about his heroes, Adolf Hitler and Joseph Goebbels. Irving's claim is that millions of Jews did not perish in Nazi Germany. The crematoriums did not burn their bodies. The Jews were not gassed in Auschwitz. In fact, he proudly declared in a 1991 speech in Calgary, Canada, "More women died in the back seat of Edward Kennedy's car at Chappaquidick than ever died in a gas chamber at Auschwitz."[220]

Deborah Lipstadt, an expert on the subject of Holocaust denial, had informed her readers about the anti-Semitic teachings of Irving. The arrogant Irving sued Lipstadt and her publisher, Penguin Books, for libel in an English court. Irving lost. But the problem continues to grow throughout the Arab Middle East, across Europe, and in many areas around the world. Anti-Semitism and Holocaust denial are on the rise.

In a poll commissioned by the leaders of the European Union, it was learned that the residents of Europe appear to the lead the way in harboring appalling sentiments toward Israel and the Jewish people. "Shockingly. Israel was rated first with 59% *ahead* of Iran and North Korea."[252] This statistic should send shockwaves around the world and inform every interested reader as to the bias that molds the views of Europeans. They appear to be following the lead established by the Arab nations and the Muslim leaders of the world. This does not bode well for world Judaism or the prospects for peace in the Middle East.

It is Not Academic!

The problem of ignoring the revisionist lies being disseminated about the Holocaust is reflected in the U.S. and many other nations. The problem will not be corrected by pretending that it does not exist. There is a growing tendency in the academic world to promote doubt as a virtue. It is now in vogue to reject previously held theories in order to make room for newer, often more farfetched proposals about the past. This is the "current fashion in academia associated with the trend in criticism known as deconstruction. Brought to the world's attention by Paul deMan (himself an apparent Nazi sympathizer in his native Belgium)."[222] Holocaust deniers have turned the revisionist deconstruction of history into an art form of hatred. Jack Fischel, himself associated with the Millersville University Department of History, has offered this warning to students of history:

> To students and faculty unfamiliar with the lies and deceit used by the deniers, such arguments can be persuasive. It is couched in the language of moderation and, after all, who can be against listening "to another point of view?" If, with all of the documentation that envelopes our knowledge of the Holocaust, the deniers can still find a public willing to listen to their distortion of history, what future does this portend for the craft of history? Professional historians have not made a sufficient connection between the denial of the Holocaust and the potential to negate or distort other events of history . . . Professional historians must become more vocal and far ranging in combating the deniers, if only to protect the craft from professional liars who distort and pervert history from their perspective of conspiracy and bigotry.[223]

Europe's Denial

A 1992 public opinion poll in Italy revealed that ten percent of the population reject the fact that the Holocaust occurred.[224] In France, deniers of the Holocaust teach in Universities, write books, distribute literature, and one of their adherents, Jean Marie Le Pen, won 14.4 percent of the popular vote in their 1988 presidential election. Le Pen came in fourth. The organization headed by Le Pen is known as the National Front. Le Pen has publicly questioned the existence of gas chambers by the Nazis. "The National Front head (Le Pen) compounded his slander of the Six Million Dead with this: 'I am not saying the gas chambers did not exist. I could not see them myself. I have not studied the question. But I believe it is a minor point in the history of World War II.' "[225] Le Pen's coy, cold, and crass responses to one of the worst tragedies in history is appalling. Fully aware of the degree to which modern Holocaust deniers have taken their claims, Le Pen has given the pseudo-historian anti-Semites reason to rejoice. He stood with them and asked this question, "Do you want me to say it is a revealed truth? I say there are historians who are debating these questions."[226] At one point, Le Pen's popularity reached as high as seventeen percent. In the first round of the French presidential campaign of April, 1988,

> Le Pen's once "fringe" party, much ignored by the press from the party's inception in October, 1972, startled experienced observers by winning four-and-a-half million votes, only a fraction less than fifteen percent of the total in a four-way contest with President Francois Mitterand, Prime Minister Jacques Chirac and Raymond Barre, a former prime minister.[227]

Le Pen could not have generated such support for his campaign or his organization, the National Front, if a strong anti-Semitic base did not precede his efforts. Though France is proud of their national motto, *"Liberte', Egalite', Fraternite'* (Liberty, Equality, Fraternity), it appears obvious that Jews are not expected to experience those benefits as other Frenchmen. The French may have a language of love, but they tolerate hatred and the rhetoric of bigotry. France has long been friendly to the views of the enemies of Judaism. Bookstores freely distribute anti-Semitic literature. Revisionist theories of history are welcomed in French thought.

> Such Judeophobia was the theme of Jean-Paul Sartre's analysis of Jew hatred in his *Reflexions sur la Question Juive*. Pondering the silence of his compatriots regarding Jews at the end of the war, he wrote: "Today those Jews whom the Germans did not deport or murder are coming back to their homes. Many were among the first members of the Resistance; others had sons or cousins in Leclerc's army. Now all France rejoices in the streets . . . Do we say nothing about the Jews? Do we give a thought to those who died in the gas chambers at Lublin? Not a word. Not a line in the newspapers. That is because we must not irritate the anti-Semites."[228]

The silence felt by Sartre was certainly felt by the Jews of France. With horrifying accuracy Sartre identified the sentiment that would continue to prevail in France. The silence did not help France correct itself. Two decades after the war, France was still not free from its delusional views toward Jews or Judaism. "By the mid-1950s over half of those who identified with the Right denied that the Jews were authentically French. According to another poll in the mid-1960s, 20 per cent of the population was anti-Semitic in orientation."[229] The politicians of France have a tradition of bigotry to uphold. Perhaps Le Pen is merely an extension of what others before him have felt but have been afraid to speak. Perhaps his predecessors have spoken but few listened to what they said.

> After the Six-Day War in 1967, the French President Charles de Gaulle referred to the Jewish people as an arrogant, elitist, and domineering group. Such views evoked the image of Jewish power and domination . . . At the time the Jewish political commentator Raymond Aaron accused de Gaulle of making anti-Semitism respectable, yet the President was simply expressing a traditional prejudice deeply rooted in the French psyche.[230]

It appears that France maintains only a thinly veiled disdain for Jews. This was again shown by the political leanings of the nation. Instead of being shunned for his anti-Semitic behavior and censured for his infamous 1987 remark that the Holocaust was merely "a detail of history," Le Pen was rewarded with a stunning political upset over all but one of his French political opponents in the 2002 presidential election. "Right-wing leader Jean-Marie Le Pen placed second in the country's presidential elections . . . and ensured Le Pen a runoff against President Jacques Chirac."[231] Perhaps in selecting the lesser of two evils, Chirac remained president of France. However, conditions for French Jews have continued to deteriorate. "More than one-quarter of the Jews want to leave France after suffering from more than 300 anti-Semitic attacks in just over one year alone. The latest fire-bombing target: a Jewish school in the Paris suburbs."[232] There is a steady stream of French Jews leaving the anti-Semitism of France to take their chances living with the Muslim *intifada* in Israel.

France continues to line up against Jews and the Jewish nation of Israel. Zionism, as a philosophical position, is not tolerated in France. Perhaps that is why France was so outspoken against the U.S. led war in Iraq. It supports the enemies of Israel and stood against the coalition forces that toppled Saddam Hussein. France is no friend to Israel or America.

Is the world safe for Jews?

The World Jewish Congress reported that "Jews are facing a dangerous surge in anti-Semitic passion around the world: Bombings. Mass murder . . . 2004 may become one of our most difficult and pivotal years."[233] They reported that 24 Jews were killed at synagogues in Istanbul, Turkey. In Casablanca, Morocco 45 were killed by suicide bombers. The Prime Minister of Malaysia "urged the world's 1.3 billion Muslims to unite for 'final victory' against the Jews."[234]

There were 205 anti-Semitic attacks in 2003. The problem of anti-Semitism and Holocaust denial is a growing problem for Jews in Canada, England, Germany, Croatia, Slovakia, Belgium, Austria and the list grows. The world is not a safe place for Jews!

Asian Anti-Semitism

"A Japanese edition of the *International Jew* by Henry Ford was prominently on display in the economics section of Tokyo's leading bookstore chain."[235] Tokyo is an unexpected repository of anti-Semitism. Jews are nearly invisible in the Japanese census . . . "with 120 million people—there are little more than 1,000 Jews."[236] Though it would seem impossible, given the vast base of current knowledge, the myth of Jewish wealth, control, and power persists and seems to be spreading across the globe. "A current edition of a mainstream newsmagazine, 'Sapio,' . . . chronicles over several pages the alleged control of the Jewish community over global banking and the international media."[237] Rabbi Abraham Cooper examines several painfully cutting issues in a recent letter printed by the Simon Wiesenthal Center:

> Imagine a place in the world where there exists nary a Jew, yet millions of people are subjected to the canard that <u>a Jewish conspiracy controls their economies</u>. Where even with no direct exposure to Jews, they are expected to accept as fact that Jews are dishonest and cannot be trusted. . . . The place I am referring to is Asia, the fastest growing region—both in population <u>and</u> in economic strength—on Earth. I'm writing today to alert you to the seriousness of the growing problem of <u>antisemitism and vicious hate-mongering in Asian countries</u> like Japan, Malaysia, Thailand and Indonesia . . . ugly mythology and

stereotypes about Jews have been propagated by a spate of dangerous antisemitic books, newspapers and tabloids that are available everywhere. [238]

Rabbi Cooper's observations should not be ignored. His efforts, along with those of the Simon Wiesenthal Center, help to identify the growing trend toward anti-Semitism in America and abroad. Their vigilance will not prohibit hatred; however, they can focus attention on the efforts of hate groups before they become deadly national movements. Cooper's personal experiences and observations provide valuable insight for those interested in the attitudes of foreign nationals toward Jews in areas of the world with negligible Jewish populations.

> During a recent stay in Japan, I personally was able to purchase the infamous *Protocols of the Learned Elders of Zion* in my hotel gift shop . . . But most surprising of all is the emergence of a new book, featuring Adolph [sic] Hitler's photo and a swastika on the cover and written by a respected leader in Japan's Liberal Democratic Party. It is entitled *Hitler's Election Strategy: A Bible for Sure Victory in Modern Elections*! Each chapter of this appalling work begins with a quote directly from Hitler's *Mein Kampf*—including one that opens with, "My slogan is . . . exterminate enemies with emergency measures."[239]

The trend toward open anti-Semitism in Asia is disconcerting. "Bestselling writers have borrowed Hitler's anti-Semitic propaganda, claiming that Jews control the world through "international conspiracies."[240] Books that have become popular in Japan include such titles as: *If You Understand Judea*; *You Can Understand the World*; *The Secret of Jewish Power to Control the* World; and *The Jewish Plan for Conquest of the World*. These texts were not written by radical Communists or revolutionaries. "The authors include Eisaburo Saito, a member of the Japanese parliament, and the well-known writer, Masomi Uno, who regards himself as a Christian.[241] Japan's errors are not unique. Other areas within Asia are experiencing equally disturbing resurgence of problems that many Americans may believe to have been extinct. Anti-Semitism is not gone. It is not even hidden. Normally, it is not discussed. Perhaps that is the strength of the infection. It does not receive much publicity until it reaches epidemic proportions. Consider the following observations from Rabbi Cooper:

> In Malaysia . . . the internationally acclaimed, Oscar-win-

ning motion picture "Schindler's List" was banned by Malaysia's government, which labeled the film "propaganda" . . . In Thailand . . . at a popular amusement park near Bangkok, visitors are attracted by a show featuring mock-Nazis wearing swastika armbands and knee-high boots as they defend a World War II German military camp. After the applause, audiences rush toward the actors to have their pictures taken alongside the uniformed Nazis. In Indonesia . . . Muslim youths recently thronged the gates of the U.S. Embassy in Jakarta and the U.S. Consulates in two other cities, screaming and waving posters emblazoned with the slogans, "GO TO HELL JEW" and "JEWS CAN'T BE TRUSTED."

As the leading Moslem country in Asia, Indonesia is a key target of radical Islamic Fundamentalists aiming to spread hatred. Some of the books and articles surfacing there accuse Jews of "calling on the supernatural power of Satan" when they worship in synagogues. The "Protocols" are widely presented in mainstream newspapers as accepted fact, and local bookstores prominently display titles like *76 Characteristics of the Jew* . . . One book even proclaims that "the descendants of Israel kept performing evil deeds, so finally they met with the horrifying retribution of Hitler's slaughter"![242]

Russia's New Freedom to Hate

Jews cannot be safe in the former Soviet Union because of political uncertainty and the constant undercurrent of violent anti-Semitism. After the 1967 Six-Day War, official Soviet anti-Jewish policies came out which were upheld for two decades.

In the late 1980's, the world rejoiced at the introduction of *Glasnost*. That policy of Soviet openness was not beneficial to all Soviet citizens. The Soviet Jews were not benefited. As freedom expanded across the oppressed nation, the application of one newfound privilege was damaging. Freedom of speech was expanded to permit and encourage anti-Semitic activists. Disaster could come to the Jews of Russia directly from changes in government policies or indirectly from the planning and implementation of actions by the *Pamyat*—a national hate group committed to destroying Jews. They intend to focus the hatred of the Russian people toward the Jews as they attribute the blame for Russia's problems on Russian Jews.

Pamyat's form of violent anti-Semitism is terrible and dangerous. "It feeds on economic troubles and uncertain future, fears that drive ordinary people to look for simple answers and easy scapegoats."[243]

Pamyat people believe that the Jews killed Christ and Czar Nicholas II. They say Jews organized the Bolshevik revolution, and masterminded Stalin's terror. They see glasnost and *perestroika* as a conspiracy to allow Jewish capitalists to regain control of the country.[244]

Pamyat poses a real threat to the well being of all Jews. Jews in Russia are accused of many forms libelous behavior. The damage that has been done to the reputation of the Jewish people by vocal proponents of anti-Semitism will never be completely understood. Henry Ford will not be forgotten, neither will the echoes of his poisonous journalism cease to ring in the ears of those who look for reasons to hate Jews. Preposterous data, when printed, becomes fodder from Hell to be gathered by disciples of anti-Jewish propagandists. The Jerusalem Post recently printed an article with the headlines "It's official: Moscow judge rules 'Protocols" a forgery." In it the reporter notes that the

Protocols was written by Czarist agents at the turn of the century, and despite periodic exposure, has been a favorite of antisemitic propagandists around the world to 'prove' that Jews are plotting to dominate the world . . . Despite the fact that the *Protocols* has been correctly labeled a 'warrant for genocide' by historians, the book remains a bestseller from the Middle East to Japan.[245]

Were it not for the efforts of thinking, concerned, doggedly committed protectors of freedom like Rabbi Abraham Cooper, the Russian hate group, *Pamyat*, would have not been deterred from spreading the lies contained in that forgery. The rabbi "presented the court with 150 pages of historic and contemporary information showing how the *Protocols* was used by major antisemites in the 20th century from Adolf Hitler to Louis Farrakhan."[246] This defensive effort to slow the work of *Pamyat* is not in vain. Those Jews are at great risk that remain in Russia. After the blood bath in the Russian Parliament, reporters from the Associated Press described the chaos that transpired in the wake of the violence. As has happened in so many centuries, the Jews have been blamed by mobilized vocal anti-Semites. The Jews of Russia are filled with a realistic fear of what might yet be in their future.

In the wake of a second violent attack against Moscow's Choral Synagogue, Jewish leaders have reported that the Moscow Jewish community no longer feels safe. In spite of numerous calls for protection for the synagogue, authorities have not responded.[247] The general feeling of fear has been known to many Jews of Russia. The realities of anti-Semitism and violence have compelled the majority of the Jews of Russia to leave. Most have emigrated to Israel, while many have come to America. Those who remain in Russia live at risk. That is why the *Passion of the Christ* is such an issue for Jewish people. Many understand how these passion plays have inspired Christians to perpetrate terrible crimes against Jewish people. "In Russia, for example, the czars supported both the production of the plays and the pogroms they inspired."[248]

The impact of the horrid history of hatred among Russians has been exported. Impossible as it might seem, Russian Neo-Nazis have now been transplanted into Israel. "According to the Information Center for Victims of Anti-Semitism in Israel, more than 500 anti-Semitic incidents were reported over the last three years. 'It is a sad irony that Jews who immigrated to Israel because of the anti-Semitism in the former Soviet Union are now harassed by anti-Semites here.' . . . 'But we have to remember that a full 75 percent of the Russian immigrants arriving in Israel over the past three years are not even Jewish'."[249] This is the shocking result of immigrants being permitted with only distant connections to Jewish relatives under the Law of Return. Many are atheists and some are nominal Christians. The problem is that the immigrants include growing numbers of skinheads. These hooligans are causing many problems and Israel realizes a response is needed. They have been poisoned by hatred and lies from deceived Christians for many generations.

How will the Church respond? What steps will be taken to insure the protection of the Children of Israel? The error of Holocaust denial surrounds an event that first-hand witnesses can still refute. The error surrounding Christian anti-Semitism is much older, much denied, and much harder to prove. It is, however, a serious problem. Whether it is accidental or intentional, when an imbalance exists in the Church's perspective on Judaism, for the security of Jews and the well being of Christians it should be addressed.

---

214 Deborah Lipstadt, *Denying the Holocaust, The Growing Assault on Truth and Memory* (New York: The Free Press, A Division of Macmillan, Inc., 1993), 5.

215 Ibid.
216 Ibid.
217 Charles R. Allen, Jr., *Reform Judaism*, "Patrick J. Buchanan: Master Holocaust Denier," Winter 1996, 27.
218 Ibid.
219 Ibid.
220 Eric Silver, *The Jerusalem Report*, "The Holocaust on Trial," (February 28, 2000), 28.
221 Rabbi Abraham Cooper, Editor, *Response*, "EU Poll: Israel #1 Threat to Peace", Fall/Winter 2003-04 Volume 25, Number 1, 6.
222 Fischel, 10.
223 Ibid.
224 Lipstadt, 12.
225 Forster, 395.
226 Ibid.
227 Ibid., 396.
228 Cohn-Sherbok, 215.
229 Ibid.
230 Ibid.
231 Vivienne Walt, *USA Today*, "Right-wing leader qualifies for run-off in France," April 22, 2002, 8a.
232 Edgar M Bronfman, quoted from his letter sent from the World Jewish Congress March 2004.
233 Ibid.
234 Ibid.
235 Rabbi Abraham Cooper, Editor, *Response*, "Why is this Book a Best-Seller in Japan?", Fall/Winter 1993-94 Volume 14, Number 3, 2.
236 Alan M. Tigay, *Hadassah Magazine*, "The Jewish Traveler," October 1988, 46.
237 Rabbi Abraham Cooper, Editor, *Response*, "Why is this Book a Best-Seller in Japan?", Fall/Winter 1993-94 Volume 14, Number 3, 2.
238 Rabbi Abraham Cooper, "Project Asia," letter published by the Simon Wiesenthal Center, Los Angeles, CA, 1.
239 Ibid.
240 Forster, 400.
241 Ibid.
242 Cooper, "Project Asia", 2.
243 Tom Mathews, Rod Norland, and Carroll Bogert, *Newsweek*, "The Long Shadow: New Fears of Anti-Semitism in Eastern Europe and the Soviet Union," May 7, 1990, 35.
244 Ibid.
245 Tom Tugend, *The Jerusalem Post International Edition*, December 4, 1993, 3.
246 Ibid., *Response*, 3.
247 Ibid.
248 Liel Leibovitz, 35.
249 Aviel Schneider, Editor, *Israel Today*, Jerusalem, October, 2003, 7.

Chapter XIV

The Pope, Nazis, & Israel

As has been shown, many passion play presentations seek to place the primary guilt for the crucifixion on the Jews, while alleviating the weight of Roman responsibility. There is the possibility that modern Rome has this view in common with the "theologians" of the caliber of Gerald L. K. Smith. This tendency to ascribe guilt to the Jews, such as the drama in Eureka Springs, is dangerous. Far more problematic than a bigot in Arkansas is the manner in which the issue was addressed in the most recent writings from the pontiff in Rome. The Pope wrote after quoting from John 18:37:

> "What is truth?" (Jn 18:38), and here ended the judicial proceeding, that tragic proceeding in which man accused God before the tribunal of his own history, and in which the sentence handed down did not conform to the truth. Pilate says: "I find no guilt in him" (Jn 18:38), and a second later he orders: "Take him yourselves and crucify him!" (Jn 19:6). In this way he washes his hands of the issue and returns the responsibility to the violent crowd.[250]

The Pope may have removed the "Threshold of Hope" he desired to cross. According to a *Newsweek* magazine report from October 31, 1994, 1.25 million copies of the Pope's book, *Crossing The Threshold Of Hope*, arrived in bookstores simultaneously in thirty-five countries. The article rightly says, "Even some of the faithful may be mystified by the pontiff's new book."[251] The article informs that the publisher claims the pope "speaks to people of all faiths," however, they suggest that "Muslims, Jews, even Protestants may find his calls for 'dialogue' empty."[252] A better description of the book may have suggested the dialogue leads to "intense concern."

There is a dangerous implication in the Pope's writings that should not be overlooked. In no fashion could Pilate have returned "the responsibility to the violent crowd." The crowd had no authority to crucify Jesus. The Pope's specific reference to the crowd being "violent" is not mentioned in the text he selected from the writings of John. Neither John, nor any of the writers of the three other Gospels described a "violent crowd." Had the Pope reviewed Matthew's report, he could have easily identified that the only suggestion of any concern about the crowd's behavior was that "a tumult was made" (Matthew 27:24). The "tumult" was have been no more violent than a vocal disagreement. Luke and Mark both seem to define this erroneous charge of violence as nothing more than those in attendance at Pilate's raised their voices to inform Pilate of their concern. "And they were instant with loud voices" (Luke 23:23). Mark's assessment was similar, "And the multitude crying aloud began to desire him to do as he had ever done unto them" (Mark 15:8).

The "multitude" is never defined as violent, and as to its size, it is never defined as being larger than the group gathered by the priests. The specific text chosen by the Pope was John 19:6. It refers to the "chief priests and officers" in particular. No mention of a "violent crowd" was suggested by the apostle John. That was left for Pope John Paul II to imply. The innuendo of a "violent crowd" fits into the centuries-old pattern that conjures up images of a bloodthirsty Jewish mob screaming in unison for the crucifixion. If the Pope made an error in his interpretation, that could be understood and forgiven; however, barring a mistake, it would seem that the Pope infers the historical misinterpretation to be valid—it is not! A tumult, described at its worst as loud voices, has been turned into accusations of Jewish violence. This unfounded accusation by the head of the Catholic Church must not go unchallenged.

The ancient stereotyped mob scene is not supported by the apostle John's text or by official Church doctrine. The 1965 Declaration on Non-Christian Religions which came from the Second Vatican Council (which included John Paul II) flatly rejected that ancient anti-Semitic presupposition. The suggestion about the "violent crowd" was simply wrong. Does the Pope believe that a violent Jewish crowd is responsible for the death of Jesus? Either the crowd was violent or it was not violent. Either the Roman authorities had the power to determine guilt or the Jewish crowd was responsible. It can be understood how an Arkansas racist might interpret the text of John with an anti-Semitic twist. However, the Pope must walk more circumspectly.

Referring again to Pope John Paul's text, he suggested, "The scandal of the Cross remains the key to the interpretation of the great mystery of suffering, which is so much a part of the history of mankind." The theological depth of the "scandal of the Cross" is not in question. The Church is not to be at the roots of scandal, yet in one way, the Pope's following words are a scandal. "All individual and collective suffering caused by the forces of nature and unleashed by man's free will—the wars, the gulags, and the holocausts: the Holocaust of the Jews but also, for example, the holocaust of the black slaves from Africa."[253] In this seemingly innocent analysis, the Pope has followed a trail that has been blazed by the worst Holocaust deniers. The deniers often begin by removing the uniqueness of the Holocaust in human experience. If they cannot discredit the event itself, the next best step is to make it comparable to the injustice of others. This is horrible and dangerous for Jews.

The Pope erroneously discusses "holocausts." There have not been holocaust_s_. It is hoped that history will only record one Holocaust! No other event in the annals of mankind compares to the Holocaust because at no other time has suffering been the result of pure genocide. Mass murders and the massacre of untold thousands (perhaps even millions) have occurred in the world, but this is not an equivalency. It is unbelievably horrible, but it is not the same thing. The fundamental difference is that Hitler's attempt was not murder—even mass murder; it was nothing less than the specific purpose of wiping out an entire race of people.

Holocaust denial techniques include efforts to confuse the public about the historicity of the Holocaust. Ignorance is their greatest tool. Americans are easy prey to the doctrines of denial and revisionist lies about history. This is due primarily to the lack of historical knowledge that plagues Americans.

> Countries such as the United States, where the degree of ignorance about historical matters is legendary, are particularly susceptible to this kind of rewriting of history. In 1990 only 45 percent of Alabama high school seniors knew that the

Holocaust was the Nazi attempt to exterminate the Jews. It is telling that many of those who gave the wrong answer thought that the United States had committed the Holocaust against the Japanese with the bombing of Hiroshima and Nagasaki.[254]

I think the Pope dealt the Jewish people a great disservice. He removed the uniqueness of an event that is incomparable in human history by comparing the Holocaust to slavery. Slavery turned individuals into personal property. Slavery was an awful example of human cruelty. Slavery was a blight on the Blacks of Africa and a curse on the system that abused and dehumanized them, but it was not comparable to the Holocaust.

Somehow, Christianity learned to speak comforting words about the sin of slavery as though it had lost the knowledge of Christian slave owners. The collective memory of the Church might need to be reformatted. Black slavery was once touted as being beneficial. Pro-slavery whites, many of them Christian, promoted slavery as a positive good.

> Slavery, they claimed, was supported by the authority of the Bible and the wisdom of Aristotle. It was good for the Africans, who were lifted from the barbarism of the jungle and clothed with the blessings of Christian civilization. Slavemasters did indeed encourage religion in the slave quarters. A catechism for blacks contained such passages as:
>
> Q. Who gave you a master and a mistress?
> A. God gave them to me.
> Q. Who says that you must obey them?
> A. God says that I must.[255]

The pope was correct in identifying that black slaves were terribly mistreated. Unlike the Jews in Nazi Germany, at least the slaves maintained value to someone. Perhaps the Pope was unaware that sometimes Black slaves were given more consideration than Roman Catholic Irish immigrants!

> Above all, the planters regarded the slaves as investments, into which they had sunk nearly $2 billion of their capital by 1860. Slaves were the primary form of wealth in the South, and as such they were cared for as any asset is cared for by a prudent capitalist. Accordingly, they were sometimes, though by no means always, spared dangerous work, like putting a roof on a

house. If a neck was going to be broken, the master preferred it to be that of a wage-earning Irish laborer rather than that of a prime field hand, worth $1,800 by 1860 (a price that had quintupled since 1800). Tunnel blasting and swamp draining were often consigned to itinerant gangs of expendable Irishmen because the labor was "death on niggers and mules."[256]

Incredibly, Irish immigrants worked for the lowest wages and were often given the jobs that might have killed a slave. The entire concept is dehumanizing yet, in no way can the Pope be justified in his comparison with the Jews of the Nazi death camps. Slaves could not have been sold as lampshades or auctioned as footwear! Yet that was the incomparable fate of many Jews killed by the Nazis. Jewish men and women were often valued for the fillings in their teeth, the skin from their dead bodies (which was tanned into products like lampshades), or even their hair while still alive. "Hair is to be used in the manufacture of hair-yarn-socks for 'U'-boat crews and hair-felt foot-wear for the Reichs-railway."[257]

The Pope's Insensitivity

Have things truly changed? During medieval times, the Jews were often portrayed as a wicked character named "Synagogue," as discussed in a previous chapter. "In a collective form, the Jewish people appeared in the character of *Synagogue*, portrayed as blindfolded, with broken banner, and grasping a goat's head, a *symbol of Old Testament sacrifices and of Jewish stubbornness and unchastity* [emphasis mine].[258]

I was greatly discouraged by the recognition that the character of "Synagogue" remains in the Christian consciousness. Though considered by modern Christians to be a figment of the distant past (if they knew of the insulting character at all), "Synagogue" has been recently reintroduced to modern Catholics by a Pope. Though not belabored in his book, *Crossing The Threshold Of Hope*, Pope John Paul II reminded his readers that the Jews reject God in the human forms accepted by Christianity. Presumably, he referred to the view of God in Jesus as Savior. He named the protesters precisely: *"This great protest has precise names—first it is called the Synagogue, and then Islam.* Neither can accept God who is so human."[259] It can safely be assumed that the Pope refers to the humanness of the Messiah in his brief discreditation of opposing worldviews.

Islam is not the subject of this investigation, but Judaism clearly has a variety of views about the humanity of God. If one studies the texts of the ancient Hebrew prophet Daniel, the concept of an individual seen by Nebuchadnezzar as one "like the Son of God" (Daniel 3:25) must be considered. The most basic readings of the Dead Sea Scrolls present serious problems to the Pope's assumptions. The ancient Qumran manuscripts are unquestionably Jewish in origin. Therefore, the content boldly proclaims one historical viewpoint of that segment of Judaism. Those world-famous Jewish writings offer some very interesting comments about the human character of the "Teacher of Righteousness." It must be remembered that he is seen by many to be a messiah figure. Though I find it to be doubtful, some have even suggested that the Qumran writings are about Jesus Christ. Though specific Christian inferences are not widely accepted, the human character of their messiah can be argued from several perspectives. That segment of the ancient Jewish population had a view toward the son of God with human characteristics.

The ancient Jewish writers of the "Son of God" texts from the *Pseudo-Danielic Writings (4Qps Dan and 4Q246)*, did expect a promised Messiah and alluded to the son of God. "He shall be called son of God, and they shall designate him son of the Most High."[260] This passage, along with other texts suggesting messianic imagery (such as contained in the War Scroll) have added intrigue to the debate among historians and scholars investigating the Dead Sea Scrolls.

> There can be no denying the relation of allusions of this kind to the Lukan prefiguration of Jesus: "He will be great, and will be called the son of the Most High; and the Lord God will give him the Throne of his father David . . . For that reason the Holy offspring will be called the Son of God" (Luke 1:32-35).[261]

Ancient Jews can no longer defend their theological strengths or weaknesses. What of modern Jews? Granted, Jews and Christians do not agree on many theological issues. Nonetheless, too many unresolved considerations should cause the Pope retract his comment (its a book, not a papal bull so a reevaluation of an insensitive comment would not cross the line of infallibility). The human character of the Messiah can be hotly debated among Jews of different sects. Did the Pope's view of Judaism's inability to see God as human recognize the concept of the *zaddik*? "He is the people's way to God. The *zaddik* secures redemption for his generation. One way in which he does this is by absorption of the suffering like the 'red heifer' of biblical times, but his suffering also effects vicarious atonement for the sins of others."[262] Judaism and Jews are too diverse to stereotype or limit. Judaism has too many faces to discount the relevance of each.

Actually, when dealing with the Jewish viewpoint of God, many Jews incorporate aspects of the mystical traditions. Beliefs about the human-like attributes of God within the *Sefirot* are legion. Many Christians would view the emphasis given God within Kabbalistic traditions to be too human. Some aspects of the Kabbalah's *Sefirot* would include the following: a male/female dimension of God, the good/evil conflict within God, the sexuality and needs of God. The Pope, and other Gentile Christian writers, might wish to review their studies of Jews and the varieties of Judaism. They will discover an incredibly wide selection of theological systems among Jews. Though not as diverse as the denominational gaps among Christians, still, Gentile Christian theologians should understand how the differing forms of Judaism view God before they accuse them of being unable to consider God's human characteristics, or worse, lump their beliefs with Islam!

Guilt Crosses Denominational Lines

The Catholic Church does not shoulder the blame alone. An entire generation of Christians must seek the face of God and see the torment caused by the Nazi Holocaust.

> Hitler claimed great originality for his radically antisemitic views, but for the most part they were inherited from the Catholic antisemitism of the Austrian politics of his youth. Only the will to exterminate was new. When at his Nuremberg trial Julius Streicher, the editor of the scurrilous Nazi newspaper *Der Sturmer*, claimed that if he must stand arraigned for his views on the Jews, so should Martin Luther, he had more than a semblance of justification for his contention.[263]

Christian and Jewish thinkers of this generation have finally begun to address the theological issues surrounding the vast gulf between the questions of Jewish suffering and the answers of Christian responsibility in light of God's love. "The Nazis . . . could never have arisen without the Christian past . . . *Without the inheritance of 'knowledge' that Jews were bad, there could have been no Holocaust*" [emphasis mine]![264] It can only be hoped that future generations of Christian scholars will be led by a spirit of love and power that improves the character of Christian expression and truly grows in grace toward the Jewish people. This should not be difficult if compared to the expressions of recent decades.

> Within Germany itself the Nazis believed they were performing their Christian duty in advancing Hitler's anti-Jewish policies. Thus Heinrich Himmler declared that "by and large . . . we can say that we have performed this task in love of our people, and we have suffered no damage from it, in our inner self, in our soul, in our character." During the years of war the German Church did not issue a challenge to the activities of the Nazis, and only a few years after the war ended the German Evangelical Conference at Darmstadt proclaimed that the Jewish suffering which had occurred during the Holocaust was a divine visitation and a call to Jews to accept Christ as their Saviour. Such modern attitudes are not far removed from previous centuries of Christian contempt of Judaism and the Jewish people.[265]

Righteous Gentiles

The history of the Church has not been altogether unrighteous. Without doubt, many Christians opposed the behavior of the Nazis, such as: Dietrich Bonhoeffer, a martyred Christian saint; Patriarch Nikodemus, the head of the Orthodox Church in Rumania; the French Capuchin, Fr Marie-Benoit; Metropolitan Andreas Szeptycki, Archbishop of Lvov; Bishop H. Fuglsang Damgaard of Denmark; Raoul Wallenberg of Denmark; Corrie ten Boom; and not to be forgotten, the Gentile saint who was the hero of Schindler's List.[266] No effort will be made to produce a truly exhaustive list of Christians who defied Hitler. Obviously there were not enough to stop him.

Today's generation of Catholics and Protestants must deal with their responsibility toward Israel and the Jewish people. It is encouraging to see efforts being made by both segments of the church world, but the problems are far from being settled. As the Vatican has reviewed their position regarding the Jewish people, a broader base of Christians have made their own efforts as well. Though the late date of their effort is discouraging, at least they made a positive response.

In 1982 the (World Council of Churches) WCC statement *Ecumenical Considerations on Jewish-Christian Dialogue* was produced, which pointed out the need for Christians to abandon stereotypes. Judaism, it asserted, is not a fossilized religion of legalism, but a living tradition. Further, Christian responsibility for Jewish suffering was acknowledged: "Teachings of contempt for Jews and Judaism in certain Christian traditions proved a spawning ground for the evil of the Nazi Holocaust."

. . . Such pronouncements have repudiated misconceptions about Judaism and have paved the way for positive Jewish-Christian encounter—after centuries of persecution, the Churches have at last come to accept responsibility for the plight of the Jews.[267]

Israel, the Pope, and *The Passion of the Christ*

Mr. Gibson's film, *The Passion of the Christ*, has created an opportunity for the Catholic Church. The Pope had a great moment to bring clarity to a confusing situation. Catholics look to their pope in matters of faith. At the time of this writing, many Jewish people, including Israel's Chief Rabbi, are also watching his attitude about the film. "Rabbi Yona Metzger wrote a letter to Pope John Paul asking him to publicly reaffirm that the Jews are not to blame for killing Jesus." He used the strongest language to condemn the popular passion movie, calling it "a tendentious, malicious film," suggesting that "Many viewers may be led to believe that the Jews are collectively responsible for the crucifixion of Christ. Indeed, the film may provoke undesirable anti-Semitic responses both in the short-term and in the long-term."[268]

Mr. Gibson has repeatedly indicated that the Pope John Paul II viewed the film and was alleged to have declared. "It is as it was." However, "the Vatican later denied the quote, saying that the pope doesn't render judgments on films."[269] The Vatican did not need to act as a film critic to satisfy the Chief Rabbi of Israel. "In response to the letter, the Pope urged bishops to respect the Jews as 'elder brothers' and instruct priests how they can forestall any anti-Semitic sentiment that might result from the film."[270] One Israeli newspaper ran a front-page full color photo of the film's leading character wearing the crown of thorns on His bloodied brow. The headline read, "LETHAL WEAPON." The leader of the ultra-Orthodox Shas party, Eli Yishai, deemed the film to be a "blood libel and should be banned."[271]

The Jewish people of the world need this generation of evangelical Protestants and Catholics to successfully integrate a correct view of Jews and Judaism into their doctrines. Their anti-Semitic medieval European forefathers failed to identify the problem and thereby perpetuated the tradition that has been wrongly embraced by mid-twentieth century European fathers. To paraphrase a familiar question asked within the Jewish Passover liturgy, "Why is this generation different from all other generations?" If this question is to be answered with hope, the Church must exhibit the love of God to the people of God. Anything less warrants righteous indignation.

---

250 His Holiness John Paul II, *Crossing The Threshold Of Hope*, (New York: Alfred A. Knopf, 1994), 65.

251 David Gates, *Newsweek*, "A Papal Publishing Event," October 31, 1994, 68.

252 Ibid.

253 Pope John Paul II, 63.

254 Lipstadt, 216.

255 Thomas A. Bailey, and David M. Kennedy, *The American Pageant, A History of the Republic, Vol. I*, (Lexington, Massachusetts: D. C. Heath and Company, 1991), 357.

256 Ibid., 350.

257 Quoted by Barbara Distel and Ruth Jakusch, Editors, *Concentration Camp Dachau 1933-1945*, (Munich, Germany: Comite' International de Dachau, 1978), 137.

258 Nicholls, 252.

259 Pope John Paul II, 41.

260 Vermes, Geza, *The Dead Sea Scrolls in English*, (Middlesex, England: Penguin Books, 1990), 275.

261 Robert Eisenman and Michael Wise, *The Dead Sea Scrolls Uncovered*, (Dorset: Element, Shaftesbury, 1992), 68.

262 Byron Sherwin, *Mystical Theology and Social Dissent*, 140 as cited in unpublished manuscript provided for "Medieval Judaism" course by Spertus Institute of Jewish Studies, Chicago, IL, Summer 1994.

263 Nicholls, xxii.

264 Ibid.

265 Cohn-Sherbok, 209.

266 Readers might be interested in the fact that the Jewish man responsible for bringing *Schindler's List* to the screen had great incentive to produce his work. Stephen Spielberg is a third-generation Jewish American. His ancestors came from Odessa and Austrian dominated Polish Galicia. According to a December, 1993 *Hadassah Magazine* article "Spielberg learned to count from the numbers on the forearm of a refugee to

whom his grandmother was teaching English." The numbers referred to in this quote were the Nazi tattoos given as identification numbers to all Jews in the concentration camps. These were commonly seen on the older relatives of many American Jews who survived the Holocaust. In my youth, I recall the silence heard and horror felt when friends and relatives accidentally revealed their mementos from Hell. We tried to avoid discussing the tattoos because family members had first hand knowledge of the tragedy.

267 Cohn-Sherbok, 224-225.
268 Aviel Schneider, Editor, *Israel Today*, Jerusalem, April 2004, 22.
269 Liel Leibovitz, 35.
270 Ibid.
271 Ibid.

Chapter XV

Rome and the Chosen People

The Catholic Church has been irresponsible in the manner it has related to Israel and the Jewish people. Yet in one important effort, they have surpassed many medieval Protestant theologians. As briefly discussed in the previous chapter, the Vatican has adjusted its public position toward the Jews. As announced in the 1965 Declaration on Non-Christian Religions, Rome firmly asserts that, "God holds the Jews most dear for the sake of the Fathers; His gift and call are irrevocable" . . . the Jews should not be presented as rejected or accursed by God.[272] It is gross error to place any collective guilt for the death of Jesus on the Jewish people

> This behavior forms the basis of what is perhaps the most baneful of all anti-Jewish ideas: the notion that the Jews have been rejected or cursed by God. Allied with this notion is the belief that the Old Covenant has been voided by the New, or that the Kingdom of God has been taken from Jewry and given to the Church.

The Vatican should be acknowledged for the precision with which their scholars have addressed this issue so fundamental to healthy relations between Jews and Christians. In 1965 they took an enormous step in the right direction but they stopped short of addressing broader issues.

> Without actually proscribing or even mentioning the key word, deicide, and without any expression of repentance for

Catholic anti-Judaic ideas and actions, the declaration did nevertheless make it clear that the Jewish people could not be held corporately responsible for the death of Christ.[273]

Someday the infallibility of the pope, and therefore, the guilt of the Catholic Church, will be questioned with more openness. Then, there will be hope that the erroneous decisions made by Rome during World War II will be addressed with truth and honesty. This may be the only path that will lead to genuine repentance. This will be required eventually and cannot be eternally avoided. Christians have supported systems that have damaged God's chosen people. God will not ignore this fact of Church history.

Chosenness Discussed

Some have confused the concept of "chosen" with that of "choice." The chosenness of a people is not equivalent to their personal choices. Chosen, as in the realm of being Jewish, is unlike the choice associated with becoming a Christian. It compares to the difference between seminal descent and mental assent. Jewish chosenness is a heritage obtained by being born a descendant of the patriarchs and counted among the children of Jacob's lineage. The issue of salvation cannot automatically be equated to chosenness. Neither can it be related directly to personal righteousness. The issue of chosenness must be elevated to a matter singularly attributed to the will of God.

The Vatican, which represents a giant portion of Christendom, refused to recognize the State of Israel for decades. Only recently did Rome finally establish diplomatic relations with Israel. Although this may seem absurd to knowledgeable modern American Catholics, previously, the two governments had no ambassadorial exchanges. One Jewish magazine offered an interesting perspective on the Vatican's behavior. Their commentary was contained within a larger article reviewing a book written by Jewish conservative, Don Feder. While lambasting the views of Jewish liberals and ultra-liberals, *The Jewish Enquirer* stated the following about the Vatican's refusal to treat the Jewish nation appropriately:

> It is the Jewish Liberals who instituted the tradition of running to kowtow to popes, who for 45 years refused to recognize the existence of the State of Israel. And now, after begrudgingly establishing "diplomatic" relations with Israel (after running out of excuses for its history of Jew-hate), the

Vatican has informed Israel it's first ambassador is unacceptable, because David Rosen is a member of the *Jewish* clergy. Of course, the Vatican's ambassador to Israel is a member of the Catholic clergy.[274]

The propriety of the Vatican's history of staunch refusal[275] to accept the Jewish state, and their history of "the church's evident partiality toward the Arabs"[276] makes one wonder about their position toward the Jewish people in general. Likewise, some recognize that the Vatican has always had its own desire to control the Holyland.

Rome Sees No Evil

The Simon Wiesenthal Center correctly denounced the action of the Vatican when they honored a man known to be a liar and a Nazi. Rabbi Marvin Hier represented the Center as they

> reacted with indignation at the bestowal of the "pius Order," a high papal honor, upon ex-Austrian president Kurt Waldheim. "We are appalled by this action . . . There can be no moral justification in honoring a man who hid his Nazi past, and who later, after his lies were exposed, never found the courage to acknowledge and apologize for his actions," he added. In 1987, following a campaign by the Wiesenthal Center, the World Jewish Congress and other Jewish groups, the U.S. barred Waldheim from visiting the country as a private citizen. [277]

Many have found it to be nearly inconceivable that Pope John Paul II could have granted an audience to Kurt Waldheim. The Catholic Church honored a man believed by many to be worthy of a prison sentence as a Nazi war criminal. The philosophical ramifications are quite serious. As described in the Pope's own words, the following understanding of his incredible power and position is explained:

> Confronted with the Pope, one must make a choice. The leader of the Catholic Church is defined by the faith as the Vicar of Jesus Christ (and is accepted as such by believers). The Pope is considered the man on earth who represents the Son of God, who "takes the place" of the Second Person of the omnipotent God of the Trinity.[278]

In light of this view held by so many millions of Catholics around the world, one must ask if "the Second Person of the omnipotent God of the Trinity," Jesus Christ, would have honored Kurt Waldheim with a medal, or, would He have commanded Waldheim to repent and confess his sins. It could be construed among Catholics that the Pope's commendation of a known Nazi validates Waldheim's behavior. It could be construed among Jews that the Pope's commendation defines the "church's" beliefs about God's attitude toward the Jewish people. Philosophically, politically, spiritually, that action did not serve to improve Jewish-Christian relations.

Far worse than giving out medals to successful politicians who were known to support and participate in anti-Semitic causes, the Catholic Church once again failed to correctly deal with its own behavior. In fact, it directly supported Nazi war criminals.

Nazis: Saved by Grace or Rome?

During the initial research for this work, Sam Donaldson was featured on an episode of *Prime Time Live*. Acting on the data supplied to him by the Wiesenthal Center, the ABC news correspondent traveled to San Carlos de Bariloche, Argentina, to confront Reinhard Kops. Along with many Americans, I had the unique experience of watching an active ex-Nazi respond to Donaldson on national television. Kops immediately gave information which led Donaldson and each of us in the eager national TV audience on the hunt to an even more despicable Nazi, Erich Priebke.

> One of the highest-ranking officials of the dreaded Nazi security police and security service in Italy, Priebke headed the Gestapo office in Brescia. By his own admission, he also participated in the infamous massacre of March 24, 1944, in which 335 Italian civilians, including 75 Jews, were bound and shot in the back of the neck at the Ardeatine Caves outside Rome.
>
> Donaldson found an arrogant and untroubled Nazi. Confronted by TV cameras, Priebke made no effort to conceal his identity. Nor did he deny his participation in the Ardeatine murders.[279]

The horror of the case surrounding Reinhard Kops and Erich Priebke was astounding enough without detailing their evil behavior or that of their associates. One fact must be emphatically proclaimed. *Many Nazi war criminals could never have walked free without the direct consent and help of the Roman Catholic Church.* Aiding and abetting criminals is a crime in itself.

Asked by reporters how he made his way to Argentina, the former SS Captain replied, "I couldn't leave with my own passport so I asked for help from the Vatican. It got word to me through Bishop Alois Hudal that it was prepared to help me." . . . When he was arrested after the war, Priebke somehow managed to find his way out of the British-run prison at Rimini, after signing a confession to his role in the massacre.[280]

The decisions and attitudes of a Pope cannot be ignored. As previously quoted from his book, the Pope sees himself as the "Vicar of Jesus Christ." He "takes the place" of Jesus in the world. It is therefore presumed that the Pope acts in the fashion that Jesus would act. According to Catholic beliefs, "The Pope is not the only one who holds this title. With regard to the Church entrusted to him, each bishop is *Vicarius Christi*. The Pope is Vicar of Christ . . . one cannot consider it apart from the *dignity of the entire college of bishops*."[281] From this perspective, each Nazi war criminal helped by any Catholic bishop was vicariously applauded by his presumed benefactor, Jesus Christ. The philosophical ramifications are extremely troublesome!

One revelation of another similar incident relates to Paul Touvier, an aide to Gestapo Chief Klaus Barbie. Touvier is the first Frenchmen to stand trial as a Nazi war criminal. The Catholic Church will someday be taken to task over these matters revealed in March of 1994.

For the 45 years that preceded his arrest at a Roman Catholic priory in Nice in 1989, Touvier was a fugitive, moving from convent to monastery under assumed names with his wife and two children in tow.

The jury trial will focus on how a man condemned to death twice in abstentia managed to elude authorities for so long, and why nearly 50 Roman Catholic institutions offered him financial aid and logistical support. . . . Touvier was helped over the years by church groups ranging from extreme conservatives led by renegade Marcel Lefevre to moderate organizations such as the charity Secours Catholic, which paid him a regular living allowance.[282]

Touvier had been safely hidden since 1947. He came out after the twenty-year statute of limitations expired. "In 1971, Premier Georges Pompidou pardoned Touvier at the behest of leading church officials."[283] It is possible that Touvier would have quietly been permitted to forget his past. If it were not for the efforts of vigilant resistance groups and Jewish survivors the matter would have been closed. Many were incensed by the pardon. No justification should permit a known Nazi war criminal to go free and even be helped by the Church. The new evidence against Touvier sent him scurrying back underground until 1989 when he was arrested at the Roman Catholic priory.

Conflicts of Conscience?

Without doubt, the Pope's audience with Austria's Nazi, Kurt Waldheim, was easier to justify than a previous Pope's posturing during the Nazi extermination campaign. Christians around the world failed to join together to involve themselves in saving the Jews. A few could have made a big difference. Many continue to wonder what would have happened if the Catholic Church had taken a strong stand on behalf of the Jews in Europe. One awful example from that previous generation must be a reminder to Christians of future generations.

On June 2, 1941, France enacted vicious anti-Semitic laws. The French Vichy government asked Pope Pius XII if he would take a stand on the issue? His response expressed the Pope's lack of concern for Jews. He said, "In principle, there is nothing in these measures which the Holy See would find to criticize."[284] He was also asked by Dr Eduardo Senatro, the Berlin correspondent of *L'Osservatore Romano*, if he would offer any protest to the Nazi extermination of Jews? The Pope replied: "Dear friend, do not forget that millions of Catholics serve in the German armies. Shall I bring them into conflicts of conscience?"[285] The answers from Pope Pius XII could have impacted millions of Jews. The Vatican could have been a powerful force for good toward the Children of God during this test of faith. Instead, after the war, the Vatican and others close to it helped thousands of war criminals to escape from Germany.

Without doubt, conflicts of conscience must now exist. No effort today can justify or restore yesterday's tragic losses. Only confession and repentance will bring peace. One can only pray that the Christian conscience will be so seared that churchmen will be forced to submit to the heart of God and properly love God's chosen people as He does!

272 Banki and Strober, 13.
273 Nicholls, xxiii.
274 Chavah Halevi, *The Jewish Enquirer*, "Book Review," Volume I, Number 2, HaChodesh HaAshiri, 35.
275 According to Pope John Paul II, the recent efforts to reach peace accords in the Middle East have permitted the Vatican to establish diplomatic relations. This seems rather odd since peace treaties, plans, accords, and various schemes have been being negotiated for many years. Nonetheless, the pontiff says on page 100 of *Crossing The Threshold Of Hope*, "I am also pleased that as a result of the peace process currently taking place, despite setbacks and obstacles, in the Middle East, and thanks also to the initiative of the State of Israel, it became possible *to establish diplomatic relations between the Apostolic See and Israel.* As for the recognition of the State of Israel, it is important to reaffirm that I myself never had any doubts in this regard." This sounds somewhat hollow and belated, yet, it is important and gratifying to know Israel was finally recognized by the Vatican.
276 Forster, 411.
277 Rabbi Abraham Cooper, Editor, *Response*, "Deadliest Attack in Diaspora Since the Holocaust," Summer 1994, Volume 15, Number 2, 8.
278 Pope John Paul II, 3.
279 Rabbi Abraham Cooper, Editor, *Response*, "The Ghosts of the Ardeatine Caves," Summer 1994, Volume 15, Number 2, 3.
280 Ibid.
281 Pope John Paul II, 13.
282 Marilyn August, The Associated Press, *The Oregonian*, March 16, 1994, A6.
283 Ibid.
284 Cohn-Sherbok, 208-209.
285 Ibid.

Chapter XVI

Passionate About the Passion?

Are you passionate about the passion? I mean that in the richest sense. Are you passionate about the contemporary passion film by Mel Gibson? Are you passionate about the actual passion of the Christ? Are you passionate about God's love and His passion to draw people to Himself? Or are you just reading this because you wondered whether a Jewish man who believes in Jesus would give the film a "thumbs up" or "thumbs down" review? If that is your concern, I gave the film both. I loved the film and I hated the film. Those of you who read the *Prologue to a Jewish Guy's Concerns About The Passion of the Christ* already knew that. It was too complex to limit to one emotion.

This chapter was saved till now because the patterns of error in earlier passion play presentations appear to have informed certain elements of the script used by the contemporary film. Please do not presume that I am suggesting the scriptwriter, or the producer, or any of the consultants to the production plagiarized or even viewed other passion play presentations. I have no way of knowing that. Though I assume from the typical pattern displayed, they must have been aware of what audiences expect and provided the required heroes and villains. I am definitely suggesting that important elements of the drama were presented through the eyes of individuals who had been influenced by the same incorrect interpretations evidenced in the earlier dramas described in this book. These same incorrect interpretations are what have led to the massive public outcry against the film by many Jewish leaders. Their concerns are not unwarranted. Polls "indicate that one quarter of professed Christians in the U.S. support the charge of deicide against the Jews."[286]

The film has recorded both stunning successes and failures, if these can be measured by the extreme impact it has had on audiences. The intensity of the presentation apparently caused the pastor of the Lovingway United Pentecostal Church to advertise the unloving sign on his church marquis that boldly declared, "Jews killed the Lord Jesus." On the other end of the spectrum, it was reported that the film had such a positive impact on one viewer that he went to the police and confessed to having committed a murder that had been previously ruled as a suicide. Perhaps the pastor got the innuendo in the anti-Semitic pattern of the film—the Jews are responsible for the death of Christ. Whereas the murderer got the message—Jesus suffered as our atonement—forgiveness is available. Letters to editors around the nation exploded in columns proving that viewers were both elevated and depreciated. Faith was built in many lives and faith was assaulted in many lives.

There is no doubt that when compared to recent attempts to present the life of Jesus in blasphemous terms, this film was obviously driven by a desire to reveal the divine nature of Jesus—a perfect revelation of God's perfect love. I was extremely gratified to hear of one outstanding Jewish man, Rabbi Daniel Lapin, who spoke out on behalf of the film. He appropriately made the comparison to *The Last Temptation of Christ* and scolded those opponents of Mr. Gibson's film who failed to speak out against the blasphemy of the *Last Temptation* or *The Priest*. He wisely reminded angry Jewish critics that their voice was lost in this matter if they refused to speak out against prior films that blasphemed Christianity. It was hypocritical of some Jewish critics to defend films that publicly mocked Jesus under the guise of free speech, then attempt to censure Mr. Gibson due to their dislike of the film. Constitutional rights cut both ways. It is not limited to the purview of those who want to demean the Christian faith. Christians have the same right to declare what they believe as boldly as others might voice their disbelief. This film is a strong declaration about the faith of Mr. Gibson. His faith was well represented and it had the desired positive effect on countless throngs of spectators. Perhaps the filming of *The Passion of the Christ* serves to remind us that Christianity is not a spectator sport.

Actors on the set declared that their participation in the project deepened their faith and brought them closer to God. Some were reportedly struck by lightning and lived to tell about it. Mr. Gibson also was touched in many ways during the filming of his epic (and I do believe this is a proper term to describe this marvelous cinematic presentation of the suffering of Jesus Christ.) The cast had the opportunity to enjoy Catholic Mass every morning during the creation of the film. Mr. Gibson felt this important because, "We had to be squeaky clean just working on this."[287] My personal view differs from Mr. Gibson in that I believe our efforts to get clean through religious activities are insufficient. Rather, it seems to me that Jesus brings His righteousness to the party and thus, He provides the atonement. It is exclusively thereby that we can be "squeaky clean" in the sight of God through the sacrifice revealed in the film. Of course, that is just a Jewish Protestant's spin on the theological gap that differentiates Mr. Gibson and me.

As I declared above, I had mixed emotions about the film. I am like the fella who had one hand stuck in a pot of boiling water and the other buried in a bucket of ice. When asked how he was feeling, he answered, "On the average, I'm fine." The movie touched me too deeply to be just fine. My feelings are informed by my love for the Messiah with a deep appreciation for what He endured on my behalf. Yet my views are also invested in the centuries of suffering endured by my people due to the accusation of deicide resulting from the wrong interpretations of passion presentations. Therefore, in seeking the views of others, I looked beyond the local and regional opinions.

I was interested in how my people in Israel responded to news about the film. There was an immediate outcry against the film and it was banned in Israel. As one might expect, many Jews in Israel had more global concerns. There were many who rightly expected much of the Muslim world to embrace the film in spite of their blatant religious rejection of the Crucifixion. Islam promotes an odd view that Jesus was not crucified, and that rather, someone else was executed in place of Jesus. However, Palestinian leader Yasser Arafat viewed the film at his West Bank compound with some Catholic leaders. One of his aides reported that Arafat was quick to compare the suffering of Jesus to the suffering of the Palestinians. According to the April 9, 2004, edition of The Christian Science monitor, an aide reported Arafat said, "The Palestinians are still daily being exposed to the kind of pain Jesus was exposed to during his crucifixion." Obviously, both were alleged to be at the hands of the wicked Jews. This was the emotion stimulated among many Muslim viewers. And there were very, very many viewers in the Arab world. That same article reported, "*The Passion of the Christ*, is breaking box office records across the Middle East . . . posting record sales in Lebanon, Egypt, Syria, Qatar, Jordan, and the United Arab Emirates." Some Muslims have chosen to equate the death of Sheikh Ahmad Yassin with the Jewish call for execution that killed Jesus. Of course the difference should be obvious. Jesus was a Jew who gathered a peaceful, godly, loving group of tender disciples and He gave His life to buy our freedom. The sheikh was the founder of *Hamas*, a terrorist organization dedicated to destroying Jews.

KRON, channel 4-TV reported that a Muslim viewer in Jordan believed the film "unmasked the Jews' lies and I hope that everybody, everywhere, turns against the Jews." However, some Muslims will not be allowed to see the film. Some Islamic nations banned the movie in theatres because it was deemed to violate Islamic *sharia* (religious laws). One Muslim regulation forbids the depiction of the prophets of Islam. Jesus is considered to be such a prophet and therefore the film was considered unacceptable. At the time of this publication, Kuwait was still debating the issue. A significant argument raged between Sunni Muslims who opposed the airing and Shiite Muslims who favored permitting the film to seen. Ayatollah Mohammed Baqer al-Mehri, a top Shiite cleric in Kuwait requested their government make an exception to permit the Mr. Gibson's film to air because it "reveals crimes committed by Jews against Christ." On the other hand, Bahrain and Malaysia adhered to their beliefs that it was wrong to release a film showing a prophet. Therefore, they did not permit the airing in their nations.

In contradistinction to all the negative propaganda generated by the film in Islamic nations, the power of the Word of God should never be devalued or underestimated. It was very exciting that some Arabic-speaking people found a connection to the Aramaic language spoken in much of the film. The film also posed a wonderful new opportunity to counter the false teaching about Jesus that is common throughout Islam. This film presented a unique opportunity for many Muslims around the world to learn about important aspects of the New Testament that have been hidden from them. Many were completely unfamiliar with those aspects of the life of Jesus addressed in the film. I am confident that as a result, many Muslims who had never heard the true Gospel will be touched and changed by the powerful presentation of God's love expressed in the depiction of the suffering of Jesus. Let us pray that millions of Muslims find the true Jesus of the New Testament as a result of Mr. Gibson's effort. The film boldly declares the love of God revealed in Christ and I would encourage every

Islamic person to see the film and reach their own conclusion.

Though I am fascinated with the Muslim response to the film, I must return to the concerns shared by Israelis. They are typically quite well informed about issues that impact Jews around the world. They are also very sensitive about developments that have the potential to create added tensions for Jewish people living in non-Jewish areas. It is for this reason that Israeli critics have been very vocal about their views on the film. They resent Mr. Gibson's implications if you attack the film, "you attack the Scriptures themselves."[288] It is often not the film in particular that is at issue. Rather, it is the results of previous examples of similar presentations in Church history that concern Jews. Many of the critics have not seen the film. Nonetheless, they are aware of the atrocities committed by Church folk after passion plays had been presented in other eras. Christian scholar Bernard E. Olsen was quoted by *The Jerusalem Report* saying, "The crucifixion drama is regarded . . . as having played a prominent part in Jewish disabilities through the centuries as well as providing a major cause of negative attitudes towards Jews today."[289] The problem is neither new nor unknown. It is simply ignored by those who wish to believe it does not exist. Jewish writers in Israel are quite correct in their assessment of the danger.

> Throughout history, mainly in medieval Europe, the passion plays' powerful evocation of the deicide charge sparked violent outbursts against Jews, so powerful that passion plays were banned in Rome in 1539 because they were regularly followed by murderous raids on the Jewish ghetto.[290]

Are the Jewish critics from Israel over-reacting? Consider this: Hitler returned to enjoy the Passion Play at Oberammergau during its run in 1942. He spoke to the "adoring masses and stressed a direct link between his vision and the tradition of the plays. Quoting Matthew 27:25, 'his blood be on us and on our children,' Hitler said, 'Maybe I'm the one who must execute this curse . . . I do no more than join what has been done for more than 1,500 years already. Maybe I render Christianity the best service ever!' "[291] From there, it became well known that Hitler began using multi-media presentations to educate his constituency about the changes he brought to Germany.

> The Nazi regime utilized anti-Semitic movies in a way similar to that in which the passion plays were utilized for cen-

turies, with similar, if far more terrible results . . . those movies were used as a propaganda piece and were screened to the Einsatzgruppen before they were sent out to kill Jews.[292]

The film has been both praised and panned by film critics, letters to the editor, rabbis, priests, pastors, Christians, Jews, and most flavors of religious folk in between. My synagogue (a Reform Temple) presented a lecture on "How to Respond to *The Passion of the Christ*: A Training Session." I love my rabbi and look forward to discussing his views on this book after I can give him a copy. We disagree about the messiahship of Jesus, but I assume we will find much in common about the history of the genre of passion dramas.

I think it fair to say that my rabbi and I might both enjoy some of the works of Mel Gibson. I also think we would find agreement on Mr. Gibson's troublesome handling of his father's alleged Holocaust denial. I believe he could have resolved the matter with much less controversy. For example, millions of people across the nation saw the Diane Sawyer interview with Mr. Gibson. When asked about his father's Holocaust denial, the reply was rather abrupt, "Leave it alone."[293] Certainly more could have been said to diffuse the problem. His father, Hutton Gibson, has made his views well known. They are in the public eye. Had they been kept private, it would not be necessary to comment, but this cat is out of the bag and there is no chance to put it back under wraps. "In a recent radio interview, the elder Gibson repeated his contention that the Holocaust was 'all—maybe not all fiction—but most of it is'."[294] The media helped promote the terrible lie of Holocaust denial by promoting the skewed beliefs of Mel Gibson's father. Will the sins of the father be shared with the son? It seems possible if the lie is not renounced. One cannot sugarcoat this poison pill and expect it to be swallowed without grave consequences. The film was too popular. The producer was too popular. And now, the sinful view of his father has been made too popular.

Gibson was interviewed by Peggy Noonan of Reader's Digest. He was asked a very straightforward question. "You're going to have to go on record. The Holocaust happened right?"[295] It would seem to me that the obvious correct answer would have been a very simple, YES! Instead, he launched into a story about knowing people with numbers on their arms. He spoke of many atrocities of the war and suffering by a variety of people groups. This depreciates the uniqueness of the Nazi Holocaust. It also equates it to a laundry list of human ills. I agree with his analysis. However, he never just said, YES, the Holocaust happened. Six million Jews died in the genocide. Perhaps he has said this in other venues. I hope so. I can appreciate his unwillingness to disassociate with his father. However, he can love his father and disassociate himself from his father's errant views.

Of course I realize that one's view of *The Passion of the Christ* is justifiably influenced by one's view of the New Testament. Jewish people that deny the validity of the account in the Gospel narratives tend to reject the awesome quality of the film's presentation revealing the love of God depicted in the suffering of Jesus. They often shift focus to the terrible violence levied against the hero of the story brought about by the villains—the Jews. In contrast, Christians who believe the New Testament, find the love of God revealed in the film's dramatic expression of that love through the suffering endured by the hero—Jesus. Hence, this is why Christians tend to respond positively to the violence and Jews often respond negatively to the same suffering. Christians saw the love of God expressed through the identical vehicle in which the Jews saw the presumed hatred of our people against the love God. It should not be difficult to understand why the Jews feel like the villains. It is also easy to identify why they were presented as the twisted, bloodthirsty, inhumane enemies of the hero. Dramas need heroes and villains. Greater heroes and worse villains create more intense drama. Many people were touched by the love of God shown in the voluntary suffering of Jesus. Many people were also touched by the hatred of the enemies of God (the Jews) shown in the film. Is there any question as to why the film has polarized so many Jews and Christians? An honest appraisal of the film requires one to admit that the Jews and the Romans shared equally in the crime. Both peoples were cast in a despicable light. But I must point out that all of the Roman soldiers are long gone. Only Jewish people remain alive and cognizant of the tendency to be stigmatized.

It is disturbing that many Christian leaders dismissed the negative impact that this film has had on Jewish people. It is more disturbing that many Christian leaders ignored this aspect of the film's impact while praising the film in the media. It is most disturbing that they ignored this impact and acted as though they were incredulous that anyone could find anything in the film that might be anti-Semitic. This behavior is disingenuous or dangerously uninformed. It is particularly troublesome because the Jewish critics are so much better informed about the basic historical issues surrounding the passion play than most Christian leaders.

And with these comments now on the record, permit me to recount a few reflections from my experience viewing the film. Many of these thoughts are merely observations and should not be taken as criticisms. I will be clear about that which I found to be troublesome.

Thumbs up & down:
the film review by one Jewish guy

I enjoyed the opening Scripture selected from Isaiah 53. This important section of the Hebrew Bible is most enlightening when evaluating messianic texts from the Jewish Scriptures. Though many modern Jews reject the messianic implications of Isaiah 53, it is clearly a messianic prophecy and was regarded so by many ancient rabbis. It is also a section of the Bible intentionally left out during the weekly Jewish Bible readings. In other words, this text, though clearly canonical and messianic, is never heard during standard synagogue Bible readings. Therefore, it is probably not often heard or read by many Jews. As such, it represented one of the finest text selections the producer could have chosen to impact both Jews and Gentiles in his effort to present Christ as the "Suffering Servant." Christians rightly believe Jesus is the subject of that messianic prophecy declared by Isaiah more than 700 years before Christ.

The scene in the garden certainly took liberties with the Bible but it was handled quite tastefully. I particularly enjoyed the added element of the snake in the scene. The producer powerfully called to mind the first snake in the first garden. That snake succeeded in helping remind the audience about the first human sin. The snake in the film was treated as a fulfillment of a prophecy in Genesis given to Adam and Eve. It was a very dramatic enactment to see the "seed" of the woman crush the snake with His foot.

I was deeply saddened by the costume selected for Jesus. It was troublesome that He was not wearing the customary fringed garment or prayer shawl. This was the most intense prayer of His life, yet He was presented as having disobeyed the commands of both Numbers 15:38 and Deuteronomy 22:12. Both texts clearly demand that observant Jewish men wear *tzitzit* (fringes) in the corners of their garments. The Jewish custom remains the same today. This is one of the primary reasons why many Jewish men wear prayer shawls in synagogue and other worship situations. It is also why some Jewish men wear a smaller version under their clothes with only the fringes exposed. Jesus would not have sinned by ignoring this standard Jewish practice or donned the robes of a non-Jew. Of course, having seen a variety of prior passion dramas, my fears about this matter were quickly confirmed. Not only was Jesus portrayed as "non-Jewish" by His apparel, His sleeping disciples were also not wearing the garments of observant Jews. Then as expected, when a character was finally seen wearing the fringed clothes of a Jew, it was the typical enemies of Jesus who were portrayed as Jews and dressed according to standard Jewish practice. This is the same pattern of other passion dramas. The Jewish enemies are clad in a fashion so as to identify the villains as Jews. The Jewish Messiah, the Jewish disciples, and the Jewish supporters of Jesus are stripped of the outward appearance of their Jewishness. A false image was therefore created. It was as if the heroes and the villains were not all equally Jewish—they were!

I do not agree with the assumption of the producer that Satan was at the garden prayer vigil. Nor do I agree that Satan was aware of the true plan of God for the Crucifixion. In fact, it seems to me that if Satan had been previously cognizant of the results of the Resurrection, instead of possessing Judas to betray Jesus to the wicked priests, Satan would have possessed Johnny Cochran to insure Jesus had the best defense lawyer possible.

Since the film's phenomenal financial success, I have heard many negative comments about Mr. Gibson's motives for making the film. I have seen several critical cartoons implying that he had a greedy profit motive. I believe those rude implications to be completely absurd and probably rooted in jealousy. Nobody in their right mind would invest $30,000,000.00 to produce an entire film in dead languages for a theatrical release to people who could not understand the dialogue. I reject all of those accusations against Mr. Gibson. How many films with subtitles have ever made a profit when the actresses wore all of their clothes in every scene? No, I am convinced that Mr. Gibson's motives were pure. However, due to the film's dialogue being spoken exclusively in ancient languages (Aramaic, Latin, and Hebrew), most viewers probably missed one of the most beautiful nuances of the filmmaker's technique. I was deeply touched by the scene of Mary being troubled in the night. She woke up simultaneously as Jesus was being arrested in the garden. Mary was startled and cried out the following Hebrew words: *"Ma'nishtanah ha'lailah ha'zeh meecall ha'layloat."* These words are translated as, "Why is this night different from all other nights?" This famous sentence was lifted directly from one of the central sections of the Jewish Passover Seder.

A few hours earlier, the same words would have been spoken verbatim during the "Last Supper" when the *Feer Kashas*—Four Questions were recited. These questions have been asked and answered by Jews at every Passover *seder* around the world since the time of Moses. Just as Mary may have taught Jesus those words when He was a small boy, she recited them that night prior to His death when she awoke terrified because her son was being arrested to suffer and die for our deliverance.

Mary then made reference to the *Avodeem Chayeenu*. "We" were slaves to Pharaoh in Egypt. This familiar Passover recitation creates a first person connection to "our" slavery in Egypt and "our" deliverance discussed in the Exodus account. Jews of every era personally identify with the slaves. We participate in the event of God's miraculous redemption as we celebrate the festival commanded in Scripture.

These unmistakable analogies from the Jewish celebration were probably lost to the uninitiated non-Jewish viewers. It is unfortunate that these positive inclusions of the script were not better explained in the film because there were many other less desirable emotions stirred by other powerful images that should have been cut from the editor's final version. Nevertheless, hidden in that brief screen exchange is the urgent connection between our Passover deliverance from the temporal slavery to Egypt and that eternal deliverance from slavery to sin that Christ won for us by His death and Resurrection. In that moment, the film's depth was more powerful and positive than I can adequately describe.

Immediately thereafter, the Jewish soldiers were seen beating Jesus as they walked from the garden back to His trial before the priests. Along the walk, these soldiers threw Jesus over a wall and allowed a chain that bound Him to break His fall. There is no biblical record of such an event. It was extremely brutal and would have likely broken His back. The portrayal was an unnecessary and a particularly brutal scene from the filmmaker's imagination. But it was the scene that followed that troubled me more than most.

As recorded in the Scriptures, false witnesses had been hired to speak against Jesus. They were testifying before the Sanhedrin in a mock trial at the home of Caiaphas, the High Priest. The room was jammed with perhaps as many as 100-150 people gathered to convict Jesus before the Jewish council. In reality, the quantity of people on hand was probably much smaller than was depicted in the film. It seemed that only two stood up to question the manner in which the "trial" was being handled. Nicodemus and Joseph of Arimathea were presumably the two friends of Jesus at that gathering. As mentioned earlier in this research, it is also possible that they were not even present at the gathering. It is very likely that only a quorum of the Sanhedrin attended. The obvious supporters of Jesus would have likely been overlooked when the invitations were made. The scene could have certainly been handled in a less antagonistic fashion if there was a sincere desire to avoid alienating Jewish viewers. For example, the scene included what appeared to be a mindless idiot enthused at the thought of killing Jesus. The character reminded me of what the angry offspring of the Hunchback of Notre Dame might have looked like if Quasimoto had married Lizzie Borden. I guess the producer thought it added color. I think it added another bitter pill for Jewish viewers to swallow.

For the record, I do accept the basic premise of the scene. There is no doubt that a mock trial occurred. I also allow for the possibility that the sentiments of the Jewish leaders (and the false witnesses bribed to speak at their pleasure) were angry and bitter. However, I thoroughly reject the idea that the main body of Jews were committed to the destruction of Jesus. It is my firm belief that most Jewish people would have refused to take part in any such effort. Yet in spite of my dissatisfaction with the size of the crowd inside, it was the activity outside that I found to be most disconcerting. It was certainly one of the more awkward moments for me to watch as a Jewish viewer. I was appalled at the magnitude of the crowd that had gathered in the courtyard outside the home. The presentation of the mock trial of Jesus was typical of passion dramas. Certain dramatic elements of the scene could have been less inflammatory without detracting from the film's message. There is no record of a bustling crowd in the courtyard. I believe the scene outside the house of the High Priest was greatly exaggerated. It was visually easy to follow the growing crowd. A small group of angry Jews joined a growing powerful bandwagon of other angry Jews leading to their hateful demand of the brutal execution of Jesus. Yet the Gospel according to Matthew presents a very different encounter. The Bible suggests a significantly smaller gathering inside attended by "the chief priests, and elders, and all the council" (Matthew 26:59). There were certainly "false witnesses" also present according to verse 60. But it was primarily the crowd outside that appears to be a fabrication.

During my third viewing of the film, when I reached that scene I could not avoid reflecting on a trip I had taken with my wife. In October 2001, I hosted a tour to Israel. Everyone was quite concerned about conditions in the Middle East immediately following September 11, 2001. Likewise, many people were afraid to visit New York City after the debacle at the World Trade Center. Up until that time, my wife and I had never visited the Big Apple. We decided that we should pay our respects and show our support to New Yorkers by staying in downtown New York City for a few days prior to departing for Israel. While there, we decided to go to the very first stage play we had ever attended. We went to see The Music Man (it was wonderful). We also had the privilege of attending Times Square Church and seeing Pastor David Wilkerson (it was even more wonderful!). In prior years, I had been somewhat intimidated by the thought of going to New York City. However, our few days there after September 11 were very meaningful. I do recall being quite stunned walking around Times Square very late at night. The lights were amazing. The buildings were amazing. But one could not help but notice that a city that never sleeps seemed to be asleep. There were no perpetual crowds milling around. In fact, there were no crowds! The hustle and bustle of daytime was gone. The streets were quiet and the sidewalks abandoned! It was as though everything was shut down but the lights.

More recently, my wife and I had to go to Chicago on some business. We had an extra day in town so we stayed at a hotel in the Loop and visited a friend. We had enjoyed our first stage play in New York so much so that we decided to find a cheap pair of tickets to see a late night performance of "Beauty and the Beast." The Chicago weather was mild that night so we decided to walk back to our hotel after the play. It was near midnight and the trek required us to walk about as far as eight blocks traversing through the very heart of downtown Chicago. I was astounded at how quiet it was. The streets were empty. We were quite alone. It seemed that the only the folks out were those leaving the theatre.

The two personal stories just related were not rabbit trails. I have personally walked the streets of two of the most heavily populated metropolitan areas in America after midnight. I can only assume that if I had walked those same streets after 3:00 in the morning (closer to the time of the arrest of Jesus), they would have been even more barren. Yet it seems to me that in the film, I saw more people milling around the streets of Jerusalem as they visited the courtyard of the priest than I saw in the middle of downtown Chicago or New York City's Times Square. Contrary to the film's alleged review by the Pope, "This is not as it was." Rather, it is as it has generally been presented in the context of passion dramas. These have typically been unfriendly toward Jews and unfaithful to the Gospel presentation. They falsely create throngs of Jews who by their actions show hatred for Jesus and ignored the multitude of supporters who placed great hope in Jesus.

There is no reason to assume a massive angry crowd formed in the middle of the night in that courtyard. This was not New York. It was not Chicago. It was not even South Bend, Indiana or Lubbock, Texas. You just can't find a crowd at 3:00 or 4:00 in the morning in most small to mid-sized communities. Jerusalem may have been the largest city in Israel, but it was still a relatively small city in antiquity when compared to modern national capitals. One should also recognize that the Jews of the city had just celebrated one of their biggest festival meals. They prayed heartily, they ate heartily, they sang songs heartily, many drank a fair bit of wine, and the city went to sleep—just like the disciples! The general population was not milling around the streets in the middle of the night waiting for a parade.

A simple reading of the Gospel proves the errant interpretation of that specific scene in the film. Matthew indicated that the small group who had gathered outside consisted of Peter sitting in the courtyard "with the servants" (Matthew 26:58). How many servants did the High Priest have? How many hired hands were required to press his skivvies or polish his crown? However many it was, they were the only folks stoking the fire with Peter. Luke mentioned a non-descript "they" in his account saying "they had kindled a fire in the midst of the courtyard and sat down together, Peter sat among them, and a certain servant girl . . . said 'This man was also with Him' " (Luke 22:55). No crowd is detailed. No angry mob is implied. The jeering crowds and the angry mobs are nothing more than centuries of poor interpretations wrongly put forth by earlier anti-Semitic readings. These earlier extra-biblical, ungodly interpretations have been typical of the sentiments expressed by Christians that have plagued my people since the Dark Ages. This film did not invent the problem; it simply missed an opportunity to correct it.

I will not argue against the belief that Jewish leaders were at the helm of the conspiracy to destroy Jesus. They were. However, I do reject the belief that the average Jews of Jerusalem were in any way involved in that conspiracy. Yet this is what can be wrongly assumed when one views the film without considering the above-mentioned facts. The film presented a growing crowd of Jews who hated Jesus and wanted Him executed. They achieved their goal in the film. Coincidentally, by the time of that courtyard scene, the Jews were finally portrayed wearing fringed prayer shawls. There can be no mistake as to who the enemies were in the gospel according to the filmmaker. The rising anger was also amplified by the audio of that scene as it seemed to have more voices and noise added increasing the level of activity and commotion. The background sounds may have even exceeded the exaggerated numbers of people who were allegedly present. There simply would not have been such a large group of people roaming the streets outside so very, very late in the middle of the night. And the group continued to grow in numbers and intensity to the point that Roman soldiers were presented as being concerned about the dangerous tenor of the gathering.

By the time the scene shifted into the next trial that Jesus endured at Pilate's court, the typical passion play errors were even more recognizable. Looking out into the streets of Jerusalem from the vantage point of Pilate, all one could see through the gates of his court was what appeared to be an endless stream of angry Jews coming to the trial. The outdoor court of Pilate continued to fill up with as many Jews as could be crammed into the scene. The feeling one had as a viewer was that all the Jews of Jerusalem must have turned against Jesus. Of course, this is an untenable perspective and the growing angry mob scene was as ludicrous as most other passion dramas.

Pilate held court near 6:00 in the morning. Pilate would not have permitted a disorderly horde to bring chaos and commotion to his court. He certainly would not have tolerated a riot during his watch. More important, the Jewish leaders did not want unfriendly voices prohibiting their deceptive scheme. The film suggests the preponderance of voices were against Jesus. The actors behaved as wickedly against Christ as did the Sanhedrin and the High Priest. Yet in fact, the Jewish leaders were quite careful to handle the arrest and trial of Jesus under the cloak of darkness. They knew that the Jews of Jerusalem loved Jesus. They knew they could not afford to act out their wicked plans in the daylight when their wickedness might be identified and stopped by the massive number of supporters who loved Jesus. In all likelihood, the group in attendance was very small and intentionally limited to those involved in the conspiracy. Instead of a growing parade of Jews who followed the mob, it was more likely to have followed the course precisely described in the Gospel.

So as to avoid speculation, I will present the texts and provide a reasonable interpretation of the account from the Gospel of Luke. This will explain the enormous gap that exists between the biblical narrative and the scene presented in *The Passion of the Christ*. It will also clearly reveal why I believe the film fell into some of the same passion drama errors that have depreciated the truth about the event since this genre of theatre was developed in the anti-Semitic theological soup of the Middle Ages.

The text informs careful readers, "Then the whole multitude of them arose and led Him to Pilate" (Luke 23:1). We can be certain who led the Jews to Pilate. It was not the angry mob depicted in the film. It was not any vicious crowd of Jews who had been roaming the streets of Jerusalem. We can know precisely who inhabited the group wrongly portrayed by stage directors and film producers to create a dramatic effect at the cost of biblical truth. This scene is probably abused more than any other to the detriment of the Jewish people and Mr. Gibson's film followed the same bitter pattern. Fortunately, it is very simple to know the correct makeup of the group in question. In fact, it was the identical group that had dragged Jesus to their own mock trial at the break of dawn five verses earlier.

Luke made clear that immediately after the Jewish leaders railroaded Jesus through their own rigged hearing, the same Jewish leaders forced Him to the hearing in front of Pilate. It was this specific group that Luke identified as "the elders of the people, both chief priests and scribes." Matthew limited the group to "the chief priests and elders of the people" (Matthew 27:1). Mark expanded the base somewhat to include the chief priests, "the elders and scribes and the whole council" (Mark 15:1). It is also meaningful to here present the idea that Mark's inclusion of the "whole council" may have included less than 100% of the 70 Sanhedrin members. If only a quorum was in attendance, their decision would have carried the weight of the whole council as if they were all present. It is just as if the Congress of the United States had met in session, voted, and passed laws. The authority of the whole congress would stand behind the laws enacted just as if every legislator were present. This would be true even if many of the members were absent for the vote on the floor, provided the minimum number for a legal quorum were in attendance.

There is very little doubt as to who should have been cast in the scene. Make no mistake about their identities. It was the same clandestine group that "came together and led Him into their council" (Luke 22:66). I am confident that this is true because later in the chapter, Pilate also addressed the group in specific terms saying that Pilate "called together the chief priests, the rulers, and the people" (Luke 23:13). I believe it fair to suggest that "the people" included the scribes previously mentioned, and perhaps three other important small groups of specific individuals. There were some Jewish Temple guard soldiers involved in the initial arrest, possibly a handful of Roman soldiers to keep the mission "kosher," and the false witnesses hired by the leaders of the conspiracy. This was also the same group of people involved in the earlier trial. Since the gathering before Pilate was another legal proceeding, the Jewish leaders would have required the false witnesses to also attend in case they needed to present corroborating (albeit contrived) evidence against the defendant—Jesus. The soldiers would have possibly remained in the gathering to insure order, and more likely, to discourage any accidental uninvited participation from the supporters of Jesus.

Mr. Gibson made another major error in his departure from the Scriptures in the judgment hall scene. This is not surprising as the mistake is typical within the common patterns of passion dramas. The scene in Pilate's court is usually focused on the governor's desire to set Jesus free. He is usually unable to release Jesus because of a bloodthirsty Jewish mob. Likewise, Pilate tends to befriend Jesus. At first he is puzzled by the charismatic Jewish Messiah. Then, after a few moments in His presence, the Roman leader appears so taken by the hero of the drama that he would "get saved" if someone was to softly play Just As I Am and present an altar call. But alas, neither an organ nor a choir could be found. Mr. Gibson's portrayal was true to passion drama form. Pilate was so moved by his encounter with Jesus that it caused him to begin asking the deep questions of life. It sort of made you want to pray for poor old Pilate and quote John 14:6. But soon enough, Pilate moved to the hand-washing scene and the Jewish rabble-rousers screamed for the death of our hero. It had all of the needed qualities for a great drama, but ignored the cast of characters defined in the Bible.

All four of the New Testament writers agree as to the limits of the participants at Pilate's court. This scene was extremely disturbing. As is normal, it was extremely dramatic and horribly exaggerated to such astounding levels that one is convinced that the Jews must be hateful and inhumane. Of course it included Pilate's gracious offer to free Jesus. But as usual, Pilate, was forced to kill Jesus to satisfy the Jewish bloodlust and free Barabbas. It is true that the Scripture declares, "They all cried out at once, saying, 'Away with this Man, and release to us Barabbas' " (Luke 23:18). But who actually spoke those words? Who constitutes "they?" Mr. Gibson's version was worse than some I have experienced because of the grotesque nature of his choice for Barabbas. Someone needed to disinfect this character before he spread his disease through the crowd via his sickening, arrogant, tongue-wagging mouth. I thought he bore a striking resemblance to Shrek. Then on further reflection, I assume he was next-of-kin to Gibson's Quasimoto from the High Priest's court.

Of course, when presenting a passion drama, one rarely misses an opportunity to bring Jesus in front of Herod. For some reason, Herod is usually a homosexual, drunken, blithering idiot only interested in seeing a quick miracle so he can return to his debauchery. This is unfair. Herod had many other disgusting characteristics that were overlooked. Perhaps those highlighted were more fun for the audience.

On a much more serious note, one fundamentally confused element of the film related to the fear displayed by Pilate regarding his concern over the danger of a riot breaking out. This is also typical of the perverted misunderstanding generally presented which erroneously suggests that the preponderance of Jews wanted Jesus to be executed. The fear generally presented in these dramas tend to imply that if the angry mob fails to have its way and Jesus was to escape execution, then as a result, trouble would erupt. The bloodthirsty mob was expected to riot or take justice into their own hands. Of course nothing could be further from the truth! It was true that some Jewish leaders feared a revolt. But it was exclusively the result of the popularity enjoyed by Jesus. He was beloved among the multitudes of Jewish people. There was a justifiable fear that violence might occur if things got out of hand and the many followers of Jesus had learned about the scheme of the conspirators. The violence that would have surely shaken the city would have been for exactly the opposite of the reason presented in the passion drama. The conspirators had Jesus arrested under the cloak of darkness to insure that the mass of followers would not see them and stop their wicked plan. This was the reason the soldiers carried lanterns and torches. It was the middle of the night. The city was asleep. Nobody outside of the conspirators was supposed to know it was happening for fear of reprisals from the Jewish supporters of Jesus.

One additional commonly twisted segment of the drama was also played out in front of Pilate. This was the call for the crucifixion of Jesus by the Jewish mob. In Gibson's film, as is usual, the crowd demanded the death of Jesus in an incessant clamor of hatred. Again and again and again and again they cried for His crucifixion. It seemed like the cheerleaders of hate screamed for this a dozen times. I do not believe they were all included in the English subtitles. Nonetheless, the crowd continued to demand the death of Jesus in a scene that seemed to be unending. This most inflammatory presentation was totally inappropriate, although customary in the genre. It was another clear departure from the Scriptures.

The call to crucify Jesus came from the identical clandestine group of Jewish conspirators and their cohorts previously identified. Luke details the correct wording of the script that should have been spoken by the group, "Crucify him, crucify him" (Luke 23:21). That's it. It's all he wrote!

In the 27th chapter of Matthew, the same facts are recorded. He wrote, "Let him be crucified" (Matthew 27:22). This was also repeated exactly one more time in the following verse. Mark agrees without exception. Only John suggests any modification. His report inserts one additional cry for crucifixion following Pilate's private conference with Jesus. It is only an inherent anti-Semitic flair or the creative juices of careless drama directors who turn the scene into the hatefest typical of passion plays.

Of course as a Jew, my beef is with Mr. Gibson's portrayal of the Jews in his film. However, if I were a Roman, I would have been much more disturbed. Pilate, who was a ruthless, brutal Roman leader, would turn over in Hell if he had seen himself depicted as an indecisive type of "casper milktoast" character led around at the whim of his wife. Many of the Roman soldiers were also portrayed in a fashion that was completely unrealistic. They certainly had the capability of being vicious and violent. However, they were not disobedient to their leaders. The film indicated them to be a bunch of rowdy, uncontrollable, irreverent, murderous thugs. They seemed to ignore the clear command of Pilate merely to punish Jesus. They were absolutely under orders not to beat him to death. Pilate's order seemed to be ignored and mocked by the murderous, sadistic beating they gave Jesus. A normal man would have certainly been dead long before they changed tools of torture to flay the rest of his skin. Likewise, he would not have made it to basting the flip side, let alone, the added beating in the locker room when He received His crown of thorns. Once again, the disobedience of the Roman soldiers would have been humorous were the scene not so tragic. I find it very unlikely that well-trained, battle-hardened Roman soldiers would have ignored Pilate's specific orders. I find it terribly improbable that they would have intentionally disobeyed the governor's orders and then went ahead to get drunk on the job (as it appeared some of the Roman soldiers did). Especially since all of this was taking place while the Jewish crowds appeared to stand by and watch.

I must also add another disclaimer about the presentation of Satan in the film. I did not quite understand the ugly hairy baby (unless it was the Anti-Christ?) during the torture scene. It still seemed the devil appeared to know what was going on. Yet, she (he?) also seemed to enjoy the show. It would seem to me that if Satan really had the big picture, or understood God's plan of salvation (indicated by Satan's comments made about the inability of Jesus to die for the people), Satan would have implemented a far different plan. Instead of turning the Sanhedrin against Jesus and using Judas to betray the Lord, Satan would have given Judas a cell phone and

Passionate About the Passion?

made him call 911 before anything happened to the Son of Man. The last thing Satan would have tolerated would have been the death of Jesus if it were known that His death was sacrificial leading to the Resurrection and the salvation of the Church Triumphant.

I was greatly troubled by the typical mistaken connection made between the Jews who worshipped Jesus on Palm Sunday and those who cheered His torture on Good Friday. In Gibson's presentation, Jesus had a flashback to the prior Sunday when people were celebrating His arrival to Jerusalem. The image suggested that the same Jews had turned against Him less than a week later. This inference creates a concept that the Jews were hypocrites and easily swayed. They changed loyalty on a whim and betrayed their hero without any conscience. As I have shown, it would have been a completely different group of Jews who hated Jesus and wanted to participate in His demise. To create a visual link between the Jews singing Hosanna on Palm Sunday with those involved in His betrayal on Good Friday is a betrayal of truth.

Finally, the scene that should win the award for least likely to have reached the silver screen must go the flashback of the Last Supper. This was a classic. I can almost hear the director scolding the scriptwriter who must have said, "I forgot to read the book before we shot the scene." Permit me to simply point out that the scene was a celebration of Passover. Yet Jesus was shown preparing to "break bread" with His disciples. They served a platter of bread, in spite of the fact it was the Feast of Unleavened Bread. In Yiddish, we would say the producer had a *goyishe kop*. In other words, the passion play Passover *seder* was definitely directed by a Gentile. Ma'nishtanah ha'lailah ha'zeh meecall ha'layloat.[296] It seems to me that someone stole much more than the *afikomen*[297] at that *seder*. They stole all of the matzah along with the Jewishness of Jesus.

Is Gibson a Catholic Who Broke the Rules?

It has been widely reported that Mel Gibson is a devout Catholic. No one doubts this and the film has a variety of Catholic elements not addressed in this work because they were beyond the purview of the topic. I did not take on the task of discussing the Protestant vs. Catholic issues one might raise from the perspective of the film's composition. Whether or not Mary was given proper emphasis or the Stations of the Cross appropriate seem to be questions for others to debate. However, I am convinced that Mr. Gibson did break the established rules for Passion Play presentations endorsed by the Catholic Church.

In case you were unaware that such rules exist, do not be surprised. In this highly litigious era, one can find rules for anything. These rules, however, are wise. They were carefully crafted by informed scholars and had they been followed, much of the furor over the film and the publication of this new book could have been avoided.

The United States Secretariat for Catholic-Jewish Relations published a guideline for Passion Play presentations. He properly acknowledged that "carelessly written or produced Passion plays can become a source of anti-Semitic reactions."[298] I will herein only quote the five basic rules suggested to producers of passion play presentations designed and approved as a warning to avoid erroneous interpretations and negligent misrepresentations.

1. "To conceal the fact that Jesus is a Jew and that His friends as well as His enemies in the drama are Jews;
2. To create the impression that most Jews of Jesus' day willed His death, failing to show the secrecy surrounding much of Jesus' trial was motivated by the large following He had in Jerusalem;
3. To change the 'crowd' before the governor's palace into a screaming 'mob,' as representing all Jerusalem, and indeed all Israel;
4. To depict Pilate, whom historiography has shown to have been a ruthless tyrant, as an innocent and kindly bystander;
5. To highlight those texts of the gospel narrative that are amenable to misinterpretation by uninformed audiences."[299]

The Bishop's Committee for Ecumenical and Interreligious Affairs also provided a simple summary for scholars and educators to consider when producing materials related to the subject. One important point identified by them that was apparently ignored by Mr. Gibson was the requirement to avoid, "The misconception that the Judaism of Jesus' time was decadent, formal and hypocritical, and that Jesus' enemies were representative of it."[300]

It seems to me that if the film had been more true to the guiding concerns simply and eloquently stated by the above-mentioned leaders, the film could have been far more effective and much less offensive to those who took offense. Further, it would not have depreciated the message, the method, or the mood of the film. The love of Jesus could have been presented equally well without the vilification of the Jewish people who were not involved in the event.

286 Sheli Teitelbaum, *The Jerusalem Report*, "Who'll Bear the Cross?" (March 22, 2004), 38.
287 Bob Armstrong, Editor, *Voice*, FGBMFI, Lake Forest, CA, February, 2004, 9.
288 Liel Leibovitz, 34.
289 Ibid., 35.
290 Ibid.
291 Ibid.
292 Ibid.
293 Sharon Waxman was quoted from the New York Times News Service in the Dallas Morning News, February 29, 2004, 6g.
294 Ibid.
295 Noonan, Peggy, *Keeping the Faith*, Reader's Digest, March 2004, 93.
296 Just quoting Mary—a nice Jewish girl, from earlier in this chapter.
297 There are three pieces of *matzah* incorporated in the Passover service. The middle *matzah* is broken during the event and saved to be used at the end of the Passover *seder*. This middle *matzah* is called the *afikomen*. A child generally "steals" one of the broken halves and returns it for a ransom prior to the conclusion of the *seder*.
298 Judith Banki and George S. Strober, 20-21.
299 Ibid., citing the Executive Committee, Secretariat for the Catholic-Jewish Relations, A Statement on Passion Plays, press release dated February 28, 1968, p. 2; The New York Times, March 5, 1968, p. 44.
300 Ibid., citing the Executive Committee, Secretariat for the Catholic-Jewish Relations, Guidelines for Catholic-Jewish Relations (Washington, March 6, 1967), pp.7f.

Chapter XVII

Did the Jews Kill Christ or Was He the Victim of Identity Theft?

Consider the facts:
- The Jews did not kill Christ because the Jews could not kill Christ. They did not have legal authority in matters of capital crimes under Roman law at that time.
- The Jews were a diverse group of 4,500,000 people spread out over many nations of the world. They could not collectively make a single *matzah* ball or take any solitary decisive action for which all could take credit or all share blame.
- The Jews did not have power over God. The death of Christ was according to God's sovereign will according to the Scriptures.
- The Jews did not have control over a decision that belonged to Jesus. Jesus laid His life down. Nobody took it from Him. It would be wrong to depreciate His love by suggesting that the Jewish people, or other groups of people were responsible for our eternal salvation. After all, that is what Christ purchased through His death.

It seems to me that the folks who confuse these matters misunderstand the real character and true identity of Jesus. Actually, many people reinterpret the life and purpose of Jesus to fit their own agendas. They recreate Jesus to fit a pattern they prefer. Perhaps that is what happened in Mr. Gibson's film.

The producers substituted bread for matzah in the Feast of Unleavened Bread. Whether intentional or not, this error moved Jesus to a place outside the flow of Judaism. It is well known that Jews were forbidden to eat leavened bread during the time of Passover. To ignore this lowest common denominator that Jesus shared with the Jews of His community is to ignore that He was a faithful member of the Jewish community. If He can be extricated from His situation in life as a Jewish man in the first century, He can be recreated and recast in anyway that anyone chooses. In essence, He could be molded to fit the need anyone wished for Jesus to fill. But Jesus does not change at our insistence; we change at His. God does not change; He is perfect. We must change because we are imperfect. This may seem like an abstract philosophical concern, but it is not. It is a fundamental truth and we must let Jesus be Jesus. If we are permitted to modify Him to suit our fancy then we become God and He becomes our servant. That is why I refuse to ignore that the Last Supper was a traditional Jewish Passover. To make it less is to rob Jesus of His heritage on this earth. Of course that is the pattern for many Christian traditions. Leonardo Da Vinci had the same problem when he was commissioned to create *The Last Supper* for the Convent of Dominican friars at Santa Maria delle Grazie in Milan. If one looks carefully at this most famous religious painting, the traditional Gentile dinner rolls will become evident.

Jesus was born into the line of Jewish kings. Christians believe He is King eternal. Had He been born into a non-Jewish home, He would have been discredited from inheriting this throne. The prophetic mantle would have remained unfulfilled. Had He sinned in His dietary regimen eating food not kosher for Passover, He would have been disqualified as a perfect sacrifice and the Cross would have been pointless in the Father's plan of salvation. If we ignore the small details of the food Jesus ate at His final *Pesach seder*, it becomes easier to ignore other details, such as the clothing Jesus wore.

Consider what the poor woman with the issue of blood would have done if the wardrobe designer from Mr. Gibson's film had outfitted our Savior? She touched the "hem" of His garment and was healed according to Matthew 9:20. To the uninitiated reader, it might seem that Jesus wore Levi Docker slacks and the woman grabbed the neatly turned, starched hem of His pleated trousers gently draping over His penny loafers. Of course that would be quite ludicrous to suggest because everyone knows

Jesus did not wear slacks. Would dressing Jesus in slacks be anymore foolish than presuming He disobeyed the commands of Numbers 15:38 and disregarded wearing His *tallith* with the proper long *tsithith*—fringes in the corners? According to Jewish practice and the best scholarship, it is these fringes that the women touched. It was not the hem of His trousers, it was the borders (corners or wings) where the *tsithith* hung.[301]

If we can quietly allow Mr. Gibson to separate Jesus from His Jewish food and His Jewish dress, we can begin to disentangle Him from His other Jewish characteristics. That is why the subtitle of this book asks the question, *Did the Jews Kill Christ or Has Someone Stolen His Identity?* The Jews are not to blame for His death. I believe He lives! There is no body. The accusation of murder is a moot point in light of the Resurrection. The crime is in how Jesus is usually represented. Many groups have stolen His identity.

That is how the founder of *The Great Passion Play* of Eureka Springs, Arkansas, promoted Jesus. He presented images of a blond-haired, blue-eyed, WASP Savior. Jesus was the victim of identity theft. He stole the true identity of Jesus and created a fairy tale Christ invented in his vain imagination. The Bible commands us not to worship false gods, yet that is what happens when we worship an idea of God that is a fabrication. This can happen quite easily if we become distracted from worshipping the God of the Bible and begin to serve an illusion about God presented by false teachers.

WILL THE REAL JESUS PLEASE STAND UP?

If a heretic can separate Jesus from His own people, he becomes capable of casting Jesus as a member of any people. Yasser Arafat declared that Jesus was a Palestinian. It served Arafat's political purposes. If no one points out the lunacy of such errant claims, the alleged Palestinian Jesus serves Arafat obediently. The very thought is sacrilegious at numerous levels.

My wife and I recently visited a huge outdoor flea market. One seller had a plethora of Christian art. My favorite was the "Black Last Supper" where an African-American Jesus was surrounded by African-American disciples. Though this odd vision drifted further than Mr. Gibson's, I was at least pleased to see there was no pork identified on the table. I did comment to my wife that the dinner rolls were a nice touch. They were attractive in the spirit of DaVinci. Embracing Jesus as one of their own apparently serves the African-American community. It is always wiser to serve Jesus as He is than to expect Him to serve us as we are.

Jesus was neither Aryan, nor a Nazi sympathizer. Yet that is how He was portrayed in the 1934 presentation of the most famous passion play of Europe. It was a crime of identity theft that permitted the Oberammergau Passion Play to insure that all of the main characters were Aryans during the Nazi era. Hitler loved it and insisted it be preserved forever to show the world the menacing story of the Jews. The show still goes on! Jesus served Hitler in that presentation, but Hitler never served Jesus.

Neo-Nazis and Christian Identity adherents declare Jesus was not Jewish. The heretical proponents of British-Israelism shift the heritage of Jesus and the promises of God from the Jewish people of Israel to the Anglo-Saxon people in Great Britain. They don't want to be confronted by a Jewish Jesus. Of course, neither did the Catholic leaders of the Cathedral of Florence, when they commissioned Michelangelo to create the larger-than-life statue of King David (23 feet tall on pedestal). If you dare to peek, David was cast as an uncircumcised Gentile. In a truly classic *faux pax*, the 1988 edition of the *World Book Encyclopedia* described Michelangelo's artistry as "best known for his treatment of the human body . . . but is never false or artificial. See the picture of his statue of David with the **David** article."[302] How could they not notice? Apparently, the Church could not tolerate a Jewish hero. In their view, it was wise to recreate David as one like themselves, instead of one like their enemies. That could have been an embarrassment.

The gay community desires to paint Jesus as a homosexual. The women's liberation movement prefers goddesses to God and they have cast Jesus as a woman. The truth is that once Jesus is removed from the pages of the Bible, there is no anchor to hold people to truth and Jesus to His birthright.

Jesus was a poor, itinerant, Jewish rabbi teaching in the Galilee region of ancient Israel. Yet modern prosperity preachers would have us believe that Jesus was a well-to-do, name-it-and-claim-it faith preacher in an Armani robe, Gucci sandals and a Rolex sundial. If you listen to some prosperity-preaching charlatans with nice hair and big churches, you'd think God had dumped the poor people to shower all His blessings on the fat cats and major donors.

Perhaps you've heard that some are asking, WWJD—What would Jesus drive? Well, Jesus didn't tool into Jerusalem on Palm Sunday driving a donkey named Mercedes.

Like a famous American general, Jesus is coming back. But the Second Coming of Jesus will bring eternity. He is Lord of peace and Lord of the judgment.

This work is intended to be taken seriously so it is inappropriate to contain too much sarcasm. Yet there is a great irony that many seem to miss. Jesus does not need us to make Him more appealing to those who reject Him. We need Jesus to make us more appealing to those who reject Him because of us. Jesus is sufficiently winsome and wonderful that anyone who considers the true nature of Christ can easily identify the virtue that dwells in Him. It is only when we betray His love by representing Him reprehensibly that He seems unloving. It is only when we rob Him of His glorious character by infusing our own lack into His being that His worth is diminished and His value depreciated by our flawed transmission of His message.

I am here to declare that a crime has been committed. Jesus is the victim of identity theft. Every cause and each group has adopted Jesus as their own. They have created Jesus in their own image. It is one of the greatest crimes of history. Even the new improved mellow Saint Mel of the Passion recreated Jesus to suit his view.

Jesus loved women but not as sex objects. Although He may as well have, if you believe the disgusting, immoral, promiscuous, portrayals of some pre-Mel Hollywood representations of Jesus. *The Last Temptation of Christ* depicted Jesus fantasizing having sex with Mary Magdalene.

Jesus loved His mother but He wasn't a momma's boy. Jesus was a strong, bold, male role model. Nevertheless, when viewing the film, one nagging question refused to fade from my mind.

Surviving the Beating in the Passion?

The beating endured by Jesus in the film was so intense that it seemed impossible for a man, even a strong, bold man, to have lived through the preliminary stages of His torture. Perhaps that is why so much criticism has been leveled against the film from those who believed it to be too violent. The same critics were probably not offended by the violence in other films that included Mel Gibson. Yet some critics skewered his film of the Passion due to the graphic violence. Was the film too violent? No, I do not agree with that assessment. The violence contained in the film was certainly not gratuitous. It was a purposeful fair representation of what Jesus endured. There was a reason for the suffering of Jesus to be shown in the film. It was part and parcel of the Gospel story. In fact, some have posited that the film was not violent enough. That analysis is not unfounded based on the condition described in the Bible. One could still recognize the character playing Jesus on the Cross. The Scripture details that He was beaten beyond recognition.

Why did Jesus keep getting up? Why didn't He just stay down and symbolically cry "Uncle?" The Cross would not have been escaped. Only the added suffering would have been bypassed. What possessed Him to continue?

Could a normal human being have lived through the beating? I found it perplexing to watch Jesus continue to carry the Cross after being beaten with such severity. It was quite telling to see a strong, healthy man struggle with the same Cross. Simon the Cyrenian was drafted by the Roman soldiers to help Jesus. Simon could barely manhandle the Cross in their two-man team. It was too much for him. Jesus had lost so much blood and had so many unbearable wounds. It seemed impossible for Him to be able to move under His own power, let alone drag a heavy cross through the streets of Jerusalem. Could a normal man have endured? Could a normal man have trudged up the slope to the site of His execution? I guess the answer is dependent on the man's passion. It may have been impossible for a normal man. But Jesus was not normal. You see, Jesus was on a mission. His will to live exceeded His desire to avoid pain. His will to live exceeded the murderous intent of His enemies. But His will to live was limited to His need to live until He could die the death for which He was destined.

Jesus was divine. But this is not what separated Jesus from other men. I do not ascribe super-human strength to the Son of God. Rather, it was super-human love. Jesus would not quit because He would not fail. Jesus would not stop short of Calvary because He knew all about our need for His death. He knew that our salvation was at stake. Many men and women have been known to accomplish feats of strength beyond their natural ability when called upon in desperate conditions. Some people simply refuse to die until they accomplish their goals. Then they quietly pass on. I chose to attribute His ability to survive the beating and His choice to endure sub-human treatment to the unstoppable love He exhibited. Yet I could not remove the nagging doubt about a human's ability to endure that much physical torture. Then a country preacher cleared it all up for me.

Pastor Kerry McDaniel put the human ability of Jesus into focus on this subject. He reminded me that Jesus had no sin. Sin is what brought death to mankind. When he stated that, I had a revelation about the character of Jesus in Mr. Gibson's film. Could any man have endured such a beating and lived? The answer became clear. Yes! Any man who had no sin, because it is sin that brings death. The Jews did not kill Jesus. The Romans did not kill Jesus. I think those nasty soldiers could have beat Jesus until their arms turned into rigatoni. The beating would not kill Jesus. Not even the Crucifixion killed Jesus. He was fully human. But Jesus was without sin. Jesus died on the Cross, but not before He was ready. It was not before His mission was accomplished. My revelation was that it was just as the Bible had detailed the event. In John's Gospel it is written that "He said, 'It is finished' and he bowed his head and he gave up the ghost" (John 19:30). Jesus knew when His work was complete. He knew when He had completed the task of taking our sins away. He would not die until this task was completed. And then no man took His life. He willingly gave it as an offering for sin that we might have life eternal. Jesus could have endured all of the pain inflicted in the film and more. His love was greater than any suffering this world could inflict. His love and His life are eternal. The pain was only temporary.

The only way to make things right is to put Jesus back into the context in which He lived, died, and rose again. As I say in every radio or TV program I produce, "Jesus is Lord . . . and He vuz such a nice Jewish boy." To that, I will simply add, "Thank you!"

---

301 Edersheim, 431.
302 World Book Encyclopedia, 1988 ed., s.v. "Michelangelo."

Conclusion

The Holocaust cannot be undone, nor the six million brought back from the ashes of the crematoria. Only the dead have the right to forgive, and no one, least of all Christians, has the right to forgive on their behalf. Nevertheless, some theologians now believe that repentance for the antisemitism that betrayed Jesus and inflicted unimaginable harm on his people is a spiritual necessity for Christians themselves, whether or not it can earn forgiveness from Jews. Such repentance, if real, cannot fail to lead to theological change.[303]

"Theological change" may be the prerequisite for correcting the attitudes of Christian anti-Semites. Many Christians must evaluate the basis for their faith. The Jewish people can hardly be blamed for God's plan of redemption as understood within Christendom. The crucifixion was not an accident. The crucifixion was not a Jewish attempt to subvert God. Christian doctrine teaches that the human race had no alternatives. If, as proposed within Orthodox Christianity, man was condemned since the sin of Adam, what alternatives existed without the cross? The New Testament teaches that God planned the crucifixion before the earth was formed. No group of humans are to be credited or blamed. The Jewish people are not responsible for the genius of God. If God ordained the plan of the passion, God also insured that nothing remained undone.

Christians would do well to remember their own tenets of faith. This would help them to recall the events of the passion week as God's own effort to prepare a people for Himself, and at the same time to prepare a

Savior for His people. Jesus was not convicted and appointed to death independent of God's sovereignty. Neither did Jesus yearn to be crucified. He prayed, "Father, if thou be willing, remove this cup from me" (Luke 22:42 KJV). Apparently, God said, "No." God did not permit Jesus to regain his freedom at the cost of the human race's continued enslavement to sin. Christian doctrine is clear; it is only the view of certain Christians that is confused. Jesus obeyed the will of God. Will the same be said for this generation of Christians? Christians are commanded to love. Jesus loved. Jesus willingly gave His life. If Jesus was the Son of God, as believed by faithful Christians, Jesus was not helpless on the cross. Love, not nails held Jesus on the cross.

The passion play often ignores the goals of Christ's passion and denies the truth of the Christian text upon which it is based. There are obvious differences between modern Judaism and modern Christianity. What must always remain clear is the fact that the God of Abraham, Isaac, and Jacob, is the same God of Mary, Paul, and Jesus. What remains unclear, by God's own design, is a mystery which must be heartily acknowledged by every Christian submitted to the New Testament. This verse from Paul's letter to the Church at Rome was quoted in part concerning the Vatican's 1965 Declaration on Non-Christian Religions. Readers might do well to acknowledge that not all mysteries are able to be solved. Some simply remain a mystery.

> For I do not desire, brethren, that you should be ignorant of this *mystery*, lest you should be *unwise in your own opinion*, that blindness in part has happened to Israel until the fullness of the Gentiles has come in. And so all Israel will be saved, as it is written: "The Deliverer will come out of Zion, And He will turn away ungodliness from Jacob; For this is My covenant with them, when I take away their sins," Concerning the gospel they are enemies for your sake, but concerning the election *they are beloved for the sake of the fathers. For the gifts and the calling of God are irrevocable* [italics mine] (Romans 11:25-29).

"The Deliverer will come out of Zion." It is obvious that Jews and Christians do not agree on who He is or the estimated time of His arrival. It is also obvious that Jews and Christians do not agree on a host of other things, nor must they agree on everything. As stated, the New Testament deems the relationship to be somewhat of a "mystery." Often, those most unwise in their "own opinion" have formed the opinions that have become the standard. In conclusion, the facts that this research hopes to amplify are that the passion play, along with many expressions of Christian anti-Semitism, demean the Jewish people and promote Christian bigotry. Jews are still God's chosen people and no Christian should believe that Judaism is an evil system carrying the guilt of deicide. This form of confusion among some Christians is a sin against God and His people. In spite of any erroneous ancient Christian teaching, the Children of Israel "are beloved for the sake of the fathers. For the gifts and the calling of God are irrevocable."

303 Nicholls, xxviii.

Epilogue

This writer's personal history as a Jewish/Christian has been flooded with the emotional struggle of having been rejected by people on both sides of difficult religious issues. Falsehoods built from stereotypes have prospered. Individuals lose identity in groups. The character of the individuals are wrongly assimilated and lost as they are perceived to be like the group. Bigotry is permitted to grow when stereotypes are permitted to live.

The passion play continues to arouse anti-Semitic passions that have historically enraged non-Jews against their Jewish neighbors. This fact came home to me just prior to beginning this research. In fact, in large part it is the reason this work was done. It seemed like a small thing, but as I reflected on the incident, I realized how important it was to bring clarity to this matter. The church I was attending at that time put on an annual Easter Passion Play. My family and I went to see the production. The following day my little girl came home from the church-run school with a problem. She asked me why her little friend made her feel so bad? She told me that her friend had said that her "Daddy was stupid because he is Jewish!" I was crushed; but not because I had been insulted. At that time I was simultaneously working on multiple degrees from a respected university, an outstanding Bible college, and a theological seminary. Still, I was once again inadvertently labeled a "dumb Jew." When I cleaned toilets as a janitor in a factory, to some, I was still a "rich Jew." When I was later blessed to be able to send a truckload of food to the black ghetto in Harlem, I knew I could never escape being seen by some as a "greedy Jew." Even after high school locker room showers, I knew I would always be a "dirty Jew" to those predisposed to anti-Semitism. I was not insulted by my daughter's friend. I was hurt because the same mentality that has led to anti-Semitism in every society still exists today in this society and it existed in our Christian Church.

Is it possible that the little girl never met a Jew before? Could it be that the only influence toward Judaism she has had came from Church? If that could be true, what more could be expected? Should it automatically be different in my Church? We had all seen the presentation. We had all experienced the proverbial Jewish mob rush to insure the destruction of the Lamb of God. We had all heard the question posed to the effect: "How could those same Jews welcome Jesus into Jerusalem waving palm leaves, crying 'Hosanna' in one week, then turn on him so violently to crucify him the next?" The inference is clear, those Jews must have been evil or stupid, for why else would they have participated in the brutal murder of sweet, humble, loving Jesus?

If that little girl's early Jewish influence came from Church, she well might believe that all the Jews of ancient Israel wanted Barabbas freed and Jesus killed. That is certainly the way it appears in the passion play. Scattered sermons throughout the year in support of Israel, or things Jewish, will not erase the spectacular impact of a glorious passion play experience. That little girl probably saw many friends and relatives in that presentation. She had watched a large volume of adult role models dressed up like Jews screaming, "Crucify him! Kill him! He deserves to die!" <u>They would not lie</u>. Their play would not intentionally present falsehoods. It is difficult for a child to separate the truth taught by their Sunday School teacher in class from that expressed from the stage while dressed in a Jewish costume demanding the death of Jesus. My church loves Jews. Most churches love Jews. Philo-Semitism is currently common in church circles. None of that helped me answer my daughter, when she asked me about her problem. I said something approximating, "OK, ignore her. She just doesn't understand." That was a good enough answer for my little girl, but it was not satisfying to me. That event "set in concrete" the need to pursue this investigation. The correct solution to my little girl's problem is the same as the larger need to address this problem throughout Christendom. The Gentile Christian Church must be informed that a more excellent truth exists. The middle wall of partition has been broken down forever by the sacrifice of Jesus.[304] Why do some people feel obliged to find more blocks to rebuild the wall?

I rejoice in Christian activities where the obvious love of Christians for Israel, Judaism, and the Jewish people have shown like a light on a hillside. At other times in my Christian life I have felt brutally crushed and censured. I remember the horror I felt when I learned that it was considered inappropriate for me, as a Jew, to teach Christians in "their Church."

Although it was my church where my family and I had been faithful members. I had been an evangelist for many years. I had worked as a smuggler of Christian materials behind the Iron Curtain ministering to the Underground Church. Still, I was deemed unqualified to teach a group of high school Church kids. Coincidentally, that bruise came during the same period in my life that the synagogue to which we belonged was revoking our membership because of our faith in Jesus. I have cried many tears because of religious intolerance at home and abroad. I have seen pettiness, confusion, and hatred coming from civil authorities, Church leaders and my own people on both sides of the Cross. The joy of believing that Jesus will never leave me or forsake me heals me emotionally.

"Crucify him! Yes, kill him! He deserves to die!" One angry man relentlessly pursued Jesus. It was because of one angry man that Jesus suffered his ultimate humiliation and defeat. Jesus willingly offered Himself up to horrible suffering, disgrace, and the awful curse of the cross. He did it for a lost, dying, sinful, wicked man. This man hated Jesus. Truly, this man had cursed the name of Jesus, publicly, and in private. This man was guilty of unmentionable sins from which no amount of rehabilitation could have redeemed him, without divine intervention. Jesus enacted that intervention. While this man was yet a sinner, Jesus chose to die for him. The sacrificial death of Jesus was undeserved, for Jesus was sinless and perfect. Yet, in the perfect sight of God's love, it was the only way out for that sinful man whom Jesus desperately loved. Jesus took the punishment that was inevitably intended for another. Yes, the blood of Jesus has been shed. I confess, I did it. His blood is on my head, and on my children. I am not cursed for my share in the crime. Freedom echoes forever in His death. Jesus Christ died for one Jew. One Jew cried out for His crucifixion. One Jew was responsible for His brutal arrest, trial, and execution. He died for me! If the blame for the death of Jesus lies anywhere apart from personal, individual responsibility, the atoning work that accompanies His sacrifice is also beyond reach. If His blood is not on your head, you are condemned.

In closing this work, I will leave you with a thought from one of my Jewish heroes—the Apostle Paul. "I say then, have they stumbled that they should fall? God forbid: but rather through their fall salvation is come unto the Gentiles, for to provoke them to jealousy" (Romans 11:11 KJV). Do you ever wonder about the call of the Church? In a nutshell, Paul described it as the obligation to make the Jews jealous of our love relationship with the God of Israel. Paul expressed the debt owed by Gentiles and he also clarified the method to find satisfaction. It will never be found through alienating the Jewish people. It comes through loving them enough to express the heart of God.

The Church of Jesus Christ is appropriately the bride of Christ without spot or wrinkle, but this will never change God's choice of the Jewish people as His own. They are still the chosen of God and God is not done with the Jews.

> Oh, the depth of the riches both of the wisdom and knowledge of God! How unsearchable are His judgments and His ways past finding out! *"For who has known the mind of the LORD? Or who has become His counselor? Or who has first given to Him and it shall be repaid to him?"* For of Him and through Him and to Him are all things, to whom be glory forever. Amen.
>
> (Romans 11:33-36).

---

304 See Ephesians 2:14.

Bibliography

Allen, Charles R. Jr. *Reform Judaism,* "Patrick J. Buchanan: Master Holocaust Denier," Official Publication of the UAHC, New York, NY, Winter 1996.

Armstrong, Bob, Editor. *Voice,* FGBMFI, Lake Forest, CA: February, 2004.

August, Marilyn. The Associated Press, *The Oregonian,* March 16, 1994.

Bader, Gershom. *The Encyclopedia of Talmudic Sages.* Translated by Solomon Katz. Northvale, New Jersey: Jason Aronson, 1988.

Bailey, Thomas A., and David M. Kennedy. *The American Pageant.* Vol. I. Lexington, Massachusetts: D.C. Heath and Company, 1991.

Banki, Judith and George S. Strober. "Oberammergau 1960 and 1970: A Study in Religious Anti-Semitism," by the American Jewish Committee, (Institute of Human Relations of the American Jewish Committee, New York, 1970).

Birnbaum, Philip. *A Book of Jewish Concepts.* New York: Hebrew Publishing Co., 1964.

Bragg, Melvyn and Norman Jewison, screenplay, *Jesus Christ Superstar.* Music by Andrew Lloyd Webber, lyrics and book by Tim Rice. Universal an MCA company.

Bruce, F.F. *New Testament History.* Garden City, New York: A Doubleday-Galilee, 1980.

Buchanan, Patrick J. *Right From the Beginning,* Washington, D.C.: Regnery Gateway, 1990.

Buckley, William F. *In Search of Anti-Semitism.* New York: Continuum Publishing Company, 1992.

Charlesworth, James H. Editor. *Explorations,* " 'Jews,' 'Pagans,' and 'Christians' in Antiquity and Our Search for 'The Next Step.'" Volume 8, Number 1, 1994.

Cohen, Jeffrey M. *1,001 Questions and Answers on Pesach,* Northvale: Jason Aronson Inc., 1996.

Cohen, Shaye J. D. *From the Maccabees to the Mishnah.* Philadelphia: The Westminster Press, 1987.

Cohn-Sherbok, Dan. *The Crucified Jew: Twenty Centuries of Christian Anti-Semitism.* London: HarperCollins Publishers, 1992.

Cooper, Abraham, Editor. *Response.* Volume 14, Number 3, (Fall/Winter 1993).

Cooper, Abraham, Editor. *Response.* Volume 15, Number 2, (Summer 1994).

Cooper, Abraham, Editor, *Response,* Volume 25, Number 1, 6, (Fall/Winter 2003-04).

Davis, Robert Gorham. "Passion at Oberammergau." *Commentary* 29 (March 1960).

Dinnerstein, Leonard. *Antisemitism in America.* New York: Oxford University Press, 1994.

Distel, Barbara and Ruth Jakusch, Editors. *Concentration Camp Dachau 1933-1945.*

Munich, Germany: Comite' International de Dachau, 1978.
Dowley, Tim. Org. Ed. *Eerdman's Handbook to the History of Christianity*. Grand Rapids, Michigan: Wm. B. Eerdmans Publishing Company, 1988.
Edersheim, Alfred. *The Life and Times of Jesus the Messiah: New Updated Edition*, Hendrickson Publishers, Inc., 2000.
Eisenman, Robert, and Michael Wise. *The Dead Sea Scrolls Uncovered*. Shaftesbury, Dorset: Element, 1992.
Encyclopedia Judaica, 1978 ed., S.v. "English Literature."
Encyclopedia Judaica, 1978 ed., S.v. "German Literature."
Eusebius, Pamphilus. *The Ecclesiastical History of*, Translated by Christian Frederick Cruse. Grand Rapids, Michigan, Baker Book House, 1992.
Feder, Don. *A Jewish Conservative Looks at Pagan America*. Lafayette, Louisiana: Huntington House Publishers, 1993.
Fischel, Jack. *The Jewish Spectator*. Volume 59, Number 2, (Fall 1994).
Floyd, Marlene. *The Chosen People*, "The Rising Tide of Anti-Semitism." (March 1993).
Flusser, David. *The Spiritual History of the Dead Sea Sect*. Tel-Aviv, Israel: MOD Books, 1989.
Forster, Arnold. *Square One*. New York: Donald I. Fine, 1988.
Freeden, Herbert. *The Jewish Press in the Third Reich*. Providence, RI: Berg Publishera, 1993.
Friedman, Ina, *The Jerusalem Report*, "Talking about a Revolution (Again)" (November 17, 2003).
Gates, David. *Newsweek*, "A Papal Publishing Event." (October 31, 1994).
Gunton, Sharin R., Editor. *Contemporary Literary Criticism* Volume 21. Detroit, Michigan: Gale Research Company Book Tower, 1982.
Halevi, Chavah. *The Jewish Enquirer*, "Book Review." Volume I, Number 2, (HaChodesh HaAshiri).
Hirshberg, Charles. *Life*, "The Eternal Crusader." (November 1994).
Hitler, Adolf. *Mein Kampf*, New York: Reynal & Hitchcock, 1940.
Institute of Jewish Affairs. "Passion at Oberammergau," in association with the World Jewish Congress, Background Paper No. 15, (December 1969).
Jeansonne, Glen. *Gerald L. K. Smith: minister of hate*. New Haven: Yale University Press, 1988.
Jeffrey, D. L. *A Dictionary of Biblical Tradition in English Literature*. Grand Rapids, Mich.: W.B. Eerdmans, 1992.
John Paul II, His Holiness. *Crossing The Threshold Of Hope*. New York: Alfred A. Knopf, 1994.
Josephus, Flavius. Edited by William Whiston, *The Works of Josephus*, (Peabody, Massachusetts, Hendrickson Publishers, 1983.

Kaplan, Chira, Editor. *Jewish Voice.* Volume 16, Number 11, (November, 1982).
Karol, Carol, Editor. *Illiana News,* (Highland, IN: The Newspaper of the Jewish Federation NWI, December 2002).
Kayess Evelyne, Editor. *Dateline: World Jewry,* (New York: World Jewish Congress May, 1998).
Kissinger, Henry. *The White House Years.* (Boston: Little, Brown and Company, 1979).
Larsson, Gore. *Fact or Fraud? The Protocols of the Elders of Zion.* (Jerusalem: AMI-Jerusalem Center for Biblical Studies and Research, 1994).
La Sor, William Sanford, David Allan Hubbard, and Frederic William Bush. *Old Testament Survey.* Grand Rapids, Michigan: Wm. B. Eerdmans Publishing Co., 1982.
Leibovitz, Liel. *The Jerusalem Report,* "Putting 'The Passion' in Perspective," (March 22, 2004).
Lindsay, Gordon. *Acts in Action* Volume I. Dallas, TX: Christ For The Nations Institute, 1985.
Lindsey, Hal. *The Road To Holocaust.* New York, New York: Bantam Books, 1989.
Lipstadt, Deborah. *Denying the Holocaust, The Growing Assault on Truth and Memory.* New York: The Free Press, A Division of Macmillan, 1993.
MacDonald, Gordon G. "The Biblical Doctrine of Election," *The Grace of God, The Will of Man.* Clark H. Pinnock, Editor. Grand Rapids, Michigan: Acadamie Books, 1989.
Margolis, Max L., and Alexander Marx. *A History of the Jewish People.* New York: A Temple Book, Atheneum, 1973.
Mathews, Tom, Rod Norland, and Carroll Bogert. *Newsweek.* (May 7, 1990).
Matthews, Basil. *The Jew and the World Ferment.* New York: Friendship Press, 1935.
National Board of Review of Motion Pictures, Inc. *500 Best American Films to Buy, Rent or Videotape.* New York: Simon & Schuster Pocket Books, 1985.
Nelson, Jack. *Terror in the Night, The Klan's Campaign Against the Jews.* New York, New York: Simon & Schuster, 1993.
Nicholls, William. *Christian Antisemitism, A History of Hate.* Northvale, New Jersey: Jason Aronson, 1993.
Noonan, Peggy, *Keeping the Faith,* Reader's Digest, March 2004.
Phillips, J. B. *The New Testament in Modern English.* New York: Macmillan Publishing, 1972.
Rabinovich, Abraham. *The Jerusalem Post International Edition*, "The Judeo-Christians in Israel." (December 11, 1993).
Robertson, A. T. *A Harmony of the Gospels.* San Francisco: Harper, 1950.
Schauss, Hayyim. *The Jewish Festivals.* New York: Schocken, 1974.
Schaff, Philip. *The Creeds of Christendom* Volume I. Grand Rapids, MI: Baker Books, 1993.
Shakespeare, William. *The Works of William Shakespeare.* London: Studio Editions, 1993.

Schneider, Aviel, Editor, *Israel Today*, Jerusalem, January 2004.
Schneider, Aviel, Editor. *Israel Today*, Jerusalem, April, 2004.
Schneider, Aviel, Editor. *Israel Today*, Jerusalem, October, 2003.
Seif, Jeffrey. *Origin of the Christian Faith.* Dallas, Texas: JSM Publishing in cooperation with Christ For The Nations Institute, 1992.
Silver, Eric. *The Jerusalem Report,* "The Holocaust on Trial," (February 28, 2000).
Smith, Gene. *American Heritage.* Volume 45, Number 7, (November, 1994).
Sparks, H. F. D., Editor. *The Apocryphal Old Testament.* Oxford: Oxford University Press, 1990.
Strober, Gerald S. *"Jesus Christ Superstar: The Rock Opera" and Christian-Jewish Relations.* The American Jewish Committee, Institute on Human Relations, 1971.
Tallakson, Kent, Executive Producer. *The Great Passion Play.* Fayetteville, Arkansas: Elna M. Smith Foundation, 1992.
Teitelbaum, Sheli. *The Jerusalem Report,* "Who'll Bear the Cross?" (March 22, 2004).
Thompson, Frank Charles. *The Thompson Chain-Reference Bible.* Indianapolis, Indiana: B. B.Kirkbridge, 1988.
Tigay, Alan M. *Hadassah Magazine,* "The Jewish Traveler." (October 1988).
Tugend, Tom. *The Jerusalem Post International Edition.* (December 4, 1993).
Tull, Charles J. *Father Coughlin & The New Deal,* (New York: Syracuse University Press, 1965)
Vaughan, Curtis. *The Bible From 26 Translations.* Grand Rapids, Michigan: Baker Book House, 1988.
Vanderkam, James C. *The Dead Sea Scrolls After Forty Years.* Washington D.C.: Biblical Archaeology Society, 1992.
Vermes, Geza. *The Dead Sea Scrolls in English.* Middlesex, England: Penguin Books, 1990.
Walt, Vivienne. *USA Today,* "Right-wing leader qualifies for run-off in France," (April 22, 2002).
World Book Encyclopedia, 1988 ed., S.v. "Michelangelo."

About the Author

Randy Weiss, Ph.D. is the founder and host of the international radio and television program *CrossTalk*. He was raised in an observant Jewish home in Gary, Indiana. In the mid-1960's, Randy joined a rock and roll band. He soon embraced a lifestyle of heavy drug use and illicit behavior.

Randy released his first solo record in 1972. In January of 1973, he eloped with a lovely young Italian girl and left for their honeymoon/record promotion tour across the United States. Within a couple of weeks, his new wife climbed out of their hand-painted 1964 VW bug and left him.

While still on their honeymoon, Randy read, "The Late Great Planet Earth." His life was forever altered and his marriage was healed. He and his wife have boldly proclaimed the truth of their Jewish Messiah since that day in 1973.

Friends, relatives, and the people he cared for the most were devastated by his transforming choice to serve the Lord. Nearly two years went by before his family would communicate with him. At that time, his father desired to legally change Randy's name. As you can imagine, it was a painful situation for all concerned. Randy agreed to "go study with the Rabbis" to satisfy his father's wishes. As a result, he later earned a Master of Science in Jewish Studies degree from a well-respected Jewish institution. In that process of specialized study, Randy also learned about the Jewishness of the Early Church. It drew him deeper into faith and education where he earned multiple undergraduate, graduate, and post-graduate degrees. He also established the Jewish Studies Department at Columbia Evangelical Seminary and became an adjunct faculty member of Global University.

This academic involvement has served him well in Christian TV and given him skills to disarm skeptics and share the simple truth of the Gospel. Randy's Jewish wit and humor are mixed with a deep sense of his Jewish heritage and an unshakable faith in the God of Israel.

Randy and his wife reside near Dallas, Texas close to their four sons (who also serve in local ministry), two daughters, three daughters-in-law, and their seventh grandchild is "on the way." Randy remains committed to his family, his ministry, and most important, his Jewish Messiah.

Introduce Others to *CrossTalk*

Give your friends and relatives, both Jew and Gentile, a chance to receive a **FREE** teaching newsletter. Give them an opportunity to get involved with a ministry that can help to teach and share a deeper understanding of the Scriptures. Just fill out their names and addresses below. Use additional sheets of paper if necessary. Then drop in the mail to our ministry address: **PO Box 2528 Cedar Hill, TX 75106 USA.**

Please circle: Mr.   Mrs.   Miss   Rev

Name_____
Address_____
City_____State_____Zip_____
Country_____Phone_____
Email_____

Name_____
Address_____
City_____State_____Zip_____
Country_____Phone_____
Email_____

Identify me as the gift subscription donor.   (This is a required courtesy.)

My name is: _____

1-800-688-3422
www.crosstalk.org

Order Your Friends a Copy of

The Passion Conspiracy:
Did the Jews Kill Christ or Was He the Victim of Identity Theft?

Suggested donation: $12
Order Code: PCB

Here are some other products you can order from *CrossTalk* International

Does Jacob's Trouble Wear a Cross?
Dr. Weiss discusses the historical Jewish connection to the Christian faith. He also documents the tragic history of Christian anti-Semitism from the era of the Early Church to Colonial America.

Suggested donation: $9

Order Code: JT

In Search of a Lost Jewish Atonement
This book provides a brief, but in-depth understanding of the biblical Jewish festivals of *Rosh Hashanah* and *Yom Kippur*.

Suggested donation: $2.50
Order Code: ATONE

Videos and Other Materials

A Clear Witness to Israel - 3 part series

Learn how to be a clear and acceptable witness to the Jewish people. Dr. Weiss will give you these insights from his Jewish perspective and personal experiences.

Suggested Donation for video: $15 CD: $12 Cassette: $9

Order Code: Video – CLRWTV   CD – CLRWTC   Cassette – CLRWTAC

Days of Awe - 4 part series

Dr. Weiss teaches about the Jewish High Holidays of *Rosh Hashanah* and *Yom Kippur*. These biblical festivals are the most holy days of the Jewish year.

Suggested Donation for video:$20 CD:$15 Cassette:$10

Order Code: Video – AWEV   CD – AWEC   Cassette – AWEAC

Israel, Islam, & a Crisis in America
4 part series

Since the attacks on September 11, Israel and Islam have become very troublesome issues in our society. Dr. Weiss teaches about the history of Israel and the contention that exists with Muslim neighbors.

Suggested Donation for video:$20 CD:$15 Cassette:$10

Order Code: Video – CRISISV   CD – CRISISC   Cassette – CRISISAC

Myths of Islam - 4 part series

Dr. Weiss informs his viewers of the discrepancies and false teachings within the religion of Islam as well as the nation of Islam within the United States.

Suggested Donation for video:$20 CD:$15 Cassette:$10

Order Code: Video – MYTHSV   CD – MYTHSC   Cassette – MYTHSAC

Islam: The Margin of Terror in the Middle East - 8 part series

Dave Hunt of the Berean Call, and Dr. Randy Weiss dialogue and teach about the historic roots of the current situation of Islam in the Middle East today.

Suggested Donation for video: $30 CD: $20 Cassette: $15

Order Code: Video – MOTV   CD – MOTC   Cassette – MOTAC

LOGOS Bible Study Software

A computer library of various Bibles and books including *Augustine's Confessions*, *Pilgrim's Progress*, and Dr. Weiss' *Does Jacob's Trouble Wear a Cross?*

Suggested Donation for library: $29

Suggested Donation for upgraded library: $99

The Dead Sea Scrolls Revealed

This Logos Bible software takes you back to the writings of the Dead Sea Scrolls. You will learn where, how, who, and when these historical writings were made. This software is packaged with a video and printed teaching about the Dead Sea Scrolls by Dr. Weiss.

Suggested Donation: $29

Lest We Forget:
A History of the Holocaust

This Logos Bible software teaches of the atrocities that were done to the Jewish people during the Holocaust. This is packaged with a 2 part video series from Israel's *Yad Vashem* Holocaust Memorial.

Suggested Donation: $29

NOTES

NOTES